Wild Kinship

Biophilia, Inner Knowings and
Our True Nature

SORAYA

Edited by Shari Johnson
Book cover design by Soraya
Book cover formatting by Asim Tanveer

To support the writing journey visit:
Patreon.com/wildroots

ISBN 978-0-578-34493-5

To Pokey and Persia.
With honor and love.

CONTENTS

PREFACE

From the age of five I have felt a strong connection to—and deep love for—the natural world. This book, however, represents so much more than just my own love of Nature and animals . . . it represents my life.

Throughout my life, I have struggled to adequately inspire others to regard the living world beyond themselves as part of themselves. As a born naturalist in love with the *whole of Nature,* I believe that the spirit of the naturalist exists at the core of who we all are.

Many years ago, I began writing down my thoughts and observations about the natural world. As I shared some of these thoughts with others, I was often told that I should write a book. My memories were special to me, but I never thought it would go beyond that.

Over time, *Wild Kinship* began writing itself through the memories of my experiences with wild Nature. In illuminating the ways in which our present human story intertwines with our ancestral past, I relate personal connections and encounters I have had with plants and animals, both domestic and wild, from childhood to the present.

I have chosen to capitalize "Nature" and some other nature-related words to emphasize the importance I place on our natural world. It is my deepest desire to inspire a sense of this relationship in you.

1

The Beginning and the End

Pokey's Story

"I will never get over her loss. By removing her from her home I took her life. My sister held me back and made it clear for me to stay away so that I would not be able to see my dear friend's dead body. As my sister took care of her remains, I sobbed, heartbroken."

My grandmother's home rested in the countryside of the Tularosa Basin, in the Chihuahuan desert where the Sacramento mountains could be seen strewn at great length in the distance. One day, around the age of six or seven, I wandered the perimeter of my grandmother's property as I usually did. To my surprise and delight, I came across a wandering box turtle. One of the adults in my life, most likely my aunt, assisted me in catching it to place the dear turtle in a cardboard box. Every day I fed the little turtle lettuce and other vegetable scraps, absolutely charmed to watch as the sweet creature enthusiastically chomped into the grub. Because she would "poke" her head in and out of her lovely ornate shell, I named the turtle "Pokey."

Sometime after finding Pokey, there was some news that I was going to be moving. I had been spending, it seemed to me, a lot of time at my grandmother's house. But now it was clear that my family would be moving across the country to Ohio. I remember the emotional experience of saying good-bye to my grandmother and to all the little creatures I loved in her backyard farm. It was the most familiar place I had come to know up until that point of my life. I remember sobbing while sitting in the car, waiting to leave. The only thing that made me feel somewhat better was knowing that Pokey was with me. I held the box she now lived in on my lap. After a rather dream-like road trip across the country we ended up at the country house we called home for the next few years. It was a very different setting. Lush green grass carpeted the front and backyard. Beyond the edge of the lawn was a field for growing corn and beyond the field were beautiful, thick, verdant woods.

I don't recall how much time had passed since we first arrived there and a camping trip we took to a cabin in the nearby woods, but my companion Pokey was still in my life. At the new home Pokey and I had wandered about our new green lawn, as there was a lot of exploring to do. We spent a lot of time together and now we would be going camping together—of course I had to take Pokey along. My older siblings and I explored the area around the cabin where we'd be staying. I had set Pokey free to browse and explore, naively thinking she'd remain within eyeshot. A short time later, I heard some distressed chatter among the adults and my sister. My sister came to me and said that Pokey had just been run over by someone in our group who was camping nearby. I burst into tears and cried uncontrollably as I realized that she was gone forever. My sister held me back and made it clear that I should stay where I was—she didn't want me to see my dear friend's dead body. I sobbed as she took care of Pokey's remains. I was heartbroken.

Pokey's death created a shift within me. I felt that I would never get over her loss. Even now, as I write about the loss of my turtle friend I feel a clenching in my throat, and there are tears in my eyes.

I know *now* that Pokey was in fact a female. I haven't even a photo of her, yet I can still remember her stunning yellow-brown eyes, not red, which indicated she was a female, not a male. Pokey belonged to an incredible species of turtles called Ornate Western Box turtles. Her scientific name, *Terrapene ornata*, was as beautiful a name as she was in my eyes. I had done then, as a naïve, dumb kid, what so many others have done. Box turtles across North America are experiencing a significant population decline caused mainly by habitat loss and fragmentation, and removal for exotic pet trades or personal pets. Although not thought of as exotic as some other creatures, we have fragmented their habitats immensely, removing so many individuals from the wild that we risk losing her kind to extinction also.

By removing Pokey from her habitat, I took her life. And I did so because I loved her. But Pokey taught me so much about my love for the wild and the natural world. She taught me how to truly love all the creatures I would continue to cross paths with during my life. She taught me that to love the wild is to protect and keep the wild, *wild*.

~ ~ ~

As far back as I can remember, I had a fascination with Nature and her living beings. I began making observations about Nature and her wondrous lifeforms at the age of five. Somehow, I knew even then that I was going to become a biologist—long before I even understood the term. I loved every creature I ever met and as I grew older, this fascination with life turned into a deep-rooted obsession. Nature and the outdoors became my temple, and my university. The world brimmed with all kinds of wonderful creatures and amazing natural things waiting to be discovered, experienced, and understood. My world was endlessly fascinating.

I have never questioned this immense fascination, perhaps because I feel there has never been a reason to. In science, there is always a desire to know and understand more. While answers to the *wheres, whats, whens* and *hows* are discoverable through empirical investigation and experimentation, the *whys* ultimately tend to fall away to speculation, philosophy, and imagination, as well as purely irrelevant. These are the truths that are to be answered and understood only by oneself. And while these truths are inevitably to be found, there may be no singular means by which we discover them. Yet the truths answered only by each of us are intriguingly simple and foundational to the wholeness that makes up this life-giving sphere. These are the inner workings of Nature working through us, and are the inner workings of the place we call *home*.

This book is intended to be intuitive as well as scientific, drawing from personal experiences with wild Nature and musings about our place within our precious and endangered living world. I will explore not so much the whys of Nature, but the things that just *are* . . . in all that is kin. I will also explore the many facets of our true humanity as defined by innate biological behaviors that are inherent to our own species, and why we are not experiencing the wholeness of humanity, which I believe to be a natural part of the human experience. In exploring this, I will weave into each section a special connection I have made in my life with an animal or with an aspect of wild Nature. I will also explore the many ways our kindredness with all that is, is naturally apparent; the scientific aspects that give light to these connections; and some not so apparent reasons why we might feel a kinship to life beyond our own species.

In my life thus far, I have often battled between the two possible scenarios of our true human nature: the first being human nature's tendency to be an ecological wrecking ball, and the second, humanity's incredible ability to foster great kinship through nurturing inner knowings—a sense of place and an ability to thrive alongside an equally thriving natural world. My intention for this book is to focus on the possibility of the latter aspect of our humanity. In my stories you will find that I swing between the contextual meaning of the word "wild" as both literal: *untamed, natural, feral, native* and *free*; and figuratively: as an *intense* or *impressive* sense in illustrating the truly wild aspects that ultimately encompass our own true nature as human animals. In my quest to understand the nature of Nature more deeply, I have discovered many of our own wild abilities—inner knowings deeply rooted in the unconscious of our species . . . abilities that I have found to be profoundly wild.

Biophilia: A Love of Nature

First coined in 1984 by Edward O. Wilson, one of the greatest figures in conservation biology, the term "biophilia" refers to his hypothesis that humans evolved to be intrinsically infatuated with other living beings with which we share this planet and with Nature itself. This instinctual bond is driven by our genes as a result of evolving nearly 3 million years alongside the natural world. Before the rise of modern civilization and the formation of large populations and modern cultures, our innate appreciation for natural settings is what ultimately allowed us to thrive for so long.

Being hopelessly stricken with biophilia myself, my deep love of Nature has granted me an ability to deeply appreciate the *realness* of the natural world and the miracle of life of a living, breathing animal on this incredibly diverse earth. Knowing the air that I breathe, the water that I drink and the native earth that I walk upon, is one in the same for *all* of Earth's living beings. To love life is a living breathing part of who I am. I was a born naturalist. It is who I am. It is who I believe we *all* are.

My admiration for wild creatures is particularly immense. As a kid, I was enraptured by creatures of all kinds. Even before Pokey, the sweet Western Box Turtle came into my life, I relished my earliest friendships with many other critters. Such as the white turkey on my grandmother's backyard farm who walked diligently by my side seemingly everywhere I went; the ants that crawled busily across the back porch; the silly goats with whom I shared my snacks; my many pet cats and dogs; and even the sometimes intimidating, territorial rooster whose threatening charges and fly-kicks I often barely escaped! I loved them all and was fascinated by everything they were. Whether I could interact with them closely or not, I considered every animal my friend. My earliest animal meetings set me on the trajectory of an endless love of all things natural. That was only the beginning of my journey to fully understanding this love. Many wild encounters, wonders and insights into the natural world were yet to come.

I never really questioned why it was easy for me to make such "friends" or why I felt so connected to earth's creatures. Animals were easy to get along with. It was just something that felt natural. My love of life carried on to later childhood indulgences of catching bull frogs in ponds, discovering wildlife tracks along waterways, finding salamanders under weathered logs and to the delightful discovery of an endangered Luna Moth in my own back yard. Eventually that love for *life* carried me further toward a degree in Biology in which I concentrated my studies in ecology and evolutionary biology.

I felt connected not only to animals, but to the wild character of all things. Plants, mosses, fungi, the movement of water, starry night skies, *everything* associated with the pure and natural. As a young child it was apparent that the world brimmed with fascinating life-giving forces! The great sensitivity I felt toward that life made me realize the importance of the wild. I realized also that the natural world in which humans and non-human animals alike occupied was simply *habitat*. Habitat for all life. In my early days I became incredibly concerned with defending and protecting that habitat. Believing in the preservation of wilderness and *wild*-ness—that which is untamed, un-dominated, uninfluenced, and uncontrolled by anthropogenic means, as much as possible. It was evident that ecological systems left to their own natural agency was the only way sustainability for all could ultimately be achieved and maintained.

Because of the pace of modern human advancement and the interconnected nature of ecological systems, it is now clear that all things still considered *wild* could easily be considered threatened if not endangered—from the preservation of dark night skies to the native ground beneath our feet. If we are to live a fully wholesome existence here on this truly awesome Earth, we must reconcile our relationship with nature through remembering, respecting, and reconnecting with our human-earth connection, our *true* human nature. But first, we must recognize what that nature looks and feels like. I believe the curiosity, wonder and excitement of a child is a great model for this, but there are other ways we can come to recognize this deep connection.

~ ~ ~

"Come here! Come here!" my mother exclaimed as she led us to the front-yard garden where she had spotted a garter snake. Filled with giddy admiration, we smiled and

laughed as we watched the incredible, legless creature. I felt lucky to find such a creature in our very own garden. For some time after that first sighting, we began seeking the snake on a somewhat regular basis, or at least we *believed* it was the same snake. My mother called the little garter "Nikki." We loved Nikki. Oftentimes I would lie on my belly to watch Nikki move about the grass, captivated by that sweet little face and flickering red-black tongue.

One day I discovered a neat "trick" Nikki could do. While lying on the grass I twirled a leaf from its stem that caused Nikki to periscope slightly. Seemingly mesmerized, Nikki swayed side to side at the sight of the spinning leaf. Enamored by this behavior, I eagerly showed my mother and siblings, which brought a smile to all our faces. Nikki was great fun to have around.

On another day, Mom rushed us over to the garden to see that the garden was suddenly alive with slithering baby garters. Nikki was a mama! It seemed that she liked our garden enough to have her babies there and for this I felt incredible joy. Bedazzled as ever by the many natural marvels that could be found in one's own yard, it is in these moments I remember feeling nothing but pure happiness.

~ ~ ~

The love I felt for the natural world seemed as innate as breathing. In wanting to understand the world and her creatures more deeply, I remained as close to wild Nature as I could, in any way I could. This love affair brought about an ability to recognize truly wondrous things when others around me seemed not to notice. With many of the aspects of Nature I found so deeply fascinating, my words failed to fully express their true wonder; just as they will ultimately fail to fully encompass them in this book. In Nature, I could recognize the connections revealed only to those who often commune with nature, but I am sure we have all made connections in our lives   for which there are simply no words. While I can't do justice to all of these connections, I can speak about the things we can all appreciate as marvelous.

Curiosity and wonder are not things allocated only to the delight of children. Though they do often begin in the eyes of children, all humans who carry great curiosity in their hearts can appreciate more of what the natural world offers us. Our nomadic ancestors must have been endlessly curious, always learning about the wheres, whats and whens of valuable resources. Sometimes just the sheer delight in the discovery of little wonders is all that curiosity gives us. Nevertheless, it is natural for human animals to be curious investigators of our world. Such curiosities turn into knowledge, allowing us to detect food sources, mates, and even points of danger. This eventually carries us toward greater understanding of our environment.

~ ~ ~

I've always been intrigued by the "superpowers" that plants and animals seem to possess—those adapted traits in species, including humans, that reveal unique abilities and keen awareness, often taken for granted or missed entirely.

Over billions of years of evolution, these abilities in many ways and in all species point toward the nature of our true selves, establishing the direction of our own paths.

Last June, an almost unearthly brilliant greenish-blue glow caught my eye among the leaf litter. It was a glow worm! Exploring the property further, I discovered several more glow worms hiding about the grass and rock crevices. In the previous summer I found only a single glow worm in the yard, and before then I had never seen one. Now there were several of them. Growing up in the Midwest, fireflies were a normal delight of summer nights, but I had not had the privilege of making memories with glow worms. One never tires of the illuminating whimsy that fireflies breathe into this world, and the same could be said about the glow worms. Bioluminescence is one "superpower" that has evolved in certain species of insects, marine life, and algae, gracing these species with incredible uniqueness . . . a superpower I will always regard as remarkable, and one that many of us can observe in our own backyards.

~ ~ ~

One morning while sitting outside with my dog, I witnessed a superpower of hers. As she lay curled up in fallen leaves half asleep and facing east while enjoying the mid-morning sun, delicate winds drifted in from the west. From a distance behind my dog and to the west, a roaming black cat emerged from the bushes who didn't seem to notice us as she veered north on her journey. Just as the cat disappeared, my dog lifted her nose upward and sniffed the air intently toward where the cat had emerged. Content and warm, she recoiled comfortably back into the leaves. When out on walks, I often catch her pointing her nose directly into the wind. In no hurry and with eyes half-closed, she stays in this position for many moments at a time. I often wonder what secrets the winds whisper to her. I wonder also, just how many individual scents her amazing brain can process and categorize at once. Something I couldn't even begin to fathom.

My pet cats have also amazed me with their own superpowers. I have had a particular affinity for cats, both big and small, for as long as I can remember. What I love most about our domesticated feline friends is that despite their domestication, many of their wild ancestral traits have remained undeniably intact. Similar to their wild counterparts, they possess incredible hunting abilities. This is why cat owners are advised to keep cats indoors, or at least enclosed in some way. These hunting abilities and instincts have remained so strong that cats have wreaked havoc on many small birds and other mammal species. Unfortunately, this incredible trait accounts for the loss of a staggering 25 million wildlife annually. It has been estimated that both feral and house cats have killed between 1.4 billion and 3.7 billion birds and between 6.9 billion and 20.7 billion small mammals. They are natural born hunters. Playful engagement is crucial for the development and maintenance of their instinctual survival skills. This is why you might find your cat in a fit of wild playfulness. It is simply a part of the nature of cats to be agile and efficient hunters, and play helps them to be who they truly are. One thing that tends to warm my heart is the sound of my cat galloping up and down the hallway in midnight playfulness. Cats are nocturnal and crepuscular by nature, which means that much like their wild counterparts, they are primarily active during dusk and at dawn. Possessing a superior ability to see in darkness inspires excursions of nighttime play. Cats can get by on utilizing only around one-sixth the amount of light humans need. This is due to a structure called a tapetum that sits behind the retina. The tapetum allows the cat to pick up even the smallest amount of light available in the environment. Nighttime vision is just one of many wild traits I admire in cats. From their incredible agility to the sensitivity of their whiskers, they are incredible beings.

~ ~ ~

While in the forest, I like to lie awake just before dark to watch the amazing dance of bats. While the low-light night vision in cats is indeed impressive, bats take nighttime activity to an entirely new level. These remarkable blind, winged beings are able to figure-eight swiftly around the treetop canopies to efficiently snatch fast-flying insects. The unique adaptation of echolocation allows bats to precisely navigate in complete and total darkness, utilizing specific calls for prey and different environments. Certain bat species use whispered calls when pursuing moths to avoid being detected, since moths have exceptionally evolved hearing. Some species of moths have even evolved a way to escape or interfere with the echolocation of bats by flexing their tymbal organ. This produces a series of clicks in response to bat calls, causing the pursuing bat to become disoriented. In my book, both the echolocation of bats and moth defenses are spectacular.

In fact, most creatures on this earth, from the largest land mammal to the microscopic, possess wildly unique abilities—such as the olfactory prowess of dogs, the immortality of jellyfish, the anti-freeze blood of frogs, and the regeneration of lost tails in lizards. In the wild world of plants and animals, these unique abilities are endless in the great dance of life.

Biophobia: A Death Sentence

It is very natural for me to see a wild creature as some*one*, rather than as just an animal or just some*thing*, with an innate understanding that *all* creatures—those who have come and gone, and those who remain on this earth—simply belong just as much as you and I do.

While I am generally accepting of any creature who crosses my path, including spiders, snakes, and scorpions, I can recall only one critter that caused me to develop a slight phobia. As a young girl, I was sitting in the living room one morning while eating my breakfast. It was still rather dark as the day was approaching dawn. As my eyes adjusted to the darkness, I caught a glimpse of a somewhat familiar sight scamper into view across the floor. It was a large house centipede. They were as common as daddy long-legs, so I was not fazed much by its presence. *At first.*

As I often did, I got down close so I could get a better look at the fascinating creature. It had become very still, and curiosity drove me to see it in motion again. I began to reach toward what I thought was its backend to get it to move, when it suddenly rushed *toward* me rather than away. I was shaken to the core by the mistake I had made.

House centipedes are among the many underappreciated creatures that get a bad reputation for simply looking more scary or dangerous than they are. I realize that most people who would have seen a centipede scamper across the floor would not hesitate to swat at it or run from it, or at least feel squeamish. What makes house centipedes frightening to most people are its multiple pairs of long legs, fifteen pairs to be exact, which make them incredibly speedy creatures. They are, in fact, the fastest centipede in the world! House centipedes are typically yellowish grey in color with dark dorsal stripes. And although they do have venom, it is too weak to cause any real harm to larger creatures, such as humans.

Perhaps the best attribute of house centipedes is their diet. Much like daddy long-legs, house centipedes are beneficial creatures to have around, as they feed on common household pests such as termites, flies, cockroaches and even some spiders. But don't worry, despite their name, most house centipedes live mostly outdoors in damp, cool areas.

The house centipede's basic anatomy is what caused my confusion that morning. One reason for its incredibly fast speed are its super strong legs at its rear. I mistook its rear from its front. At the end of those strong legs is a second set of even longer antenna-like appendages evolved to fool predators. Well, I too was fooled. Nature is remarkably intelligent!

After spending some of my life a bit frightful of them, I took it upon myself to learn about what had fooled me, and immediately my slight fear of them vanished. Those faux antennae at its rear indeed served their evolutionary purpose, which to the centipede's point of view, might have spared its life, though I never intended to harm the delicate arthropod.

Although it can certainly help some people, one really doesn't need scientific information about the anatomy of the house centipede to be free from such an irrational fear (or phobia). What should be apparent in our heart's knowing is the understanding that all creatures *have* belonged and *do* belong. Even those now extinct.

Biophobia, the aversion to Nature or naturally existing living things, is far too prevalent in the modern world. Without my curiosity, I might never have overcome that experience. While fear of the unknown or bizarre is normal, it is irrational fear that has led to humanity's great disassociation with Nature. This irrational fear is what has contributed to the seemingly everlasting war against the natural world and its beings. Being severely afraid of moths and butterflies is irrational, and yet these phobias exist. A person with such a phobia may not risk spending time outdoors for fear of being bombarded by scary moths. To ensure greater ecological stability, humanity must overcome such irrational fears for the sake of us *all*.

In the case of many animal phobias, this fear is often taught—sometimes unintentionally and sometimes purposefully. It can begin with parents, peers, culture and so on. These irrational fears bleed further into other living and "non-living" aspects of Nature, as with people who fear dirt or getting dirty. To others, mysterious depths of waterbodies, dense forests and other lurking unknowns evoke great fears. The more time we spend tucked into our inanimate surroundings and away from Nature, the less likely we are to overcome such fears. We literally forgo the opportunity to witness the awesomeness Nature has to offer by not embracing what it means to be a human animal, thereby denying ourselves the chance to reunite with the nature of our true selves.

The tendency to sweep aside a harmless bug out of impulse or convenience versus incessantly swatting at it with the intent to kill it are two very different ways of approaching Nature. The latter is often an unnecessary biophobic response that ultimately leads to destructive wars against nature. It may only begin with exterminating pests within a home, which then leads to fumigating one's yard. Next comes an erroneous view of how things in the world "should" be. Such as, many insects or critters that are seen anywhere, even in the outdoors, are seen as *out of place* and must be exterminated. They suddenly don't belong in our world. If not curbed, such narrow-mindedness grows into the mass destruction of nature and the endangerment of many living beings—including our own kind. Disease-causing pesticides, the decimation of pollinating species from either direct chemical extermination or the food sources for other pollinators, which in turn affect our food supply, are only a few of the problems.

This kind of behavior leads to other extremes, such as hacking back as much native vegetation on one's property as possible for fear of the lurking wilds. Another extreme yet common action is radical lot-clearing—replacing native vegetation with gravel, perhaps with the thought of creating a low-maintenance space. Xeriscaping turns into *zero*-scaping by creating dead zones that lead to erosion, noxious weed issues and biodiversity loss. All these behaviors stem from fear and a misunderstanding of how native vegetation and other organisms are not only ultimately self-sustaining, but benefit whole, intact systems in Nature. We must learn to live alongside wild Nature, because the most frightening creature of all is the nature-fearing human. It is *this* creature that undermines the very essence of life.

The Civilized Human

Oftentimes I feel as if I awakened from a multi-decades-long slumber only to witness the senseless destruction of my own kind. Anguish fills my heart upon the realization that over the course of so little Earth-time, and even in my own lifetime, we have inflicted such an unnatural discord upon our own *home* and upon each other. As I daydream about the vibrant, thriving world I know could exist, reality forces me back into the daymare of poisoned and degrading ecosystems.

Since early childhood, my own sense of security has felt as threatened as the helpless plants and wildlife by the so called "civilized" world. The many ways most of us carried out our lives just felt *off* to my young heart's perspective. The modern human way of living seemed millions of miles away from what I felt it should and *could* be. Something was wrong and no one, at least in my world as a kid, *seemed* to be aware of this.

It was clear that human civilization, simply by living our day-to-day lives of buying and producing *stuff* that we are fooled into believing we absolutely *need*, had killed, threatened, or endangered just about everything I ever loved. This *stuff* we feel we can't live without—these fabricated necessities that seem to be foundational to civilized culture, litter and threaten nearly the entire natural, living world.

Upon studying our recent human past, I have learned that our conditioning to this *Neo*-way of living runs deep, but not nearly as deep as our *true* human nature. After all, this modern way of life is still new. At least 250,000 years of typical *Homo sapiens* behavior and attributes are embedded within each of us, whether we acknowledge this or not. We are still *Homo sapiens*, the human animal whose own ancestors lived for tens of thousands of years nurturing their young as innately and completely as what we see intact in other species today. We are a species among many who felt unquestionably a part of their natural surroundings. A species who up until the relatively recent past never questioned living mostly outdoors sleeping under a brilliant, starry night sky and living within alongside the means of changing seasons. It was the only way. It was *our* way.

~ ~ ~

I once read a story about a wise old Apache named Stalking Wolf, who recalled a horrific experience that sickened his stomach and caused his heart much sorrow. From a very young age, Stalking Wolf was recognized by Apache elders as unique. He became recognized for his extraordinary wisdom and ability to understand and speak with Nature. He also carried within himself great curiosity of the natural world, often posing extraordinarily astute questions to wise elders. Stalking Wolf and his people lived a free and natural existence in the mountainous deserts away from the tormented lives of captive Native Americans. His people remained one of the last Native peoples to live free from the constraints of Reservations. Stalking Wolf wandered the deserts, mountains, and forests to learn everything he possibly could about the natural world, considered by his people to be as important and alive as human beings. Once while roaming far beyond his home, he saw something he would never be able to forget. From atop a ridge, he saw a small mining village overrun by senseless people. He witnessed staggering, drunken men carrying on without Nature in their hearts. Their raucous behavior was evident in the way they spoke loudly, laughed, and stumbled about without regard for the natural world or a sense of place. Unnatural and unrecognizable waste and garbage littered the area. Waterways that once ran clear were muddied and sick. Enormous holes in the earth further fueled the young Apache's disbelief and anguish. He noticed countless more visible scars these men had inflicted upon the earth. It was almost too much for the young Apache to bear. He had never witnessed such irreverence and destruction. Much like Stalking Wolf, I have felt the loneliness of wandering this life tainted with such marks of modernity.

In Stalking Wolf's horrific encounter with the miners' village, he noticed the men carried guns with them everywhere they went. He watched as one drunken man fell asleep on the sidewalk while clutching his gun, as if afraid of what might emerge from the hillsides. He realized they were in fact guarding themselves from the elements and Nature, insulating themselves in every way possible, from heavy clothing to impenetrable buildings and barriers. These men hadn't the privilege that Stalking Wolf and his people had—to enter this world knowing they were not separate from all that is and from where all had come, and with an understanding of nature. Wild Nature to many is scary, yet it is our birthplace as natives to this Earth.

This *knowing* and "sense of place" were innate in Stalking Wolf's people and were encouraged in the young by the elders. Many Indigenous peoples knew themselves to be inseparable from Nature, whereas the miners lived in such a way that prevented the building of a relationship between themselves and the natural world. They greatly feared wild nature, and this gave further energy to their destructive behavior. The bizarre sight of that miners' village helped define Stalking Wolf's inner truth and directed the course of his life as a living, breathing, caretaker of the Earth.

There are many times in our human history in which we unknowingly severed our relationship with Nature. From the moment we gave up our nomadic lives to establish sedentary lives, we began living in fear of Nature. Working against the elements and seasons, we established crops which we then defended against wild animals and Nature, instead of living in the abundance of seasonal food sources.

When I was a little girl, riding in the back seat of the car, I had lots of thoughts about Nature as I watched the world pass by my window. This gave me an early glimpse into humanity, or rather humanity's place here on earth. I very much enjoyed the scenic view of thick woodlands and diverse landscapes. In stands of thick trees, I often wondered about the animals that regarded these places as home. I saw these spaces for the habitats they were, feeling a sense of respect, and naively thinking they would be there forever. But my young eyes began to see some things that appeared to be wrong and out of place. While it was calming to ride through places where Nature seemed to abundantly envelope us from all around, the view in other places deeply disturbed me.

I saw things that jarred my spirit. Things that didn't seem to belong. Some of those things were, strangely enough, electric poles. When I took notice of their presence I could no longer *un*-see them. One after another, after another, after another would *zip* by. They were *everywhere*! They presented themselves as unsightly blemishes on this earth. I was annoyed by their presence. But I am certainly not laughing at that younger version of myself. I giggle, a bit out of frustration for her and a bit out of fondness for the sentiments.

Upon this strange realization I began to easily notice other things like litter, construction and so on. What I saw next absolutely baffled me. I noticed "For Sale" signs for large swaths of natural woodlands, which were eventually bought up and cleared for houses and shopping plazas. In my young mind, this felt wrong—*Nature couldn't be sold*, let alone developed so carelessly.

As the list of man-made things got longer, it filled not only my view of modern reality, but my greater consciousness. I felt threatened by the things I saw. They didn't seem to belong. They were in contradiction to natural order. I couldn't help but sense they were not only wrong, but excessive. Over time, my awareness of these things was too much for my younger self to accept. It clearly wasn't for the best. Then why did humans engage in unsustainable behavior? We are after all, *Homo sapiens*, the "wise" humans. Yet, just about everything in the civilized world isn't sustainable or at all *wise*.

~ ~ ~

For someone as deeply taken with wild Nature as I was as a child, it is difficult to simply overlook the scars of civilization that so widely litter the landscape. Looking upon any landscape, whether considered "natural" or heavily influenced by man, my imagination shows me just what any wild or prehistoric landscape might look like, and in my heart, I know what could be, instead of what might presently be. In fierce defense of the natural world, I cringe every time I hear someone say that a particular landscape is ugly, because it wasn't inherently so. Usually, they are referring to a landscape blotched with human-made *stuff*. Streetlights, electric posts, traffic, ever-widening asphalt highways, cold sterile buildings, sidewalks, etcetera.

Once, I was driving along I-10 in the stunning desert of the southwest when someone in the vehicle made a comment about how ugly the desert was. Irritated, I asked him to try to see the landscape in a new perspective. The area we were driving through was mostly natural desert landscape marked with highways, cars, billboards, and buildings. I told him to use his imagination to visually remove each of the man-made components, one by one. First the cars, then the billboards, then the buildings and last, the highway. What the mind's eye should have been left with were the open desert plains and varying mountain ranges. Then, I asked if he still considered the desert ugly. He shook this head and said "No, not anymore..." It was not the desert itself that he found ugly. It was all the man-made minutiae sprawled about the landscape.

~ ~ ~

Surprisingly, what may be our worst evolutionary trait is our large brains. Touted as our greatest attribute, our amazing cognitive abilities may be the feature that not only greatly reduces our own long-term survival, but those of other species as well. The negative impact on our environment is a direct result of such intelligence. Anatomically, larger-sized brains are a physical characteristic rarely seen in other animals. However, larger brains tend to produce consequences. For one thing, human beings began to regard ourselves above all else and above all other living beings, whether those beings contributed to our survival. We have a lot to pay for our smarts.

Biophobia isn't solely an aversion to Nature or natural things, it also encompasses a disregard for anything that does not directly serve us—a tendency to affiliate only with environments and things that serve human interests. I find it hard to think of any characteristic trait that would be more destructive than this point of view. It is a response to our uncertainties of natural environments, and is ultimately the reason we are so riddled with things like Prozac and excessive light pollution. If a sidewalk isn't lit brightly enough for one to read a book, it is deemed unsafe and unacceptable. Fear of the darkness, or rather fear of what lives within the darkness in the scary depths of wild Nature, drives the development of these modern security blankets. Many people fear even their own backyards at night. But it is not just darkness that people fear, it is being in unfamiliar spaces. These biophobic responses to natural environments and other natural things stem simply from not knowing one's environment well. The child who never delights in roly-polies or explores wild Nature, perhaps because his or her parent displays such an aversion to such things and forbids it, may never learn to embrace the wonders of Nature.

2

The Human Experience

Wood Sorrels

One day when I was around eight years old, I was exploring the wonders of the backyard and nearby woods when I noticed a plant with clover-like leaves and bright yellow five-petaled flowers. These particular plants were quite abundant and yet unassuming, spread about other wild, verdant kin. For reasons unknown to me, I often found myself drawn to this delicate plant. Perhaps it was simply because I spent so much of my time close to the ground observing the world of microcosms, flipping logs, rocks, and other debris to find out what little beings might be hiding beneath. Roly-polies, also known as pill bugs, were always a favorite. To the little isopods, the stalks of these delicate plants were like towering rainforest trees. I was in the woods, but the isopods were in *woodlands of woods*—a forest within forests, a system of systems. At this young age I too was in woodlands of woods. Lost in the micro-world, I was yet unaware of the awesome macrocosm in which I was living.

One day while sitting beneath a tree I grabbed a cluster of these yellow flowers and instinctively brought them to my mouth. They were both sour and sweet, and I loved the taste. They became an occasional treat when I was exploring outdoors. This was another layer of the understory I was becoming familiar with—another piece of a puzzle within a puzzle. In other times of the year, I snacked on the green pods produced by this plant, and they had the same tantalizing flavor as the flowers. In fact, the whole plant was delicious!

It wasn't until later in life I learned what that plant was. As a child exploring nature and led only by curiosity, there was no one in my life at the time who provided names for many of these wonders, although I often didn't ask. I simply pieced together my own understanding of the things that crossed my path. Parents might say to their kids, "*Look, those are Roly-polies!*" but may not know the names of all plants. When I later learned the plant was named Yellow Woodsorrel (*Oxalis stricta*), I was surprised that the name "sorrel" stems from the high German word *sur,* meaning sour. Upon further reading I learned that these plants have been used as garnishes for salads and other foods, and that apparently, they were a great source of vitamin C! How could I have known this plant was safe for me to eat when no one taught me this?

It makes perfect sense that toddlers would come to learn of their world from the ground up, giving the most attention to what is within their reach. Incrementally, as a child grows, more and more things come within reach whether tactilely, visually, or with other senses coming into play.

To this day, this plant remains a special friend of mine. Where I currently live, the common Yellow Woodsorrel is replaced primarily with Alpine Woodsorrels (*Oxalis alpina*).

Quite similar anatomically, Alpine Wood sorrels also have clover-like leaves, made up of three green hearts, but the flower is purple instead of yellow. I still swoon at the sight of them. Savoring a handful of them reminds me of my earliest days spent with Nature, and a sweet delight in the awesomeness of an inner knowing that showed me the usefulness of this plant.

There are natural ways we can come to understand and know our world. When we are not taught by *wise elders*, we are nonetheless backed by millions of years of evolution. I will explore some of these other ways of knowing in this book.

~ ~ ~

With digestive systems similar to those of our closest primate kin, the orangutans, chimpanzees and even monkeys, it makes sense that our pre-historic diets were primarily made up of fibrous plants as well. Animal meat was eaten, but it only made up a small portion of our primarily insect and plant-based diet. If our guts had evolved to be more that of pure generalists (such as animals like raccoons that can eat a variety of foods and can live in different environments), we would not need the use of fire to help make starches found in roots and grains more digestible; starches that became more widely consumed as a result of the agricultural revolution. Our bodies would have relied on the more readily available plants, fruits, and nuts. And since we could not easily cook while on the move, we would simply grab-and-go, picking and eating seasonally available plant foods as we traveled. Plant-, fruit-, and nut-based diets are more aligned with what our bodies themselves, without the aid of cooking, have evolved to eat.

Given the anthropological evidence of the diets of our ancestors and the anatomical evidence of our intestines, it makes perfect sense that one would *test* different leafy edibles found in Nature, as I did as a small child with the Yellow Woodsorrels. Until recently in the evolution of humans, we largely browsed vegetation for possible edible fruits, nuts and even insects. We also spent a lot of our past scavenging what top predators such as lions and hyenas left behind. Meat scavenged from carrion was more likely an occasional, even rare treat than a main feature of our diets. Although speculative, the rotting meats of such carrion *may* have even made whatever available meat more digestible to humans. Multiple evidence points to the more likely scenario that early humans scavenged more than they hunted, as it was more energy efficient and less dangerous.

As for browsing for edible plants and fruits, we developed an instinctual sense of taste. Alongside our sensitive taste receptors, plants too have evolved chemicals to either "allow" a grazer to graze or ward them off with toxins. Humans, much like many other animals, utilize both their senses of smell and taste to determine safe food sources—an incredible and truly wild ability. Our senses of taste and smell have evolved to detect bitterness often associated with poisonous foods. When I tasted Yellow Woodsorrels for the first time, my taste receptors were met with a pleasant sweet and tangy taste, so I continued to consume the plant. Had my receptors been met with an astringent, bitter taste, I might have spat it out and never mentioned it again. It is incredible how our senses can keep us safe. Small trials and errors made us resilient animals in nature. And as one's lifetime goes forward, a catalogue of "safe versus dangerous" is acquired. If these things were not passed onto us by our caretakers and other *band* members, it is nice to know we were evolutionarily built to figure these things out. But because modern humans rely greatly on what is available at the supermarket, we no longer make any effort to determine what foods are safe versus poisonous, since they have already been selected, grown, picked, washed, and staged on shelves for us to buy.

Lost Senses

Wild animals utilize all the senses available to them, which allow them to adequately respond to their environment and to thrive. Some animals are more adapted visually, some auditorily and some tactilely. When there is no choice, humans do the same. As a young child, I would chew on the pithy inner parts of woody stems of certain plants. I loved peeling away its woody exterior layers to reveal the sponge-like medulla, or pith. I chewed on the spongy interior, which made my mouth water, then I would spit it out after it lost integrity. Much as with the wood sorrels, I didn't know why I did this. It just felt nice to do so at times. One of our closest relatives, the chimpanzee, has been observed chewing the inner pith of bitter plants as a pharmacological remedy to relieve an upset stomach. Behavioral scientists know this because the chimpanzees who chewed these bitter piths had a nodule worm infection that caused their upset stomachs. Chewing the pith of the *Vernonia amygdalina* plant was correlated with a noticeable increase in appetite, and a decrease in malaise, constipation, and diarrhea. Several hours after chewing the bitter pith the chimpanzees were relieved of their painful ailments. This was confirmed by the measurement of significantly decreased nodular worm eggs found in their feces. They also chewed the piths at different stages of the plant's development. Chewing the bitter pith of younger shoots tended to relieve symptoms more quickly than the pith of older stems. This is because the bitter juices and medicinal properties produced by the younger shoots were more potent.

The piths of many plants known to be eaten by animals and ancient humans hold a multitude of properties. Some are simply food sources; peeling away the outer parts of certain plant stems reveal tender edible centers. I did this also as a child, but mostly stuck with thick stemmed, barley-like grasses. The tender centers weren't much in terms of food, but they were tasty snacks, nonetheless. Since the plants I chose tended to be at older, woodier stages, they were not particularly bitter or juicy. This meant that their toxic levels, if any, might have been greatly decreased or not as potent. Recalling this now, for whatever the reason I simply found the texture of the dried inner pith pleasing. Although I do recall these piths made me salivate slightly more. Perhaps that is something meaningful, though I may never know. The point is, human animals are naturally inquisitive about their environment, and through instinctual and intuitive means we find great value in Nature's abundance—not just in food sources, but in other helpful dietary aids as well. Through trial and error and instinctual inner knowings, we find ourselves in a world of incredible abundance.

Another reason some might surmise that kids are drawn to certain plant *chewables* is that for most of our evolutionary history our pre-historic diets consisted of much higher concentrations of fibrous plants, which generally took longer to chew. We were indeed quite the chewers before cooking came along.

~ ~ ~

When we take the time to interact with our environment, the many subtleties of Nature's secrets and abundance that are sometimes hidden in plain sight guide our senses through simple responses and stimuli. The language of Nature is something we're often not consciously aware of— especially in modern times. Yet the language of Nature *is* recognized often by a deeper knowing, expressed somewhere by our most ancient subconscious. Our abilities to sense these subtleties may come more effortlessly than we realize.

Often overlooked and of little use to us humans is the language of pheromones. Both animals and plants use pheromones to communicate with each other and their environment. Pheromones are a silent but volatile language spoken in the form of chemical-ladened vapors. They are used for much the same reason as other more obvious cues of Nature between plants and animals, which is ultimately to maintain homoeostasis in an ecosystem. Carried by air currents, pheromones evolved to achieve many remarkable things—from attracting a mate, alarming others of danger, establishing territories, leaving a trail for others to follow such as with ants, increasing a bond between mother and offspring, and much more. Another truly awesome form of communication is bioluminescence. This is crucial for fireflies, glow worms, algae, and many other marine organisms. Bioluminescence in Nature is used as a general means of communication, a defense mechanism, to attract mates, or to lure potential prey.

Living underground are highways of mycorrhizae, thin fungal filaments, that interconnect tree roots to one another and to all else, carrying messages and important nutrients from tree to tree, analogous to neurosynaptic impulses. In exchange, tree roots return the favor by supplying these fungi with carbohydrates. This is one of the wildest forms of kinship in an ongoing effort to enrich ever-depleting soils. Without this extraordinary network, soil health would decline and would not be able to support the plant life we so cherish.

The model for reciprocity is widely found in Nature. Our great intellectual knowledge of the many ways we benefit from these natural relationships doesn't seem to be enough to convince us that a reorientation toward Nature is necessary. We must go deeper in our engagement with Nature to bring home this crucial message of our greatest wild entanglement with all else. I am personally convinced that learning the languages of Nature is more profound when we can immerse ourselves in Nature versus reading articles, guides, and textbooks.

I cannot fully explain why or how certain aspects of Nature make themselves apparent to me, aside from the knowledge that I was given through my education, from personal observation, and from others. Knowledge also seems to be acquired from simply allowing oneself to be a part of all else. Our evolved guidance systems are still intact, but they may not be as engaged as those of our ancestors. This is what innate animal behavior is. If you allow yourself to be a part of everything else, there are things you will come to "know" about the nature of Nature; things that you will just know are true. You may experience insights from which there seems to be an obscure origin. You may even find it difficult to explain the connections you have come to recognize in our limited spoken languages. I have always felt that Nature was my first teacher, and if one chose to listen, Nature would reveal to us many things worthy of our attention and engagement. In fact, Nature was the first teacher of us all. It is amazing what the human animal can learn simply by living alongside it. By doing so, you will find that Nature will whisper her secrets to you.

The Owl

I was hiking with my partner in an area we frequently visit when I felt a sudden sense I couldn't explain. Only the word "owl" came to my mind. I began looking around, scoping a large juniper not far from us, and there was a Great Horned Owl perched on a limb, half enveloped in the juniper's greenery. I quietly pointed the owl out to my partner and after a few moments the owl flew away. Feeling a bit befuddled by what had just happened, I pondered more deeply about the "senses" less talked about.

By drawing conclusions from previous experiences, we can create all kinds of unique connections in Nature. Living as modern beings we have distanced ourselves from experiencing Nature as extensions of ourselves. In experiencing it, we can make connections we didn't even know were possible. These lost and forgotten ways of knowing and sensing have atrophied under the umbrella of modernity. But they may not be entirely lost. We evolved to have these ancient, almost tangible skills. I believe that with deeper awareness these innate skills can be reawakened.

Our brains are constantly assimilating complex information about our environment, piecing together conclusions about what is being assimilated at lightning speed. We are not consciously aware when this is happening because it tends to happen so fast. But it is a part of our evolutionary makeup and is a large part of why our ancient ancestors survived so many conditions in so many environments for hundreds of thousands of years. Consequentially, it may very well be the case that these ancient skills are not as atrophied as we may have been led to believe, since these "senses" are a part of who we inherently are as human animals. Rather, we may have been simply using these skills somewhere in our modern every-day lives instead of in the natural world. And in doing so, we fail to see how we can relate this to living in and with Nature.

All species on this earth have evolved complex ways of understanding their environment through unconsciously reading multiple natural signs and messages; even plants and fungi as mentioned before. Again, reigniting these other sensing abilities may not be as far out of reach as we think, simply because they are a part of our evolutionary nature.

To deepen our awareness of these ancient ways of knowing we can make our more naturally *unconscious* abilities more *conscious*, through practice. As time passes, innate abilities begin to arise more and more effortlessly as we experience Nature by spending more time in natural environments.

My experience with the owl may have been as simple as having great familiarity with the landscape. Although I had not seen an owl along that trail before, I know they live there. Not only because I am a trained field biologist, but because I simply spend a lot of time in certain natural areas. But what is most amazing is that my brain picked up all the other puzzle pieces in the environment more quickly than my critical thinking mind could piece them together. With all these components pieced together, my brain sent me a message of what it could possibly mean. And that is when the word "owl" came into my mind. These are wild abilities we all possess.

Many of our actions today suggest we are not as wise as our classified namesake of *Homo sapiens* "wise humans," deems us to be. But is that really true? Modern humans do tend to undermine the very principles that uphold our existence by holding ourselves in higher regard as productive beings, rather than beings of natural order. In doing so we nearly work ourselves to death in the great race of productivity. We've grown so accustomed to engaging our critical thinking skills to maintain a level of productivity that we don't often embrace our more unconscious inner workings. But . . . we may be wiser than we know.

There are three parts of the human brain that have established themselves over the course of our species' evolution. These three parts of our brain have established multiple interconnections that influence each of the other parts. But while they do not operate independently, it may be worth knowing how they vary from each other.

The R-complex, also known as the reptilian brain, is our oldest brain and is responsible for maintaining homeostasis by controlling the basic autonomic functions such as blood pressure, heart rate, breathing, body temperature and so on. The reptilian brain is often very rigid and compulsive. The reptilian brain also encourages immediate reward processing.

The limbic system is the part of the brain responsible for the fast, subconscious learning and thinking that is critical for survival. This is the part of the brain I find most fascinating.

And finally, our newest part of the brain, the neocortex or neo-mammalian brain, is responsible for non-instinctual processing such as developing language, analytical problem solving, storytelling and self-awareness. Arguably the neocortex is perhaps what has caused us the most trouble in our modern history, as it has given us our extraordinary imagination. In having this ability, we have created all sorts of imaginary things that guide our lives today in the civilized world. Many of which are quite harmful.

According to neuroscientific studies, what the brain perceives consciously is a result of neurons coalescing and firing together in different parts of the brain. These groups of neurons compete with one another, suppressing other groups of neurons, dividing attention resulting in differing perceptions. These collections of neurons fire and wire together where they coalesce. This happens all across the brain. Subliminal messages group together in non-conscious patterns in the brain first before activating conscious processing. An information processing theory suggests unconscious integration precedes conscious awareness.

It is worth knowing that since modern humans favor fostering the traits of the neocortex, which tend to outshine the inner workings of the R-complex and limbic system, we often dismiss the unconscious involuntary processes leading to a false belief that we are always in control of our actions.

It is also worth noting that our three-brain system does not necessarily work well together. This is why we sometimes find ourselves in trouble—forever swinging between our so-called "animal-ness" (our impulsive, wild and free selves) and "human-ness" (our deliberate, rational and abstract thinking selves).

If our more instinctual reptilian brain takes the *front seat,* our conscious thinking abilities attributed to the neocortex can become overpowered, making it difficult to redirect the controlling reptilian brain. When the reptilian brain is fully engaged it can overwhelm the intellect and impair judgement. Therefore, some large public demonstrations intended to be peaceful take a turn for the worst. Small triggers excite the reptilian brain, then suddenly our actions take over. While working simultaneously, the three parts of the brain are competing with each other. This constant opposition lays a framework for much inner conflict. This happens unconsciously, of course. In fact, much of the neural processing occurs beyond conscious awareness, as renowned neuroscientist Heather Berlin points out.

While the neocortex responsible for conscious thought is trying to make sense of the world, the limbic system, sometimes referred to as the "animal brain," may already be several steps ahead in the game. Although we need all three brains to fully function, the limbic system is our ally in establishing a deeper sense of the natural world. Its ability to quickly and unconsciously piece together information in our environment may be the key to feeling a greater kinship to the living world, revealing abilities we never knew we had. This is the wisdom of Nature's intelligence found in all living beings.

While backpacking with my partner in a favorite wilderness, we set up camp in a seemingly random nook in the trees a short distance from the river. Although I couldn't discern any tracks in the sandy, leaf-littered substrate, something about the space made me think that animals might frequently visit—perhaps as a corridor of some kind. I wanted to ensure that a deer or other animal wouldn't come trodding through our sleeping area, so I scattered more of the leaf and twig litter not far from where our feet would be, maybe to sound an alarm of a wandering animal. It was partly experimental and partly intuitive, but I didn't fully understand why I did it. This wilderness is very familiar to me, but something inside told me I should do this on that night.

It was clear and warm, so no tent would be pitched. While sleeping, I thought I heard something. My mind went from deep-sleep-mode to semi-awake. I often hear wandering beings scampering about at night and so I simply brushed aside the sound of something I just *thought* I heard. After a few moments I bolted upright and grabbed my headlamp. I pointed it toward the litter boundary I had made at our feet, and I saw the profile of a retreating lone Mexican gray wolf. It leaped into the forest slightly uphill and to the right of us. My breathing stopped and my senses heightened as I peered into the dark forest with my headlamp. The wolf stopped just beyond the trees, as though trying to make sense of our presence. I could see only the glow of the eyes as they peered back at me from behind a tree—first from one side of the tree trunk and then the other as it turned it's head. With one last turn, the wolf was on its way, disappearing into darkness.

I had for so long wanted to see the wolf in this wilderness. Never did I imagine it would be as close and exciting as this. I stood in the dark forest reflecting on the incredible encounter, knowing it would be an experience I will cherish forever.

Intuition and Instinct

What I had not realized was that I was *reading* Nature after we had selected the camp spot—subconsciously so, but nevertheless the hunch I felt was something real. Just like the owl encounter. Even though there were no discernible tracks or obvious trails to be found among the forest ground, somehow, I *knew* this was a corridor of some kind. Seemingly just a random sliver in the forest of trees, the characteristic of this space "spoke" its truths to me. Little did I know that a part of myself could understand its language.

Sitting, watching, listening, and engaging with Nature, we can come to understand so much more than we ever knew possible. I believe this is how natural intuition is born. It happens subtly and yet profoundly. I still find it difficult to express in words some things I have learned about the nature of Nature simply by immersing myself in the living world. In my desire to remain oriented to this sensing animal mind to know my own world better, I may have been unintentionally exercising the muscle for these lost senses.

I believe we can develop great awareness about the world we live in, and to me that sounds endlessly fascinating. For those who believe or say that it does not come naturally for them to really *feel* these connections, is both unfortunate and untrue. As long as we remain shackled to the "imagined realities" of civilization, we may never be able to rekindle or foster these forgotten abilities—and that seems like a greatly missed opportunity.

There's nothing mystical about these experiences. They are naturally evolved abilities. Even sensing imminent dangers may be within the grasp of the human animal. The fully engaged human animal is just as incredible as any other fully attuned wild animal.

I learned to trust my most primal instincts—to trust this fantastical thing called *intuition*. I truly believe they are one and the same; two sides of one coin. Instead of a "hunch" or a "sixth sense," which may sound too mystical and otherworldly, we could regard these abilities simply as inherent behavior, our *primal intuition*.

~ ~ ~

The fact that you can read and comprehend the words on this page is in itself, astonishing. Yet as the part of the brain capable of comprehending abstract things such as these words is allowed to dominate, another part of the brain rides along in the *back seat*; not as engaged with comprehending what you are reading, but nevertheless understands so much more than we might give credit to in the moment.

While I was developing an understanding about my world as a child, I was literally riding along in the back seat. Although at the time I felt I was also *figuratively* in the back seat and unimportant. I was compiling all kinds of information about our relationship with the natural world, thoughts I felt were worthy of attention and expression, but whenever I *did* express my feelings, they were dismissed and discounted as childish and naive. Maybe because of my young age I hadn't grown as accustomed and involved in the modern things that so entangled the adults in my life. Instead, I was simply a young human animal trying to make sense of my world—a young girl who happened to love Nature and who felt intrinsically threatened by the things that didn't seem to make as much sense as natural things did.

Our forgotten wild senses also operate in the *back seat,* so we don't give them much attention. Yet understanding how this part of the brain works can be our ally in providing the opportunity for us to deepen our intuitive senses.

Brain on Nature

Why do we find the beauty of Nature so alluring? A warm sunrise pouring into a landscape glistening with dew. Vibrant wildflower meadows alive with dancing butterflies. The sight and sounds of a roaring waterfall, and trickling springs with deep green mossy banks. These are just tiny morsels of the delectable sights that nature offers to us. Why is it that so many of us find views of mountains, deep green forests, or turquoise waters so deeply captivating? It may ultimately point to our own evolution, something deeply rooted in our species' unconscious and an inner knowing about where we really belong.

While researching this phenomenon, I spoke with neuropsychologist, Dr. Ian Frampton of Exeter University for some clarity. Dr Frampton's primary research methodologies involve functional neuroimaging as well as clinical evaluations for creating intervention programs for children and young people dealing with health challenges. When we discussed what he has learned about the neurological effects that Nature has on the human brain, the findings were astounding. Frampton's studies involved measuring different kinds of neurological patterns on subjects who were given images of living natural landscapes to look at versus those who were given images of "dead" urbanized landscapes. What Frampton and his team found pointed toward extraordinary evidence that our brains may be hardwired to feel at peace and tranquil in Nature. In the subjects looking at images of natural landscapes, areas of the brain associated with deep calm were highly activated, as though they had entered a state of deep meditation. Conversely, neurological patterns of the brains of those looking at urbanized landscapes were found to be associated with anxiety and confusion, revealing that human brains may be struggling to keep up with the ever-changing landscapes as we turn more toward urbanization.

The findings are incredibly significant given how rapidly *un*natural environments are enveloping us every day across the globe. Only very recently in the history of our species have we fully embraced dead urbanized environments as normal. These neuroimages reveal that these recent changes to our environment lead to harmful, deep-seated feelings of threat, confusion, and angst. Our brains may be signaling "WARNING," perceiving urbanized places as unsafe environments. We are, in fact, still our ancestors, standing on that mountain ridgeline looking down into the miner's village trying to make sense of the world that now restrains us. Whether we are aware of this, urban environments may be stealing our sense of peace, security and belonging, thus fueling a life of unease. Since Nature tends to highlight beneficial aspects of our neurobiology, those who spend more time communing with Nature are likely to be healthier overall.

Even though humans may appear to be adjusted to urbanization, evolutionarily our brains haven't caught up with a more natural or healthy response to such unnatural environments. To our brains, these environments just don't make sense and may actually be harmful for our well-being. The negative consequences of this stimuli may be our brains telling us that we are in danger, or perhaps even endangered, as feelings of insecurity flood our neural networks.

Spending some time observing natural areas without trying to think too much about what you are looking at is all that is takes. This could take place in a nearby park, your yard or your closest woods or mountains — anything that is devoid of manmade minutiae. In fact, Frampton's research revealed our brains to be so sensitive to natural images that even a photograph of Nature can encourage feelings of peace and security. Because of this, Frampton recommends setting your computer's desktop image to a natural one. Knowing just how sensitive our brains are to natural things means we have an opportunity to take back our sense of wellbeing . . . even in our urbanized places. Redesigning our infrastructures by incorporating more natural things such as plants and parks can alleviate the stresses so commonly associated with urban living.

When you find that a sense of peace fills your being, sit with this feeling for a while and recognize the benefit you are receiving. It is an incredible, built-in mechanism designed through our own evolution to feel secure in Nature. We belong in that state as part of the healthy, thriving landscape. This is an environment that supports not only our livelihoods with clean water and air, but our psychological wellbeing as well. I believe when we see a natural and healthy landscape, a deeply rooted knowing tells us that what we are really looking at, is *home*.

Nature's Breath

Several years ago, my dog and I spent a weekend in the foothills of the Organ Mountains located in the Chihuahuan Desert. After hiking for most of the day we scouted for a place to set up camp. As I flung open my tightly rolled tent, my senses were met with an intense forest scent. Not long before this, I had taken a trip into the deep green forests of the San Pedro Wilderness. As the trapped fragrance of spruce, pine and fir were suddenly released from the folds of my tent, an odor-evoked memory transported me to a place of great serenity. I was suddenly in that forest again, though I was now in the desert. It was a magical transportation, and one I will never forget.

That experience reminds me of just how important our sense of smell is for an enriched life as a human being. The impression that forest scent left upon me was one of deep calm. Although the desert has its own set of aromatics, the contrast of being in the desert might have made the forest scent from my tent much more intense.

I can also remember the first time I smelled the Creosote Bush (*Larrea tridentata*), native to the Chihuahuan Desert. I was nearly swept off my feet by its intense, fresh, rain-like aroma. Its uniquely scented profile was like nothing I had ever experienced. It took my breath away. The scent of the Creosote Bush has remained one of my favorite scents of all time.

Much like the trees in the forest, the fragrance of the Creosote Bush results from a combination of volatile oils including terpene, limonene, camphor, methanol and 2-undecanone. Its complex scent is especially intense after a good rain.

It has been discovered that exposure to these kinds of compounds found in Nature can enhance human natural killer cell activity—cells that are responsible for boosting immunity and warding off various forms of cancer. When exposed to natural environments, the stress responses in the body naturally decrease allowing for the formation of greater natural killer cell activity. When exposed to a forest or even lake side environment, these effects have been shown to last for up to a month in the body. With this information, and perhaps because of fewer environmental pollutants as well, we can only speculate that our pre-modern human ancestors may have experienced less cancer. They were also much more physically active, and there was no such thought that being outdoors wasn't normal. It was life.

Inhaling plant terpenes and other compounds that ride along air currents, such as soil bacteria and bacteria that live on water, has shown to boost immune function and reduce stress levels due to a reduction of cortisol. Indoor air today is often very stagnant—*dead*. Or worse, filled with harmful chemicals and artificial fragrances. While humans have a relatively poor sense of smell when compared to other animals, it is still an important sense. In trying to keep my sense of smell acute, whenever I am outdoors, I intentionally try to sniff out things I might not have recognized by scent before. It's a fun and challenging way to get to know a natural space in a different way.

Not only does a room filled with artificial fragrances of candles, perfume, and cleaning products *mask* other potential odors, these chemically manmade scents can be harmful to one's health because of the many toxic chemicals they contain. This is one reason I have eliminated unnaturally scented products in my home.

~ ~ ~

If we were not meant to spend most of our time outdoors, why then would our neurobiology take these cues to boost immune function and beat stress? We belong in the outdoors. Our biology says so. If spending our time in and around Nature weren't so vital to our species, why does it prove to make us so healthy? As more and more sprawling urbanization ensues, we are finding we are losing this aspect of the human-nature experience.

In our world today we need Nature's healing diversity more than ever. Being outdoors is not only good for the soul, but for our physical health as well. More natural space would allow for more healing time in nature. Breathe in those terpenes and other naturally occurring volatile oils wherever and whenever you can. With this in mind, we can transform our cities to be more Nature-centered by planting more native trees and plants in our public spaces.

Many people have a familiar scent that reminds them of home. Usually, this scent is a trademark of a fond childhood memory, place, or person. It could be the aroma of grandpa's pecan cookies, or the unique smell of grandma's house, or even the scent of a special cat's fur. I always loved the way the nape of one of my cats smelled. These biological responses lead me to believe that perhaps we humans have an intrinsic knowing of our ancient home in natural spaces. It certainly makes me speculate: *Why else would these volatile oils found in Nature highlight such beneficial aspects of our neurobiology?*

Our brains' rapid response to scent-based stimuli evolved as a survival mechanism to protect us. Perhaps we feel intrinsically attracted to these places because they have served as our home for more than 95 percent of our human history—places where our ancestors felt secure, for it was everything to them. It is perhaps, in a very primal way, a reminder that wild Nature *is* our home.

3

Lost Natural Inheritances

Seeking to escape the contrived glamor of civilization, I can feel the pressures of dominant culture. But like a wild animal wanting to be set free, I know there is a better way. I think there is a deep sense of this in all of us, although often these feelings manifest in ways we don't fully understand. For myself, there is a deep longing to experience even a glimpse into the world that I know *could* exist—the natural world that used to exist. I long to gaze upon a brilliant night sky like those I have come close to on backcountry adventures—those rich, dark skies our ancestors had known so well, and to see those skies exist free and clear above us today; to experience the real quietness of nature free from unrelenting noise pollution that has stolen so much of Nature's serenity; to walk in natural, self-governed spaces rich with diversity. Places deemed natural today, such as many of our remaining public wildlands, have become overgoverned and overmanaged. Nature has proven time and time again that she is a self-governing force that needs little management from us. She needs only for us to embrace her generous spirit of abundance.

These deep-seated aspirations even follow me into the world of dreams where I have walked pristine wildernesses vibrant with natural song and brimming with deep verdancy. Wildernesses I have experienced in reality, although stunning, have only come close. The hawk, cougar, turtle, and even mountains, have come to speak with me in my dreamworld. They all had a message for me: The hawk encouraged me to follow my inner truth and to lay bare my love of Nature. The cougar voiced an urgent message, telling me that time is of the essence. The turtle reminded me to remain ever curious, and the mountains whispered, take your time and enjoy, there is still so much to explore and discover. These are, of course, deeply personal experiences that I alone can attempt to make sense of. Regardless, the kinship I so deeply feel with the living world is one I simply cannot ignore.

Solitude

It is nearly 6 p.m. and the rest of the crew has left for the weekend. My camp is near the base of Chicoma Peak in mountains considered sacred to the Puebloan peoples. At nearly 9,500 feet, my tent is nestled along the tree line where I am blessed with expansive views, which include views of the mountain's summit. As I eat my dinner, I look out toward the grassy meadow where I notice a lone figure sitting very still. It's a bobcat. At first glance it could easily be mistaken for a tree stump. He sits there, in no hurry to leave, around 200 feet or so from where I am. As he turns and looks about, I find myself captivated by his passive beauty. He begins to walk through the open plain toward the trees where I am camped. He hasn't noticed me. As he walks westward, I begin to quietly walk parallel to him. There is a run of trees between us and periodically I spot him through the trees as I walk. I stop when he stops and continue when he continues. He still hasn't sensed me. He turns slightly and is going to intercept the course ahead of me. He disappears for a moment before emerging on my side of the trees. I stop. Now he is directly ahead of me, no more than 20 feet. I can hardly believe it. He stops, still unaware of my presence, then turns his head toward me. Already crouched, I kneel down even farther, hoping to offer him no threat. We look at one another, frozen in time. I look into his eyes, and he looks into mine. Wonderfully clear markings on his face give him his individuality and are beyond breath-taking. I am awestruck and can barely believe my eyes. After a momentary gaze, he turns, bolts into the forest and disappears. I breathe, smile, and walk back to my camp feeling deeply grateful for the incredible chance to come face to face with the bobcat. My heart is soaring.

Few of us have the privilege to experience a meeting of this kind. Wildlife are not exactly a common sight in most of our daily lives. Aside from sightings of occasional wandering urban wildlife, some people might live out their entire lives never experiencing a wild encounter such as this. Connecting to Nature through experiences of this kind, coming face to face with a wild animal in its natural environment, is in many ways a lost tribute. This very special bobcat encounter took place in the beautiful Jemez Mountains near a site I was working as a restoration biologist, living out of my tent for two seasons. The restoration area was around 2,000 feet below where I was camped. The work was deeply rewarding, enabling me to witness incredible restoration successes in just one season to the next. It was a chance to give back, by nurturing an ecosystem largely damaged by the hand of man. I took the bobcat encounter as a "thank you" from the mountains; a gift for the work I had been a part of.

These experiences are rare in part because of Nature's intelligence. Wild creatures of all kinds have evolved to stealthily avoid all kinds of potential threats, including humans. With keen senses engaged, they are often several steps ahead of us. Another reason is our insistent modern nature to be overly noisy, social creatures. Even though humans are indeed social creatures, we fared better as quieter creatures in pre-historic times. A survival trait on which I will later elaborate.

Solitude in Nature is becoming rare. But when given the opportunity to experience this, one inevitability begins to understand a kind of *oneness* and harmony of things. There comes an inner knowing that we are all bound by the same Earth. Many people today feel an unease in wild places. By being afraid of this kind of solitude, one gives up a fundamental facet of the human animal that our ancient ancestors may have been able to master.

When we embrace solitude in nature, we come to understand that one can never be alone. We exist only as part of everything else. There is no "self," just all that is in the greater symbiosis of life on Earth. We could not *be* without the rivers, oceans, mountains and all the elements that make us who we are.

When in wild isolation, I do not feel isolated at all. But in the city, I feel very much alone. Where forests, animals and native earth are replaced with inanimate things such as concrete, asphalt, buildings, and lights, I feel quite lonely.

These are all dead things to me; not real. I miss the *alive*ness of the forest, mountains, or deserts—where the *real* things are. Not a single day passes that I do not long to be in the mountains or forests. It is only in these places where I feel most aware and most *alive*. The term "isolation" implies being away from one's own kind, not necessarily from all else. Sometimes we are fortunate enough to be out with others who are equally aligned with that which surrounds us, but not often. I sometimes backpack with my dog, though in the backcountry I prefer to be alone. I adore my four-legged companion immensely, but I know there are things I can experience in wild places without her. In times when I do backpack with my dog, I simply accept the fact that it will be a different kind of backcountry experience. No less enjoyable, just different. Although I have seen plenty of wildlife with my small companion at my side, I expect I would have seen even more if I had been hiking alone. I know this because she is nearly as inquisitive as I, which has led to many missed opportunities. Just as soon as I steer my attention to, let's say a butterfly on the trunk of a tree, picking up on my curious excitement she will soon be nose-first into whatever has my interest. But this is also another reason why I love her so much. We are very much in tune with one another. When I stop, she stops. When I'm looking about, she looks about. When I try to sniff out something, she does the same. This deeply attuned relationship has its advantages as well as disadvantages.

Once, while hiking deep into the forest with my dog, I was able to get a good look at a foraging black bear up ahead of us. Because my dog has a low profile and habitually trails right behind me on longer hikes such as this one, she had not yet noticed the bear and the bear hadn't noticed her. I paused, which caused my dog to also pause. She stood behind me while I got a good look at the bear in the woods ahead of me. A short while passed before the foraging bear became aware of my presence and retreated. Because of the thick brush, my dog didn't get to witness the bear visually—only by scent when we later traversed through where the bear had been.

Although domesticated wolves and their descendants have been our traveling companions for nearly 20,000 years, they are still often a discord upon the rhythms of Nature. In wild places, Nature operates in attunement with all else. Nature behaves sensibly. Unfortunately, our domesticated companions do not. Opportunities to get a deeper glimpse into wild animal behavior is greatly reduced when we take along our domesticated friends. To be able to witness and gain a deeper sense of what makes up wild Nature, we must brave the deep, dark, and lovely woods alone and embrace solitude.

By embracing wild solitude, I was able to have that beautiful chance encounter with the bobcat. The heightened awareness that both the bobcat and I experienced while looking into each other's eyes, is a special and rare thing. No words are sufficient to describe how meaningful that encounter was to me. The memory remains as alive within me today as when it occurred.

~ ~ ~

Not only do wildlife possess incredible sensing abilities, they live their wild lives dependent upon these abilities, sensing things we may not be able to. Wildlife are often well aware of our presence before our paths cross. Most humans simply lack a degree of grace when walking through wild spaces that perhaps our ancestors had known how to do. Wildlife sense this lack of grace by the sound of our discordant, bipedal footsteps. Although I have tried, I cannot walk as gracefully as a fox, no matter how hard I try. Wildlife can also pick up our scent long before we have a chance to intercept their paths.

Oftentimes when people enter wild places they do so with other people, which inevitably causes them to create much unnecessary noise. Sometimes people do this intentionally for fear of wild things. I have often witnessed this. Sometimes people even pass me without realizing my presence because they are so caught up in trying to *ward off* wild things. But in reality, their awareness becomes deadened by inattentiveness. If they were quieter, they might have been able to sense my presence.

Solitude can help us read between the lines of the written stories of Nature and recognize the underappreciated and often-missed aspects of Nature. What is the language of the animals, trees, rocks, plants, soil, or sky? Or the rivers, forests, mountains, or even the Earth itself? *Does Nature have a language?* Learning to understand this language requires active vigilance. It is the lifesong dance that we can listen to and observe with our normal senses as well as with our deeper intuitive senses.

Solitude has helped me see things I wouldn't have been able to had I been dampening my awareness with noise. At times, it seems the language of Nature can only be understood in times of solitude, simply because solitude seems to allow one to fully engage their senses. The world literally opens up for us. There is a natural phenomenon that occurs when one silently sits in solitude in Nature. The dance of life begins to ensue as birds, squirrels and other animals re-emerge from behind the curtains of Nature—what Tristan Gooley calls *the return*. This occurrence is Nature's rhythm of life dance playing out.

One reason I believe I was able to have the incredible bobcat encounter is because I was careful to remain in alignment with Nature's rhythm as much as possible. In the moment, I tried my best to subdue the rush I felt flowing through my body so as not to give off strong energies of excitement. It wasn't until afterward that I allowed my heart to swoon in pure delight for the chance to peer into that face—into those eyes and soul of the wild. This attunement gifted me perhaps a once-in-a-lifetime experience. These are the moments in which I can't help but feel truly alive. This is the gift solitude can give us; with our senses heightened, we become aware of our breathing and heartbeats. A truly exhilarating aspect of being a human animal.

~ ~ ~

I would like to end this section on solitude with one of my favorite passages:

"In secluded forests, those places where the [enlightened ones and wise teachers] of the past found tranquility, there is nothing to make you busy, no distractions, no commerce, no fields to be worked, no childish friends. Birds and wild deer are easy companions; spring water and leaves provide good ascetic fare. Awareness is naturally clear, and ascetic concentration develops by itself. Without enemies, without friends you can be free from the chains of attachment and hatred . . .

In the perfect secluded place, deep in the mountains, everything one does is good. Even without your making any diligent efforts to practice, in such places disillusionment with [dualistic, worldly realities], determination to be free from it, love, compassion and all the other excellent qualities of the path (of non-dualistic truth) will arise spontaneously. As a result, your whole away of life can only be wholesome . . . simply because you are now in solitude . . ."

— Patrul Rinpoche,

Words of My Perfect Teacher

Around the Hearth

It is widely known that the use of tools provided our species with a greater evolutionary advantage for survival. Some might even say an almost unfair advantage. One of the tools we have utilized for the betterment of our lives has benefited us in a very unexpected way. That tool is *fire* — perhaps the most essential tool Nature has given us. Interestingly, Nature too utilizes fire to maintain homeostasis and promote life.

It is estimated our species domesticated fire nearly 800,000 years ago. The use of fire seems to stand exceptionally apart from most other tools we made use of for survival. For one thing, fire has always existed as part of Nature. We did not invent fire; it was shown to us by Nature. We only learned to control it, or rather contain it, to illuminate, cook, clear landscapes, and provide warmth. Whether by accident or observation, we learned how nature ignites fire from friction — we simply recreated the act in a conscious, more deliberate way.

One of my personal favorite pastimes is sitting around a campfire under a starry night sky. I love every aspect of it: finding the perfect location; starting the fire; building and tending it; enjoying its warmth, hypnotic glow, lively dance, and crackling song. I also really like the smell of campfire smoke, when it is not directly in my face, of course. I often refer to the scent of campfire smoke as my favorite natural incense and love how it permeates my gear. It is an all-around feel-good, relaxing activity for me.

I had no idea at the time that researchers have studied the relaxing effects hearth and campfires have on human brains. Turns out, when exposed to all the components of a fire, the *crackling sounds, light, warmth,* and *smell,* one experiences enhanced relaxation, lower blood pressure and increased sociability. Researchers compared the physiological effects of the multiple variables that make up a fire. They found that people tended to be calmer and behaved more tolerably during fireside interactions. But not so when one or more of the components were missing, like say those charming crackling sounds, which might be missing in an electric faux fireplace heater. The hypnotic effect fire seems to have on us is just one physiological effect of being fireside. As our bodies enter a more relaxed mode it may also produce a decrease in blood pressure. Research suggests that fire-watching may have even influenced the evolution of our brains. As we spent more time mesmerized by flickering flames, we may have been inadvertently entering meditative-like states. This state allows us to think more clearly, improve memory, make more conscientious plans, and inspire new ideas. It's wild to think about. Fire watching as a practice our ancestors took part in may have made us better thinkers by altering regions in the brain. And because the smarter, good-humored person with a more peaceful disposition would have been better tolerated and more mate-worthy, this alteration in the brain would have more likely been passed on to future generations.

Many of the effects from being fireside remain apparent today. Being fireside is analogous with creating an atmosphere of togetherness, so we tend to create gathering spaces around fires. Fire has played a profound role throughout the entire course of our species' existence. Fireside exposure may affect you in subtle ways you don't even realize. Some people might relate the scent of hearth-smoke to fond memories of their grandmother or other relative cooking on a wood-burning stove. It was common for humanity to commune around and cook on fire for much of human history. Gathering around the hearth then was as common as perhaps curling up on the sofa with a blanket, a warm cup of tea, or a book is today. It is a practice that runs deep in the memory of our species.

Soil

The world beneath our feet is comprised of a community of billions of diverse microorganisms and organisms. These organisms have evolved alongside one another for millions of years, creating a living matrix of nutrients and substrate. It is this matrix that breathes life to the world above . . . our world. All that we know and love thrives upon this matrix of living organisms. In fact, entire ecosystems and civilizations were built from this matrix. The world, of which we are a part, would cease to exist without it. This matrix is soil.

We only understand a fraction about this crucial natural component. Basic knowledge about how healthy soils rich with microbial life nurture the very plants we eat still somehow fail to convince us to change the ways we modern humans ultimately treat the living breathing matrix beneath our feet. In this gross lack of understanding we spend billions of dollars on pesticides, herbicides, and fungicides, thus compromising that which directly sustains us. For when every beneficial microorganism, insect and bird is killed by the application of these poisons, surely we will find that our own lives will also come to an end. Of course, we wouldn't let this happen. We wouldn't allow the world to come to that. *Would we?* We may already have.

The state of our soil's composition will ultimately determine the course of our future. Since the abandonment of our nomadic way of life and due to the crude misunderstanding of the role soil plays in our lives, much of our earth's soil has experienced severe degradation. As we carry out our modern lives centered around enterprises that survive from deforestation and mega-agriculture, we continue to endanger this crucial life sustaining component in tremendous ways. Truly healthy soil is alive, and just as with any other living thing, when we compromise the living soil component, we influence the chain of interdependent life sustaining components associated with it. As a finite resource, the misuse and abuse of our soils could ultimately cost us our very own existence.

A startling estimation reveals that nearly 33% of the world's land surface has experienced a loss of natural topsoil due to poor farming practices, wetland draining, and forest clearing. This includes nearly all of the United States. These practices have led to the severe depletion of nutrients, erosion, over compaction, and contamination. Today, as native forestlands continue to be cleared for agriculture at unprecedented rates, the unremitting erosion of healthy soils shows no signs of stopping—leading to a distressing trend of desertification. In fact, desertification is the most prevalent and critical global issue humans will have to face if trends are not reversed. It is estimated that over two billion people live in drylands, most of which are man-caused deserts created over many decades of misusing and abusing the earth.

Although ocean levels are rising, this water is unavailable to us. By establishing regionally appropriate plants we can help secure inland fresh water sources. Establishing crops and other plants that do not naturally fare well in some regions stresses the demand for water for both humans and plant life. Plant re-establishment and restoration of abused lands is a gradual process, but ground-covering plants, apart from unnatural lawn grasses, are our allies in creating and nourishing soil, *and* for freshwater security. "Leave no land bare" is an excellent motto to live by. Areas of bareness or soil-free zones are entry points for erosion and flooding that can undermine entire ecosystems, thereby contributing to more soil loss.

Since it takes anywhere from 100 to 500 years to build just one inch of topsoil naturally, depending on different environmental variables, on a large scale it is estimated to take around *two centuries* for soils that have been degraded in North America to regain healthy pre-Columbian soil levels. For regions with even more degradation, it could take longer. This would require an unwavering diligence of restoration efforts. The sad reality is, nearly all civilizations across the globe live in ways that compromise their soils, rather than regeneratively caring for their soils. However, India and China are leading in massive reforestation and greening efforts. This is incredibly encouraging and are excellent examples of how we can create change when policies change. With greater green zones on Earth, we allow trees to store carbon in wood and roots, *creating* more soil in the process. In fact, when we plant plants, our goal should not be to solely plant plants, but *to create healthy soil.*

Soil itself can store three times more carbon than forests. Given the substantial value of soil, it is clear that we must restore this crucial element.

~ ~ ~

The components required for soil life have been distributed throughout our earth's crust over millions of years of geologic and biologic processes. The development of particle debris that make up soil's most basic composition is called weathering. Shifting tectonic plates, wind, rain, rivers, and other waterbody influences cause rock to ultimately break down. Mosses and lichen growing on top of rocks also contribute to the breaking down of rock material. Over vast geologic time, the cumulation of these weathering processes created a suitable environment within our earth's crust for which we, and all living beings, have had the privilege to evolve and thrive upon. While soil gets some of its bulk from broken down rock, this life-giving matrix is also a matrix of *life* itself that depends upon a reciprocal relationship with the life it supports. That life includes us and all other living organisms.

Truly native earth is made up of a diversity of organisms including plant roots, intricate webs of subterranean fungi, bacteria, protozoa, invertebrates, nematodes, and minerals. The sheer amount of soil biota found naturally in healthy soil is almost inconceivable. Tens of thousands of microorganisms can be found in just a single gram of healthy soil, and microorganisms numbering more than the human global population can be found in a single teaspoon of dirt. The pure complexity of life within soil is what gives this underrated resource its resiliency against deterioration from both natural and unnatural forces. The more diversity of microorganisms, the healthier the soil. And since healthier soils retain more moisture, healthier soils can help to resist the effects of drought and other influences of extreme weather. Drought-resisting soils can also resist erosion form harsh winds, fast moving currents and rain. In a world that is becoming drier and more fire-prone, it is important to recognize that healthier soils can increase the fire resiliency of the world's forests and grasslands as well. Soil *is* sustenance, not only for us, but for the Earth itself. And as we lead our lives more and more distanced from Nature, the health of our soils is deteriorating at terribly alarming rates.

~ ~ ~

Since the birth of agriculture, humans have been defined as rulers of the earth. If not through cognitive thought, humanity's battle to control and manipulate the earth speaks for itself. As humans reoriented away from the laws of Nature, we gradually began to lose perspective about the realities from which humans were once inseparable. The distinction between humans versus wild Nature soon became the newly ingrained paradox by which humans led their lives. This realignment with newly invented conveniences blurred our understanding of humanity's once unshakeable sense of place within the natural world. The disconnect and manipulation of the earth bred a new way of life, aligned with fabricated principles instead of our once fully innate biologically driven ways of subsisting from the earth just as it was. Thus, the sedentary life of early agriculturalists paved and plowed the way to an unfathomable modern world riddled with ailments.

An often-overlooked culprit for poorer human health is our massively genetically modified diet that is made up of mono-culturally grown foods designed simply for increased yields and larger-sized produce. While this ongoing *Frankensteinian* breeding accomplishes goals of supersizing our produce, evident by the enormous (and often tasteless) tomatoes found so readily in our supermarket produce aisles, the practice comes at a cost. As tomatoes doubled or even quadrupled in size after each succession of breeding faster-growing, more pest-resistant varieties, nutrient levels dropped. In addition to this, mounting evidence has found that plants experience a further depletion of nutrients as carbon dioxide levels continue to rise due to modern human activity. When grown naturally in healthy soils free from pesticides and chemical fertilizers, plants are better at maintaining their levels of nutrients and antioxidants. When plant varieties are left to deal with pests and natural threats by their own defense systems, they establish themselves in areas more favorable to their species. In the end they are stronger, more adaptable varieties. Many of these same properties contribute to their higher nutrient value. In genetically modified varieties of plants, these natural defenses are often diminished, leaving plants more vulnerable to threats such as droughts, pests, or diseases. Consider wild blueberries vs. GMO blueberries that we see in stores. The variety in stores are less nutrient-dense and often less tasty than the flavorsome wild blueberries. Wild blueberries are also less likely to be exposed to excess pesticides and have been grown in thriving and diverse soils. Given the evidence, it would seem any fruits or vegetables grown in healthier conditions devoid of such chemicals would be healthier for us. To change the trend of soil nutrient depletion and erosion, we must now do what so many profit-oriented lobbyists would consider as radical: *free our soils* from the onslaught of chemical fertilizers, herbicides, fungicides, and pesticides and eat those small or "ugly" tomatoes. I promise you, they are superior in flavor, and *flavor = nutrients*.

Since nutrient-depleting practices have become normalized, the foods that are meant to sustain us contain fewer nutrients than ever before. But while the intake of nutritious food is indeed crucial for a healthy existence, we should also consider the nutrients we humans and other animals need to thrive that extend beyond the simple ingestion of the food. In our *separatist* views of Nature, we often overlook many other sources of sustenance necessary for healthy life. Many of the ailments that plague modern life could be avoided by reintroducing the other naturally existing sources of "nutrients" our ancient ancestors thrived upon, such as sunshine, exposure to clean air, and those remarkable antibacterial, antifungal *phytoncides*—nutrients we can only gain from interacting with Nature.

Regular exposure to healthy soil is another "nutrient of life" in which we are severely deprived. Biota-rich, healthy native soil comes loaded with the microbes that have been found to boost moods, fight cancer, and even boost our immune systems by affecting our gut similarly to the action of probiotics. The aroma that arises from such rich soils is produced by different kinds of naturally occurring bacteria. The inhalation of these aromatic compounds is found to have effects comparable to those of antidepressants by stimulating the production of serotonin, which tends to make people feel more relaxed and happier. The aroma that arises from terpenes found within the bark of mature trees has also been found to have relaxing effects on the brain. One soil bacterium being studied for its natural anti-depressive, anti-anxiety and even anti-inflammatory effects is called *Mycobacterium vaccae*. It is quite possible that many more strains of soil bacteria produce similar effects, and they are being investigated for their potential to improve cognitive function, rheumatoid arthritis, and Crohn's disease.

As a consequence of depleted soil biota, our inner ecosystems, or gut biomes, have also experienced an imbalance due to an excess of harmful bacteria that outcompete our beneficial gut bacteria. With so many people opting to reach for over-the-counter supplements and probiotics to treat and manage their gastrointestinal issues, it is remarkable that these disorders could easily be avoided by simply eating a varied diet of fiber and nutrient-dense fruits and vegetables. This is because processed foods can't even compete to nurturing us in the same way, lacking the nutrient profile of naturally grown fruits and vegetables. When food comes into the world grown in rich, diversified soils teeming with billions of life-giving microbes, the food will be inherently good for you and arguably more flavorful. How could it not be? It is the way we obtained our nutrients for 95 percent of our human history.

By simply playing in Nature, exposing ourselves to living soils, we could benefit from these beneficial microbes and experience better gut health. Spending regular time in Nature makes you healthier from the inside out. Not only does our sustenance in the form of food come from the soil—soil *is* ultimately our sustenance.

The Barefoot Human

Modern idealism denies us many of the things once inherent to our existence, and touching the earth is one of those things. Many of us will spend most of our lives having never really touched the native earth. Something as basic as letting our feet touch the native ground is routinely avoided without thought by the countless barriers placed between the soles of our feet and the earth. Despite what we might think, when we *do* go barefoot, we rarely touch *native* earth. As the world continues to grow in an abnormal fashion, we find ourselves bound to not only a world of artificial earth-covering barriers, but serious alterations of the natural earth itself. These countless man-made barriers are designed by today's modern standards to insulate ourselves *from* the earth and Nature—from the shoes we wear to various types of flooring, and to dead, overly abused degraded natural ground. Sprawling urbanization isn't helping as our disconnect continues to fuel societal norms. While some of us may spend a good portion of our time barefoot on surfaces deemed "natural," such as green lawns, these too are man-made and can be quite harmful, as they are often sprayed with harmful pesticides.

One winter I took a short midday walk, deciding to leave my shoes behind. The graveled ground of the driveway felt unbearable to the soles of my tender feet. The coldness of the wintry day added to the discomfort of the jagged rocks. Not wanting to feel limited, I continued walking until I could bear it no longer. As I walked back toward my home, I recalled just how much more physically resilient I seemed to be as a child, barefoot and playing outdoors.

Feeling burdened by the limitation, I decided from that point I would walk barefoot every day, no matter what. Gradually I became reaccustomed to the earth beneath my feet. But it took some time. I can even recall being able to run over gravel as a child. What made me so sensitive now? There were many reasons I wanted to regain my barefoot-walking abilities. For one thing, it *feels* good and is incredibly freeing. I live in a transition ecozone, somewhere between desert and forest, in an area that is typically very arid. Most of the natural ground I walk upon might be considered quite formidable to most, although it truly isn't. It took a few months of easing into it, but now I am even able to hike barefoot. There are many benefits of walking barefoot. For me, I wanted to *feel* my resilience in being able to do so, even in the desert. Also, it was a way for me to honor the Native ground upon which we all live—and owe our lives.

As the soles of my feet grew stronger, walks in the native yard turned into walks in the Native lands surrounding the property where I lived, and eventually into longer and longer hikes. Barefoot walking has taught me much more about the natural world than I would have thought. I have learned to observe and respect the limitations of my feet, but also how strong they can be. I have learned more about what "earth" really is and the differences between just "ground" and *Native ground*. I have learned how comfortable it is to walk on Native earth and how *un*comfortable and displeasing it is to walk on ever-pervasive concrete and asphalt, which I tend to avoid.

Unexpectedly, walking barefoot taught me about a particular native grass growing near my home that I had never before identified, the Purple Three-Awn (*Aristide purpurea*). The Purple Three-Awn is most stunning during springtime when you can see the still soft reddish-purple fronds' seedheads swaying with the wind. I learned of the Purple Three-Awn when I quite literally stepped into it. The native grass had gone to seed, and the seeds were prolific and quite conspicuous to the strong, yet still sensitive soles of my feet and I remember discovering several seedheads clinging to my long dress as I walked. Its name describes its seeds perfectly. The sewing needle-thin cylindrical seedhead is approximately a centimeter and a half in length with a tiny triangular barb on one end and three long equally distanced awns that fan out equally perpendicular to the seed on the other. It is a beautiful native grass I have now come to appreciate more than ever. The experience of stepping into the Purple Three-Awn gifted me a bit more understanding of the world in which I am living, and with each additional morsel I learn more about my world, and the more connected I feel to it.

I have also learned how the earth beneath my feet transforms with the changing seasons and after varying types of weather. I quite enjoy walking across the Native earth after a ground's frost has thawed, where crystallized frost expands the earth, fluffing the upper substrate after remaining moisture is wicked away. Walking upon pillowy earth leaves behind perfect footprints.

Something interesting when becoming accustomed to barefoot walking; even though your soles become stronger and tougher, one can still feel the earth with great sensitivity. You can literally read the earth with your feet. You may be able to walk upon rocks, sticks and other natural debris, but your body will still maintain enough tactile sensitivities necessary to keep you safe and aware.

Walking barefoot slows your pace naturally, giving you more time to take in and appreciate your surroundings. It is a practice I have adopted indefinitely; an experience that has nurtured a new kind of resiliency, a natural ability that we human animals have largely abandoned. I now *long* for more time in which my feet are in contact with Native ground, dreading having to wear shoes for longer than is necessary. I am enjoying the time I spend literally walking on this Earth.

A long time ago while camping in a forest, I found myself relaxing into the serenity that comes from being among the trees. Deep breaths came easily, and I was undoubtedly smiling broadly, thinking of how close to *home* I was feeling. I began softening into my surroundings when the dreamy spell was broken. Far above the tree canopy within the clouds, the noise of an airplane's engine crept its way into my peaceful experience. Taken aback by such intrusiveness, my thoughts reoriented themselves toward a new present. Naively, I thought I had escaped civilized nonsense, but the continued rumbling quickly laid that notion to rest. I was young and did not fully understand the true extent of modernity's noisy intrusiveness. Probably due to my irritation, the noise seemed to linger longer than necessary, threatening my serenity as I could not run away. It was the first time I gained a realization of the senseless noise we humans have thrust upon the Natural world. Since then, I have been on a personal quest for true peacefulness. When blessed with moments of quiet, I take notice, deeply grateful for these moments that are now a rarity.

From the time of my abrupt awakening to the pervasiveness of modern noise, I have often imagined how our prehistoric ancestors might have reacted to such an unearthly roaring beast. The blasting roar of an aircraft engine would undoubtedly cause them great angst. Noises so loud and unnatural emanating from the great beyond would not only have caused our ancestors great distress, but the wildlife would surely have found the noise outright terrifying. Those noises are now pervasive all day, every day. And for most of us, this intrusiveness is the consequence of our greatly affluent modern existence, over which we have no individual power. Whereas our premodern world experienced periods of *shutting down*, modern existence runs perpetually . . . logged on and powered up.

Sound tracker and acoustic ecologist Gordon Hempton is concerned that "silence is an endangered species on the verge of extinction." Gordon's definition of silence is actual, true presence—presence of the living Earth and all her living systems; from birdsong to crashing ocean waves. When seeking silence, Gordon clarifies that he is not seeking the absence of sound, but rather the absence of *noise*. He points out that our extraordinary need for silence is as necessary as our need for clean water and starry skies, and that "by listening to natural silence, we feel connected to the land, to our evolutionary past, and to ourselves." Gordon also points out that efforts to preserve silence are basically non-existent. His work in capturing natural sounds is meant to inspire the preservation of quiet places, "places without human-made sounds." While we are aware of efforts to protect wilderness areas, we often fail to think of natural silence as part of the natural character of wilderness.

We humans, despite our social nature, are meant to be quiet creatures and active listeners. If we were not, our hunting ancestors might have scared off their prey while potentially inviting larger, more threatening predators. This would have reduced their chances of eating a meal and increased their chances of *becoming* the meal. When we fill our space with unnecessary noise, we can become more mindless and more vulnerable. Our awareness of the happenings around us is deadened. A flood of unnatural noises in our environment prevents us from hearing the real-time stories that are being told in Nature all around us. We end up missing a great deal more than we realize—we miss an element of who we are. Humans have had no other choice than to develop deep listening skills not just for hunting, but for avoiding dangerous situations.

Wildlife are phenomenal listeners. Deer need to hear if potential predators are around while they graze. They do this by not only tuning into predator sounds directly, but to other cues in their environment as well. A chipmunk might sound the alarm from the trees, causing a deer to bolt off to a safer location. Wild animals live in full awareness of their kinship to the rest of the natural world. Their lives depend upon it.

Listening to our surroundings has been crucial for our species' survival, yet in the modern world we have grown so accustomed to senseless background noise that we end up not hearing anything at all. I often feel great angst and a deep urge to run away when I hear a cacophony of unnatural noises in my environment. Biologically this makes sense. Sounds in our environment can be a sign of danger as well. And perhaps, because I spend much of my time avoiding unnatural sounds, the many sounds associated with normal modern life have become almost unbearable, triggering a signal in my brain of *"This isn't natural. Threat! Run away."* This, I learned, is a normal biological response for our species.

To someone living in a bustling city, the forest might seem dead quiet. *Too* quiet, even though it is bustling with natural activity. We just have not sharpened our listening skills enough to hear it. Not only are we not practicing active listening skills, in many cases we are losing our hearing ability altogether. As we are berated by the many noisy things in our lives, we are an *animal* prone to losing this important, natural, life-sustaining sense if we are not careful to protect what hearing we still have.

Human inner-ear hair cells did not evolve to withstand such intense decibels, and at long-lasting durations. For many, loud noises are considered part of normal life, but we did not evolve to live in such noisy environments. Today, things like bathroom hand dryers in schools and earbuds are causing premature damage to the hearing of children. Many adults are afflicted with tinnitus a form of hearing loss, which can be caused by hearing loss from exposure to loud sounds.

A new informational bulletin of the *Occupational Safety and Health Administration* has even declared that exposure to ototoxic chemicals can cause damage to hearing. Exposure to chemicals commonly found in both household and industrial products including fumes from pesticides, paints, varnishes, carpet cleaners, gasoline, plastics, vehicles, cigarette smoke and more have been found to damage inner ear cells that lead to hearing loss. This combined with exposure to loud noises increase chances of hearing damage.

The constant ringing in the ears (tinnitus) caused my hearing damage, can drown out higher pitched sounds in nature, like bird and insect calls. While it *is* normal to lose some frequencies as we age, the hearing damage we are experiencing today is often prematurely self-inflicted, hastening our hearing loss.

If we manage to protect and maintain good hearing over the course of our lifetime, we are at an advantage. The human animal is still capable of deep listening, much like our ancestors. Our ears are for listening—to navigate and locate life-sustaining resources in our environment. Sound is Nature's way of describing the character of a habitat or landscape even before one can see it. We have been attuned to this life-preserving ability for hundreds of thousands of years to recognize which environments can give and sustain life. For where life itself is bustling with *natural* song, life-giving resources can be found.

Dark Night Skies

While backpacking in the desert surrounded by stunning desert mountains, I came close to witnessing the universe through the eyes of our ancestors. The hillsides were decorated with majestic and sacred Saguaro, Prickly Pear and Jumping Cholla. Warm colors danced across their bodies as the sun barely kissed the horizon; and when cast just right, the Chollas glowed with an alien-like aura. My camp rested along a ridge nestled among these unique cactus beings where I could catch the sun's last rays of light. Nighttime temperatures were warm and comfortable, so no tent was necessary. After evening camp chores were done, I cozied into my sleeping bag and melted into the landscape as I fell asleep. Midnight restlessness stirred an awareness as I woke to an impressive open sky of stars. My breath was snatched away in the presence of the pure awesomeness of space above me. For a moment, as if I were star-light itself, I felt as though I was no longer even corporeal. When my consciousness returned to the ground where I was standing, I gazed in the amazement of what I was so blessed to be witnessing.

In many wilderness adventures I have come close to viewing the universe in this way, through near-natural, dark skies. Yet even in places where we believe we are seeing unpolluted night skies, we do not come close to the natural darkness our ancestors had known. I often wish for the opportunity to see what my ancestors saw when they looked up into the universe—to feel what they must have felt. For them to stumble out of a cave dwelling mid-night, might have felt to us like stepping directly into the cosmos. Only my imagination can say.

As it is for many, stargazing was a natural childhood pastime of mine. I don't remember ever being told to look up into the universe. It is yet another thing that comes naturally to the young human heart. Stars have been the trusted allies of our ancestors for millennia, utilized as aids for navigation and as natural nightlights, knowing the stars as well as they knew Nature itself—as extensions of themselves. Many ancient dwellings were built oriented to celestial cycles. The eastern wall of the Kin Klesto house of the ancient Chaco Canyon ruins provided observation points for predicting and determining winter solstice sunrise. Many of our ancestors would likely find themselves utterly lost, both literally and perhaps existentially, in the modern world of artificial lighting.

Biophobia has led to an abandonment of the natural heritage of purely dark nights. All terrestrial and even aquatic life that evolved alongside unpolluted, naturally dark skies for many millions of years existed as part of the stars themselves. The stars were simply a part of their world, as much as the sun was.

Irrational fears of darkness have led us to the excessive use of artificial illumination that we see so widely used today. Though many believe themselves to be, we are not meant to be night owls, reveling in artificial lighting. Many beings that have evolved alongside natural darkness, including our own kind, depended upon the dark to survive. Not only do human beings pay the price of lost natural darkness, but by altering evolved biological rhythms, artificial lighting endangers countless organisms and ecosystems worldwide. Nocturnal animals rely on this rhythm for successful breeding and hunting. Many of our avian kin rely on starlight and moonlight for navigation during their migratory journeys. Artificial lights have been shown to alter bird migration patterns, causing them to migrate either too early or too late, threatening their chances in securing proper nesting and foraging sites. The cost of this is their overall species survival.

We humans are not exempt from damaging effects of light pollution. Today a staggering 83 percent of the world's human population live under light-polluted skies. Humans rely on the circadian rhythm to stimulate the production of the hormone melatonin. Without a natural production of melatonin, our immune systems suffer, making us more prone to sickness. Cholesterol can also rise to unhealthy levels, and organs responsible for hormone balance and regulation including the thyroid, pancreas, adrenal glands, testes, and ovaries can malfunction from stepping out of circadian balance.

The fact that light pollution is affecting our mental health as well is something in which many of us can relate. Anyone who has experienced how irritating a neighbor's security light can be when its glow floods your room through the window while you are trying to sleep can say just how disturbing lights can be to our well-being. Yet there are few if any ordinances in place that can prevent your neighbor from erecting excessive outdoor lighting. The only thing in your power, according to many municipalities, is to take it upon yourself to prevent the light from entering your space with say, heavy blackout curtains. It falls on *your* actions to rectify the situation, not your neighbor's. If this sounds unfair, it is. Try reaching out to your local county office and you'll find you have little say in these matters.

When surrounded by excessive light and noise, I feel an acute sense of disconnection from my living world. On one occasion when I was living in an area many would consider quite dark and remote, my dog needed to go out in the middle of the night. Instead of encountering deep natural darkness outside, I was met with a space flooded by security lights from neighboring properties and streetlights strung out along the horizon. I felt disoriented as I watched my dog disappear into the foggy haze of lights to find a place to pee. I squatted and ducked to try to put the lights behind the horizon of the otherwise natural landscape so I could see better, but while walking I felt nearly blindfolded.

It is important to note that there were not hundreds of lights; it only takes a few, or even just one, in the right (or rather wrong) place to cause this effect. I felt frustratingly disoriented. For one who communes with Nature regularly, the sense of disconnect is deep and real. The modern shroud of artificiality blankets us from experiencing what is real. It takes away our humanness as we live in perpetual disorientation.

Deemed as safety devices for our communities, it has been shown that excessive lighting makes places *less* safe. My blindsiding experiences of lighting can attest to this with certainty. How could one protect themselves if they cannot see? Lighting technology simply has reached a point in its development where it is no longer used simply for lighting our paths, but rather as security gimmicks. We spend of a lot of money on lighting to pacify our irrational fears of darkness.

Have you ever noticed how blinding those newer LED vehicle headlights are when facing them head-on? It is not a safety feature when it causes you to shield your eyes as you drive. They seem dangerously counterproductive.

Amid the COVID-19 pandemic, the Department of Transportation in my state was urged to keep people employed. In the area where I am currently living, they quickly mobilized to install and erect 89 massively oversized light posts along a mile and a half stretch of a once naturally scenic highway that borders wild areas with prime dark skies. The most persuasive argument for the construction was the proposed bike path that connects two distant neighborhoods along the otherwise potentially dangerous-for-bicyclists highway. The bike path would provide one neighborhood with access to a grocery store—which sounds great, considering one of the two neighborhoods is without this luxury. But instead of solely installing a bike path with reasonable path-illuminating lights, there is now light from streetlights overlapping bike path lights. This redundancy is a testament to inconsiderate planning that has led to an irritating outcome and wasted resources. One doesn't need to be a lighting specialist to see just how ridiculously excessive the installation is.

Similarly, in a city where I once lived, there is a centrally located "Nature Preserve" where people can hike and learn about some of the native plants and wildlife. While the area is not spectacularly sized, it still offered the community a chance to get outdoors in a mostly natural and native landscape. I lived in the neighborhood nearest to the preserve, and it was a space I frequently walked. On a nearly daily basis, I saw native wildlife within and around the preserve, including Gambel's quail, roadrunners, lizards, coyotes, gopher snakes, Scaled quail, Mourning Dove, gray foxes, bats, owls and more. But since then, a walking/biking path has been constructed that borders the perimeter of one side of the preserve. With that, as you may have guessed, several oversized light posts were also installed. The lights are incredibly bright and can almost be compared to stadium lights. They shine all night long into the nature park situated directly beside and below. It made me wonder: *Can the park even be considered a Nature Preserve anymore?* It didn't seem it could, since shining artificial lighting into a native ecosystem directly endangers the native wildlife and plants that forage, hunt and grow there.

The saddest part is that these measures are rarely fought to be *undone*. Once they are allowed to be installed, they will likely remain for as long as humanity stays around to power them. Unless, perhaps, we find our way back to our senses by realizing just how harmful artificial lighting is to us as well as to our local wild spaces and wildlife. The unfortunate trend of increasing light pollution seems to spell disaster for the future of both human and planetary health.

The more one settles into modern living, just as we have, the more one becomes disconnected from authentic realities such as natural darkness and the utilization of our natural senses within natural environments. These things become distant notions of how *Homo sapiens sapiens* once thrived. Unfortunately, natural darkness and quiet have become modern enemies. I for one will always have trouble settling into such places, as a deep sense of despair at the thought of losing important human resiliencies loom over me—a fear of losing what I know as real.

~ ~ ~

As a young kid, I would often challenge myself to walk through the house in the dark. It was sort of a game I played with myself that started simply by wanting to get a glass of water in the middle of the night without causing too much disturbance. I thought I should know my house well enough that I didn't need to rely on any lighting. I just wanted to see if I could do it without running into or knocking over anything. While it might sound extremely simplistic, being able to quietly venture into the darkness without damaging anything, or hurting myself made, me feel sort of like a superhuman. Besides having a familiarity with the layout of furniture and other things, I realized I could see much better than I thought I would be able to, even with the smallest of ambient lighting. Now, of course, I realize that it is the liberation one feels when they no longer need to rely on something others feel they could not live without that fueled my sense of triumph.

This is the beauty in our natural abilities which give us such resilience; our eyes can see surprisingly well, or at least better than one might expect, under certain low-light conditions. This happens across all sensing abilities. In the case for lower light situations, when you allow yourself to use this ability regularly by avoiding the use of excessive artificial lighting, you find that the range of your abilities broaden. Stargazing enthusiasts know this best of all. Although, our abilities pale by comparison to a cat or other nocturnal species, our ability is still better than what most people might realize. Since we evolved to wake and sleep alongside the rise and fall of the sun, we *do* need ambient lighting to see in darker conditions. Humans have relied on ambient lighting from starlight, moonlight, and even luminous cloud cover for our entire history. But today we often deaden our abilities by continually flooding our naturally dark spaces with artificial lighting instead of utilizing our natural *nightlights*—the stars, moon, and clouds. Our irrational fears, as well as some of our natural fears, and obvious visual limitations in true darkness are all reasons we have succumbed to over-illumination. This fear-based overreaction reminds me of a Shantideva quotation:

> *"Unruly [and fearful] beings are as unlimited as space.*
> *They cannot possibly all be overcome . . .*
> *Where would I find enough leather to cover the entire surface*
> *of the earth?*
> *But [wearing] leather just on the soles of my shoes is*
> *equivalent to covering the earth with it . . ."*

This fear of darkness represents our irrational way of dealing with threats and fears of the unknown. In the modern world, it seems as though we have opted for illuminating the darkness as far and wide as possible, instead of simply lighting our walking paths where it might be necessary. It is both wasteful and harmful to us *and* the rest of our living world. It also steals a part of who we are. This way of over-illumination certainly does not foster the use of our natural abilities. We remain forever bound by the constraints and sense of security of unnatural lighting. Any place beyond this unnatural illumination, many modern humans conclude, is too frightful.

~ ~ ~

Excessive illumination contributes to a condition called *nyctalopia* or night blindness: an inability to see well in low-light environments, precisely what I was experiencing on that night out with my dog. One simple way to prevent night blindness is to avoid looking directly into an artificial light source at night. You should also allow your eyes some time to adjust to areas of low light; 20 minutes or so is all one needs. Actively moving your eyes to scan your environment also helps keep night blindness at bay; a tactic used by many avid stargazers. In thinking about this, I recalled an experience I had when assisting a colleague as a student researcher. The project involved scouting the desert at nighttime to survey snakes. It was remarkable how much we could see under just starlight. I could see a slithering snake fairly well, even at some distance away. The affect that starlight, moonlight, and daylight have on our neurobiology is truly fascinating. The activation of certain brain cells when exposed to starlight become silenced once our eyes are exposed to daylight, which in turn activates a different set of brain cells. It is a way our brain finds a cost-effective balance of energies. This may be why we feel fatigue when deprived of true darkness. When we push the limits too far into the night or remain under too much artificial lighting during the night, we create a neurological misfiring . . . which leads to a poor production of natural melatonin.

I still challenge myself to use as little artificial lighting as possible. When awakening in the early hours of civil twilight, I try to prepare my coffee in as much natural light as possible, only resorting to using artificial lighting when necessary. Similarly, while I do take along a headlamp when backpacking, I refrain from using it unless absolutely necessary. I feel this helps me see better under low light conditions and to avoid night blindness. Utilizing these tips can help us reconnect with the wonders only found in natural darkness. Of course, the greatest wonder of all is a star-filled night sky; a wonder so many of us in the modern world are becoming deprived of.

Much like the feelings I can experience when exposed to an excess of unnatural noises, excessive lighting produces similar sentiments of wanting to *run away*. Although I realize my feelings on such things may be an exception, they do point to a critical misunderstanding of who we really are. Knowing the alternative is possible and having the great fortune of regularly seeing genuinely dark skies simply make these sentiments stronger. A light-polluted world is *not* a world suitable for human beings; it is simply not the kind of world we and many other living beings were meant to thrive in.

When I awoke to those naturally dark skies in the desert mountains, it was as if I were seeing through the eyes of my ancestors. The profound experience struck within me a sudden sense of smallness. This deep humbleness is lost when we can no longer see a sky of stars, for we would not be able to perceive our great insignificance. Stepping out of the shadows of artificial lighting and into the natural illumination of the night is at the heart of our true nature and is how we may be able to reconnect with the state of this natural humility.

Open-air Living

There are many ways humans shield themselves from Nature and the elements, rarely giving themselves an opportunity to truly acclimate to their surroundings in a deeper, more intimate way. This involves deepening your senses as well as feeling the elements. One way to be able to endure the elements more comfortably is to regularly expose yourself to them.

When the weather begins to turn while out on a long hike, I try to see how long I can endure the change without an extra layer or jacket. I do this whenever I can and for as long as it makes sense. I can tolerate the cold much better than if I continually relied on excessive artificial insulation. When it becomes too much, I simply adjust my layering. Usually, that point for me is when I lose the ability to use my hands. People have been surprised by just how much natural cold I can take, as I am thin. After some time of practicing this, you might be surprised at the low temperatures you will be able to tolerate. Although initially, acclimation does take some time.

Human animals are incredible beings. We can often handle so much more than we ever thought possible. It just takes practice and a willingness to be a little uncomfortable. I do this for the same reason I practice daily barefoot walking—to regain and maintain a form of resiliency I know is a part of my human animal makeup. By allowing the wind to sweep across our face or the nipping cold to kiss our hands and ears, we can learn to appreciate the elements of weather differently. My point here is not to be so uncomfortable that you put yourself in harm's way. I am not encouraging one to strip down and frolic in the snow. I am referring to incremental exposure. I simply want it to be possible for you to *feel* the realness of your environment in a more intimate way, knowing that these aspects of Nature also belong. When you become friends with these elements, it makes time spent in the backcountry as comfortable as being in your comfortable home. Since Nature *is* my home, I want to sensibly do whatever I can to remain as durable as possible.

One thing I have noticed from doing this, is that it is much easier to handle incremental weather changes than it is to handle blasting cold air conditioning or excessive indoor heating. After a while you will find that you can live more comfortably without as much air conditioning and heating. This durability can take us a long way. Instead of air conditioning, you may find that opening a couple of windows to allow a cross breeze is all that is needed.

Over the course of tens of thousands of years, humans have adapted to many varying temperature extremes, all without the use of artificial cooling. Albeit we did utilize fires for cooking and warmth, we were certainly capable of withstanding greater temperature variances than today, simply because we had to. At the very least, we can opt for more earth-friendly measures such as using layers for warmth, or by utilizing north-facing areas in your home in hotter times of the year, and south-facing areas for cooler times of the year. Wild animals consistently do this by alternating southern and northern slopes throughout the year, I am almost certain that our ancestors would have as well.

It has always been the *realness* of being in Nature and wilderness that I deeply cherish. And being exposed to the elements is part of this reality. While most of the modern world is caressed by artificiality and insulated from Nature's elements, the hardships I've experienced in the wild, which include dealing with extreme heat and cold, have been the things in my life that make me feel most alive and my senses most acute. An Indian proverb puts it perfectly: *"If you want to live by the river, you better make friends with the crocodile."* If you want to experience the wonders of the outdoors, you will have to make friends with the elements. Well, you don't *have* to, but it sure makes outdoor living more enjoyable. The saying certainly can be applied to many aspects of Nature. If you want to live on the edge of wilderness, you better make friends with the wolf, for the wilderness cannot exist without them. The wolf encounter I experienced was also a time when I felt deeply alive.

When I speak of wild encounters, I am not only referring to encounters with wildlife. Wild encounters can be experienced with plants, entire mountains, rivers and even the elements. I have encountered a towering alligator juniper believed to be over 800 years old and *Juni,* a grand old One-seed juniper of an unknown age with whom I've fallen in love. I have spent time resting beneath and admiring both of these magnificent tree-beings that I consider just as incredible as wild encounters with animals. One can also find themselves face to face with wild elements—encounters that are often difficult to forget. Some of my most memorable and rewarding moments spent in wild nature were in inclement weather at high elevations. It is the feeling of aliveness after emerging from these experiences that point to our ability to endure. We are truly as incredible as our wild counterparts and as our ancestors might have had to be. We can survive with far less than we ever thought possible. We can handle things a bit cooler and a bit warmer. But not so much if we consistently bury ourselves in artificial insulators that keep our bodies inadequately conditioned and ill-adapted to the elements.

There is a Norwegian concept of optimizing time spent in the outdoors called *friluftsliv* (pronounced "free-loofts-liv"). Its rough translation: "open-air living." It is a concept long embraced in Norwegians' heritage. It is a celebration of time outdoors, no matter what kind of weather. Open-air living may also ward off infectious disease since terpenes and other volatile compounds in Nature are natural antimicrobial agents that act as air purifiers. Many Norwegians consider open-air living as simply a way of life. Not too long ago, this was a way of life for *all*.

Wanderers No More

Today we have backyards to play in, but for most of our life here on this planet humans had the whole natural world open to explore, ramble about in, forage and hunt—of course with the exception of some boundaries here and there, whether physical boundaries such as rivers and oceans or territorial boundaries set by animals using pheromones. But even within these boundaries there were enough open spaces to carry out our lives as the wandering humans we were.

Land that was once believed to be common to all to live on, obtain sustenance from and flourish has since been divided into individual property. Once again humanity turns against their own natural resiliency through modern prejudices or greed, unknowingly creating not a better life, but ultimately a more vulnerable life for us all. We are meant to be on the move. In fact, our bodies evolved to be mobile. The multitude of modern ailments reveal this about our evolved physiology. Historically, and still today, private property has led to division of natural resources necessary for survival of not only human life, but native plant and animal life as well. In part, it is also the reason that the modern world is made up of so many marginalized communities.

Turning from hunter-gatherers to farmers, an ill-equipped method for *ultimate* survival, farmers were at a disadvantage. First, farmers relied heavily on stationary crops that required enormous amounts of tending. Farmers also faced more famine than indigenous peoples who knew their natural world more intimately. Indigenous peoples knew where to find resources in their travels and in different times of the year. It was life. By domesticating the land and animals, we inadvertently domesticated ourselves. The domesticated human is yet another creature to be wary of, for they are like lost babes in the woods.

The Weavers

In the animal kingdom are many *weaving* beings from spiders and silkworms who produce their own weaving materials, to birds and beavers who utilize collected materials for their woven creations. The intricacy of woven bird nests from Bald Eagles to Hummingbird nests are wonders that continue to amaze architects and naturalists alike. A Bald Eagle's nest is built by both the male and female and is made up of stacked and woven branches and sticks. The nest can ultimately measure three meters wide by six meters deep; one of the largest of bird nests. Some birds such as common tailorbirds take weaving nests to a whole new level by literally sewing leaves together with plant fibers, strings and even spider silk.

Female hummingbirds begin building their nests by packing a platform with fluffy plant fibers, which are then pulled at the edges and anchored carefully into tree bark and small branches. The female hummingbird continues packing her fluffy platform by stomping in a circular fashion until a round shape is formed. She then utilizes spider silk to build up the nest walls around her. As she does so, she incorporates tiny pieces of plant material, including anything from seeds, lichen, and stringy moss, onto the walls of matted silk until her creation meets her satisfaction.

Male African weaver birds begin building their incredibly unique nests by first tying a fresh strip of grass fiber in a half-hitch fashion onto a twig. They do this by holding one part of the fiber firmly with their foot as they tie the fiber with their beak, often while hanging upside down. The integrity of all subsequent weaving depends upon this first tied fiber. The construction is continued by adding a ring of woven grass, which dangles from that first tied grass fiber where many more fibers will then be woven into. The end result is a dangling, and dazzling, teardrop-shaped nest.

Even a basic dove nest holds great secrets to Nature's ingenuity. Try weaving a small bird nest using only your hands as tools. Use twigs, grass, and other natural materials available to you. It is incredibly difficult, as our hands lack the nimbleness of bird beaks and feet to create small, tightly bound nests. You will be astounded by the delicate complexity and strength of a simple bird nest.

Beavers, one of Nature's most invaluable engineers, work tirelessly to drag various logs and branches to a selected area along a stream or riverbank. They begin building their dens by first wedging branches into the river or stream bottom as anchors. Sticks and branches are then wedged and interwoven into these anchors until the dam is built up, much like a woven bird's nest made of twigs and sticks only much larger. Mud is also used as a natural sealant, creating an incredibly durable structure.

Humans also are weavers. Across the globe, humans have woven baskets mainly for practical use and sometimes for ceremonial use. Because indigenous baskets are made of natural materials that eventually succumb to deterioration, just how far back in time the craft of weaving baskets began is left to reasonable estimations. The oldest known baskets were unearthed in Faiyum, upper Egypt. Radiocarbon dating suggests these baskets to be between 10,000 and 12,000 years old; older than any dated pottery. Traditional basket weaving carries much the same intricacies and complexities of bird nests, although of course basket creations tend to be executed at larger scales than delicate nests. The material used in weaving included yucca, willow, vines, beargrass, agave, cattail, tule, grass and more. With a wide range of complex patterns and shapes, a multitude of creations could be made to suit the needs of early humans—such as food-carrying vessels, baskets for food processing, fish traps, headgear, baby carriers and more. Typically, localized native materials were utilized, which meant that a great knowledge of one's own landscape was necessary to ensure quality creations. This bioregional knowledge aided our ancestors not only in basketry, but in survival. Little did our ancestors know that these naturally giving landscapes could suffer so unimaginably, and that their connections to these landscapes could someday be forcibly severed.

Traditional basket weavers of today continue to share their stories of losing native natural materials as land misuse and ownership impede once naturally abundant landscapes. Historical invasions and colonization, which pitted man against man, fueled land wars that ultimately led to prohibiting laws, degraded landscapes, and other threats. During early historical invasions indigenous weavers were forbidden to gather and harvest materials that allowed them to participate in traditional weaving practices. Traditional weavers today continue to be plagued with threats of pesticides, herbicides, and other threatening industries; threats we have come to accept as normal in the modern world.

Just as with any persons whose livelihoods revolved around a natural existence, a great kinship toward the giving natural world would have been highlighted in the minds of indigenous weavers. As reeds of cattail and tule come to life with bird song and dance, a shared celebration of Nature's abundance would have no doubt ripened in the heart of Indigenous weavers. As a lifelong forager of wild edibles, I am familiar with this sense of celebration. Recently I began experimenting with natural materials in cordage making and basket weaving and have been utterly floored by the incredible abundance around me. I experienced this in foraging for edibles, but I had never really sensed the generous abundance in weaving until I tried my own hand at it. A newly found respect and regard blossomed in my heart and mind and I wondered how I had not come to embrace the skill earlier in my life.

What I love most of all about weaving is the practical nature of baskets and other creations. While they can also be beautifully artful, they are amazingly functional. In my personal experimentation of harvesting and weaving with natural materials, my final pieces are quite crude and could hardly be considered artful, although for me the beauty lies in their functionality as well as in my own ability to create such a useful tool—all from the incredible natural abundance around me. I have utilized cattails, yuccas, beargrass, Baltic rush, willow, and even corn husks using a large locust thorn as an awl. The possibilities of creations are endless. I continue to put my first-ever-made basket to use collecting wild edibles while hiking. For this, the basket serves its purpose perfectly.

While certainly there is always room for innovation, Indigenous baskets represent pure simplicity, no matter how complex their designs. The jobs of baskets were to hold basic necessities for life, from food to baby carriers. But when colonialism ensued, the design of simply utilitarian baskets began to change from personally or spiritually representative to more decorative designs tailored toward commercialism. The more decorative baskets represented the loss of a people. As market-driven opportunists dominated Native grounds and requested designs less indicative to the cultures of Native peoples, these baskets began to lose their purpose and were reduced to useless novelties placed on display. Through the exploitation of master weavers who developed and upheld a craft born out of necessity, the spiritually and personally significant stories of the Native peoples from which these baskets were created is lost. For someone looking in from outside like myself, there is a deep sense that Indigenous weavers represented so much more than just people endowed with a creative hand. The Indigenous basket represented a simple and naturally aware existence.

Indigenous weavers and harvesters also had a sense of what constituted a healthy landscape, whereby great abundance is sure to be found. Living closely alongside the changing seasons and shifting resources, they did not dominate the earth to express themselves through their basketry; rather their basketry paid homage to the giving land of plants and animals around them. From basketry to pure sustenance, this awareness shaped our own ancestry and ability to thrive as part of that flourishing abundance. The way of life of weavers and gatherers had naturally insisted that they had this awareness. To continue thriving, weavers and harvesters felt it natural to teach the craft to younger generations. In a way to honor and uphold tradition, many Indigenous weavers sang to particular plants or to the Earth from which they harvested, in thanks for their blessed usefulness. Their songs embodied their gratitude for the generous spirit that moves through all things, which can only be described as Nature itself. Although not exclusively, most weavers were women—women who also gathered and provided for their families. These women became our mothers. We owe our existence to our weaving mothers, brothers, sisters, and fathers. No matter how far back in time we may go, our ancestry undoubtedly crossed paths with the craft of weaving. Without the great ecological knowledge and nurturing of our weaving ancestors, we may have never come into existence and thrived so incredibly. Their natural spirit can be found interwoven into a part of ourselves.

4

Bioregionalism

I once worked on a post-fire restoration project at an elevation of around 7,000 feet within the Jemez Mountains. The area had endured a massive fire caused by a fallen powerline in lower elevations. As the fire raced farther into the mountains it consumed the native vegetation and the soil's earth-stabilizing biotic network along with it. Incredible erosion followed this massive event after monsoonal rains caused preexisting ground to bottom out. The erosion was exacerbated by logging and overgrazing, which had caused more arid conditions across the landscape. Enormous, incised channels were created, resulting in barren bottoms made of silt and sand. Our job was to install native vegetation within these channels that would act naturally to halt and resist further erosion, as well as design and build natural erosion-control structures using native material.

One day I was able to work alongside a very skilled Navajo (Diné) man named Harold who had been doing this kind of work for many years. He was kind, had a quiet nature and was extremely observant. I felt lucky to be working alongside him that day. Harold and I were figuring out the best placement for a contour structure in relation to the channel and other surrounding natural factors. To optimize recovery, we had to be sure the placement would do its job in collecting and trapping sediment to provide a suitable habitat for vegetation to grow, while also abiding by a general "do no harm" policy. I had decided on a placement that I thought would be optimal. It included moving a downed tree into that location. Downed burned trees were regularly utilized in our work. The fallen tree required a near 30-degree rotation to be set just right. When I discussed this with him, he made an immediate observation of something I had missed entirely.

Without a word, Harold walked a few steps toward the area we had discussed, knelt down, and gently pointed out an approximately five-inch-tall spruce sapling. It was directly in the spot we were going to move the massive log. I remember how gently he caressed the still flexible sapling with his fingers, as if petting it. In that moment, deeply impressed with his ability to see the easy-to-miss, I quickly adopted a heightened awareness about all the living things growing around me. My mere footsteps suddenly felt as destructive as a logging truck.

Redundancy in our work sometimes blinds us from these little, but no less important aspects. Knowing your land can save it. I will always appreciate Harold for that simple lesson. The awareness that moment bred in me is more than he could ever know.

~ ~ ~

Although our endangered world is faced with seemingly endless ecological issues, reversing these seemingly dire trends may not be as difficult as we may think. The healing processes can begin quite close to home if efforts are made. In just about every populated part of this planet there are marks of (hu-)man; whether in the form of soil degradation (erosion), invasive species takeover or pollution, there is very likely a place near you that could use your help.

Working in riparian restoration has made me realize that there is a chain reaction of degrading effects that occurs from one region to the next when an area is severely abused. This may seem obvious, but to see it happening nearly in real time is startling. Conversely, this connectivity reveals that efforts taken to restore one region could potentially have positive effects by setting off a chain reaction in the multiple directions of the connecting cared-for regions. This, of course, would involve organized community effort. When a person becomes familiar enough with a region, that person inevitably realizes the connection to another and to another because *all is connected*. If we individually as well as communally decided to do this, we could ignite widespread ecological recovery. It took the knowledge of our land by our ancestors to get where we are today. We have had hundreds of thousands of years' worth of evolution and reasons to protect our land and come to know it well. Now we must navigate through our tremendous stores of knowledge to continue our species' survival legacy through thoughtful restorative efforts.

I remember feeling a great sense of loss when I *really* and deeply reflected on the fact that buffalo no longer roamed our lands. It was a visceral sense of loss that pierced my heart. Globally, there are very few great wild migrations left. Historically existing migratory paths have been interrupted by a host of modern reasons and remaining wild migrations continue to face countless more. Due greatly to exploitation, the agricultural revolution, the increase in private property, as well as some very unfortunate ecological blunders of our ancestors, free-roaming buffalo are gone forever.

Instead, our greater ecology has many points of stagnation where once the flow of Nature pulsated with the breath of life across the Earth. Nature is made up of multiple layers of systems—when you cauterize just one of these systems the rest follow a path of degradation. Migrating animals of land, sea, and air are components of the whole of Nature—a part of an evolved niche of regulatory systems. Where the buffalo roamed, they *danced* alongside other elements and life that existed, maintaining ecological stability. We know this now about many of our largest creatures. They are keystones to all of life. Yet modernity operates outside of the rules of natural order. Today's modern humanity seems to do everything it can to disregard Nature's inherent laws. It certainly would be less damaging to accept and abide by Nature's ruling forces by living more simply, than to cast aside these innate truths.

The journey to discovering the truths about the nature of Nature is an everlasting, ever enticing, lifelong quest. These truths could set our life journeys on a path to greater sustainability. To be clear, a simpler way of living doesn't necessarily mean easier. Many ecological blunders were made along our evolutionary and pre-historic way. Not all was perfect. Yet today we stand forever at the precipice of potentially catastrophic ecological disaster and the potential destruction of our own existence. The truth is, we have already adopted an *easier* not simpler way of living. It is the life you and I are living today. A life dependent upon modern conveniences in a relatively peaceful society. Yet the overabundance of modern conveniences has undermined our own natural abilities to create and maintain resilient sustainability.

A *simpler life* would be one of deeper awareness of our kinship to the rest of life, as well as meeting only our absolute needs. With our *species-normal* utilization of senses fully engaged, we would be vigilant in reading landscapes and patterns of Nature, thus building an awareness of what balance looks like. A simpler life would be one of greater resilience, much more skill, and an intrinsic understanding of how Nature works as part of ourselves.

When I was studying physical anthropology and evolutionary biology as an undergraduate, I was absolutely convinced that modern humans were the *least* adapted species on the planet. To survive, we have intrusively manipulated our environment instead of adapting to the laws of the Natural world. It says a lot about our intelligence, but not of our wisdom. Prevailing evidence to these thoughts continued to reveal itself all around me.

Everything we have done to live within a civilized world seemed to put us at an extreme disadvantage as human animals. We are the only animals who destroy our own kind's chances for ultimate and sustainable survival. We do this by polluting and poisoning our homes and those of our neighbors, children, grandchildren and our wild cousins, the native plants and wildlife. By reorienting ourselves toward the laws of Nature, we could redeem the dignity of our classified namesake *Homo sapiens sapiens*, "the *wise* hominids." If I could inspire even the smallest desire to reconnect with your true *humanness*…to investigate what that true nature looks like, a quest nurtured simply by a willingness to understand the simplicity of life that still exists wild and free around you, I will have achieved my intention in writing this book. The elements that make up this living sphere—the breath, perspiration, and rhythm of the Earth's pulse—thrive simply to give us life.

In understanding how the space we now occupy has evolved over vast geologic time, we can feel a connection to the life-giving spirit of Nature. Let us never forget just how different this land was not long ago in our human history. Wherever you may be, you might be standing right where a mammoth once stood, or where the buffalo once roamed, or where an incredible life-giving forest once thrived, or even where massive aquatic beings once swam. If that doesn't shake your world, I'm not sure what would. We all live upon ancestral lands.

Many people want to travel the world, yet many haven't even explored their own backyards. I am continually amazed by the wonders I find in my own back woods and nearby mountains and by the area's natural history. Our ancestors benefited greatly from knowing the land. I think we could too. Knowing what native animals and plants grew in their neck of the woods or mountains kept our ancestors from facing famine, unlike their post-agricultural descendants. We may believe this skill is no longer of use to us, but fathom just how well it aided the success of our ancestors. This is the inspiration we need to reconnect to our amazing living world.

Knowing Your Place Well

The fact that farmers experienced famine more than pre-agricultural hunter and gatherers lies in their differing perceptions of Nature. Farmers lived as separatists bound by the constraints of continually vying for control over viable land, ravaging the earth to meet the demands of expansion, and taming the wild for fears of losing their crops and herds to natural and wild elements, whereas our foraging ancestors knew themselves to be a part of their natural environment, subsisting by the ebb and flow of seasonally produced edibles and hunting. The separatist view of farming has led to the unfortunate disgrace of sacrificing many of our wild kin and keystone species for their more easily controllable domesticated counterparts. The arduous efforts made by popularized farming practices are ultimately futile, for the Earth's innate ever persistent *rewilding* process of reestablishing ecological equilibrium is a process of wild Nature that can never be tamed.

Agriculturalists laboriously toiled and worked to defend crops; our foraging ancestors hunted and gathered a large variety of animals and plants opportunistically. If, say, drought conditions prevented certain plants from producing fruit within a season, our ancestors could fall back on a multitude of other food sources. This required a great knowledge of their natural surroundings. Eventually agriculture expanded, displacing existing hunter-gatherer populations. An otherwise sustainable way of life by subsisting on the land became threatened. Free-foraging peoples have been funneled into ever decreasing ancestral lands as they try to uphold their old way of life . . . or have lost their aboriginal way forever.

The remarkable ability our pre-agricultural ancestors had in maintaining and sustaining populations over many millennia by a foraging way of life points to the incredible importance of ecological biodiversity — biodiversity that has been directly affected by the arrival of agricultural farming. The more biodiverse our mountains, forests and deserts, the more resources they provide. Sustenance for survival would be plentiful and ever accessible if one knew how to find the food. These are the skills our elders' elders once taught as part of normal — to know the land, plants, and animals with whom they shared this world. Unfortunately, it is now another lost inheritance. The loss of this *knowledge* that greatly benefited our ancestors, combined with less biodiversity, affect our ability for survival independent of modern agriculture.

If one mastered preagricultural skills of our pre-historic ancestors, one would inevitably have the advantage of a longer-term survival rate than those of our brothers and sisters who cling ever so tightly to modern "nourishment" of limited preselected sources of foods. As a hobby, I have compiled a list of wild edibles native to my region, and it is an astonishing array of delectables that seems to never end. It's a rewarding pastime that gives me a sense of resiliency.

Knowledge of the native animals and plants that thrive wherever *you* are is one way to become aware of your kinship with Nature. Not just the edible plants, but the variety of all life can teach us so much about our amazing home if done so with a willingness to understand the part those individual plants and animals play in keeping natural balance. Ask yourself, *what regulatory systems are they a part of? How do they influence the whole of Nature? How do they influence my existence?* You will find that you are not as far from the wilds as you may think.

Although they are shifting, the regulatory systems of the Earth are still in place. This is why we still have breathable air. But because of the negative impact we modern humans have had on the environment, we cannot simply return to our nomadic hunter-gatherer way of life, migrating alongside animals and following the cycles of edible plants. To our prehistoric ancestors, this was a necessary way of life. One important thing one *can* do in these extreme times of modernity, is to learn as much as possible about the premodern *Homo sapiens*, and the land upon which that human animal has thrived for hundreds of thousands of years. Also, in sustaining oneself or family, adopt a sort of *prime directive* attitude by leaving as little effect of your presence on the land as possible. One way of doing this is to learn about the natural areas most accessible to you, whether they be wildlife reserves, wetlands, beaches, woodlands, or natural parks.

What plants and animals live there? Which plants and animals are native to the region? What do they eat? Are they migratory? When in natural history did these places seem to thrive most? And why do you think that was? What is the state of these places now versus two hundred, five hundred, ten thousand years ago, or more? Imagine how *Homo sapiens* have lived upon those lands before modern agriculture. Following the natural history timeline can offer much insight into our world. What we think is normal may perhaps only be a few decades or centuries old, which on the full scale of things isn't a long time at all.

Modern humans are still more than capable of making the same connections about our environment as our ancestors might have, even when they are close to home. One needn't travel the globe to understand Nature. Those wild spaces closest to home is a good place to start this journey. In fact, it is likely to be even *more* enriching, because you could have more time to develop an intimate understanding of the areas nearest to you. Through this personal journey you will find that these spaces become a part of you. In understanding our great history and our great kinship, we find it easier to acknowledge that in every place we step, we walk upon common ancestral grounds.

No matter where you find yourself, the will of Nature is found. Simply stated, plants growing wild in a vacant lot represent Nature's will to thrive and promote life.

Although plants may seem quite autonomous, they were in many ways the extraordinary guides of our ancestors. Even now they continually communicate with surrounding lifeforms through brightly colored flowers that invite pollinating species; with soil biota; and even with humans through invitations of abundant food, other resources and stress-busting phytoncides. They provide sustenance, building material, and medicine. It is endlessly fascinating that weeds tend to grow in abundance in particularly disturbed areas. Many are medicinal or useful in some way, as if the plants are giving us what we need to be healthy in times of ecological degradation. These plants also grow in various wild niches throughout Nature, but they seem to thrive in greater abundance in distressed areas. Learning your place well by today's standards might be seen as something only for hobbyists, yet for our ancestors it meant the difference between life and death.

Shifting the Baseline

Firefly season always peaked right around the time of my birthday. As any child would, I took great delight in their arrival. It was the perfect natural gift. Young children couldn't ask for anything more magical than fireflies in summer. Fireflies provide natural whimsy and wonder free from the chains of the dreaded schoolyear. It is a time when freedom abounds—freedom to take part in the joyous *dance of summer* as children try to catch a flash of fireflies, only to be swept away into another direction at the sight of yet another flash, and then another. A summer dance to which all children are invited. The anticipatory and joyous miscalculations of firefly illuminations are un-schooling at its best.

Barefoot in the lush grass, I could be found chasing the next flicker of light from one corner of the yard to the next. I quickly learned how to hold out my hand with upward-facing palms and in a swift upward motion intercept the flight of an individual firefly, causing the flying beetle to make an abrupt landing on my hand. It was the only way I could catch them to get a closer look without causing them any harm. Trapping fireflies in jars didn't appeal to me as much as making contact with individual fireflies. I watched closely, waiting for the incredible gasp-inducing chemical reaction to illuminate my hand . . . and my heart. Soon thereafter the firefly would extend its wings and take off and I would be on my way looking for another.

The remarkably bright flashes of lights danced seemingly at random against the darkness of night. It is a natural wonder many children have experienced and many more should have. Fireflies were such a meaningful part of my childhood summers—an annual, earthly expression of natural wonder. Thinking of those joyous days causes my heart to sink a little, knowing they are now only long-past memories.

Since moving away from the Midwest over two decades ago the spirit and joyous wonder of the firefly have remained alive in my heart, as they are a part of who I am. I often wondered when and if I would see them again. Several years ago, I was thrilled to be reunited with my luminous friends while traveling across the humid south. Their presence and dance ignited the same delight and wonder as when I was a child. Reanimated with youthful exuberance, I joined the firefly dance just as I had in those liberating summer nights. I tried my best to hold on to the joys of their presence, but I realized something startlingly clear: my old friends were struggling to survive. It was a thought I had tried so desperately to push away, though I knew it was true. While their flashes remained as brilliant as ever, the magnitude of their collective dance had certainly diminished. Eclipsed by relentless light pollution, increased traffic, air pollution, and habitat loss, their populations are in serious decline.

Children of today, and of tomorrow, will never experience the large number of fireflies I did as a child, just as I have never experienced the unimaginably more numerous fireflies that generations before me did. As brilliant as they were in my childhood experience, they were said to be unimaginably more so in generations before me. I remember being told that fireflies were so abundant before my time that they were once considered a nuisance. Something I can't even imagine.

We are not only losing fireflies, we are losing an aspect of childhood wonder—a wonder I feel so deeply grateful to have experienced. It is now clear that insects of all kinds are in serious decline. New standards of "normal" are being set at alarming rates, seemingly every decade. The great acceleration that civilization has fueled is the culprit, as the changing perspectives of what is considered normal in our environment seem to accelerate with every passing generation.

~ ~ ~

I once lived near a canyon where I witnessed a disturbing decline in Scaled Quail and other native wildlife. There had been irreversible and significant changes to the neighborhood's surrounding landscape. For one, an empty lot that invited jack rabbits, cottontails, road runners, lizards, Mourning Doves, Scaled and Gamble's Quail and other various birds was sold, leveled, and prepared for the construction of an unbelievably large modern house. A multi-leveled building with steel doors and trimming now replaced the little desert refuge as it towered high above the neighboring homes. The new construction not only sat upon a place once home to the wildlife, it was situated nearby a small, but ecologically significant arroyo.

It had always been a delight to watch Scaled Quail and Gamble's Quail emerge from the arroyo to scurry about for food at dawn and at dusk. In the early mornings, the quail would forage for a couple of hours before scampering back into their wild refuge by mid-morning to escape the heat of the day. The arroyo, thickly overgrown with native vegetation, was a special wild space where grey foxes, squirrels, quail, dove, rabbits, and other wildlife could be found hunting and foraging.

One day upon returning home I was in absolute shock to find a backhoe excavating its way down into and through the entire length of the arroyo, carrying large loads of gravel that were then dumped into the arroyo. My heart sank as I watched the operator disperse his last load on top of the crushed native vegetation. My heartache soon turned into rage, although there was absolutely nothing I could do to reverse what had happened. Even in my sadness I tried desperately to understand what possible reasoning was behind this desecration, but nothing came to mind. It was, indeed, pointless. They had simply laid down truckloads of gravel, decimating native plants in the process, along with no doubt many nesting sites and other wildlife dwellings. Almost immediately after the backhoe came crashing down on their world, the quail and Mourning Doves that once visited our front yard every morning, failed to make their appearance. Nearly a decade later it still hurts when I think about this.

After that experience I began to see only a handful of Gambel's Quail at a time, and virtually no Scaled Quail when before, both species would appear in healthy numbers. What is most interesting, the lot that had been developed and the arroyo across from it were relatively small portions of undisturbed desert wildlands. Yet I had been fortunate enough to witness their ecological significance. Where passersby might not give them a second glance, carrying on as if these spaces didn't exist, I always regarded these small spaces as the wild refuges I knew they were.

In our massively growing world, even empty wild lots such as these play a significant role in the lives of our last remaining wildlife. But sadly, I have often seen birds gathering to feed in the brush of an empty lot, behaving as if the refuge would always be a place they can return to forever, and then suddenly it is replaced by a man-made structure, taking all the of the birds' natural resources with it.

In addition to this, reports showed the declination of Scaled Quail to be a disturbing trend of around 5.1% yearly in many parts of Southwest. Although populations of Scaled Quail have been declining rather steadily over the last 35 years, it was disturbing to witness this firsthand, and so quickly. Over the course of a couple of years, the Gamble's Quail numbers remained low, and the larger White-winged Doves pushed aside the smaller, more delicate Mourning Doves until they too started to decline. I no longer live in that home, although when I visited the area, I was shocked to see that not only are the quail missing, but the White-winged and Mourning Doves that once graced our mornings no longer made an appearance. Instead, they have been replaced with pigeons. Over the course of time that I lived in that home, I never once recalled seeing pigeons. Newcomers to the neighborhood will only know of pigeons flooding their yards where, in my mind, the doves and quail ought to be.

~ ~ ~

If we all paid closer attention to our living world, we would see similar transformations happening in real time, all around us. But when there is no attention given to our surroundings, these transformations aren't as clearly recognized, and we become blissfully unaware of how current baselines are radically and rapidly being redefined.

Challenging ourselves to reimagine the current natural place we find ourselves in today as though it were many years or even a few decades ago, brings about greater clarity into how we humans are shaping our world. For instance, by looking upon the lowland Chihuahuan desert, I can observe both delicate and robust plant and animal species. Upon a closer look I can also see the desert's delicate biocrust, made up of a matrix of algae, cyanobacteria, fungi and more. A crucial complex structure evolved to maintain as many nutrients and as much integrity in the desert soils as possible. The remarkably strong filaments that make up this matrix evolved to withstand blistering sun and to prevent strong windstorms from upending existing substrates. Despite their strength as an integral matrix, they are incredibly delicate to the ever-increasing unnatural inflictions. Human foot traffic, horse hooves, bicycles, or other vehicles crush the matrix that may have been over 200 years in the making. Unlike the many human-made contraptions, most of the animals who live in these deserts evolved alongside this matrix and do not pose the same amount of destruction. Hoofed animals, like the indigenous deer, bighorn sheep and peccary for example, tend to walk delicately on their *toes*, which greatly reduces the ground surface contact area. The same is true for the coyotes and foxes, who also tend to tread lightly.

Humans also have lived in deserts, though many expanding arid regions of today were not always deserts. Before becoming deserts, they were most likely rich grasslands, and before that, dense forests. Unlike multiple natural events that have either preserved or carved new landscapes, desertification is a rapid process that has come about only recently.

Modern humans have occupied the earth for a comparatively short length of time and have even shared some of that time with different species of humans. We *Homo sapiens* are still the newcomers. Grandparents of today may not even know what a "normal" landscape would have looked like prior to the onslaught of the radical changes inflicted upon the land by modern *civilized* humans, or even what it would have been like generations before them. People simply accept degraded landscapes as normal. Given how rapidly things are changing, modern humans are losing perspective. This phenomenon is called "shifting baseline syndrome" and is one of the most unfortunate afflictions of modern man. The loss of historical knowledge of previous environmental conditions and changing perceptions of what is considered *normal* is a consequence of this alarming phenomenon.

Gradually, and sometimes not so gradually, we have become accustomed to more light pollution, fewer insects, fewer fireflies, accelerating desertification, melting icecaps, shorter winters, less aquatic wildlife, less wildlife in general . . . the list goes on. This "environmental generational amnesia" is extremely troublesome given generations can never learn to appreciate what they have never known to exist or experienced. Without this appreciation comes the lack of concern to restore, preserve or protect the environmental conditions that once existed.

One of our most impressive examples of shifting baseline syndrome is the reduction of tree cover. Tree cover in forests is now nearly 50% less than when civilization first reared its forest-clearing head. An estimated 15 billion trees are lost every year to human "necessities," as well as to crop and farmland expansion. Rainforests, our oldest living ecosystems, are our greatest land-based ecological sponge; not only retaining and producing moisture necessary for life but are the treasure troves of the most biodiverse and complex life on Earth. Rainforests are home to *over half* of the world's species of plants and animals despite accounting for only 6% of the Earth's surface.

We all know how critical forests are for the wellbeing of our planet, but we are losing much more than life-giving trees. We are losing perspective. It is believed that feedback loops of self-reinforcing factors allow for the further acceleration of this loss of perspective, a process that occurs hand-in-hand with progressive environmental degradation. Having a sense of connection to our living world and wild Nature highlights this awareness, as well as perhaps a great sense of loss. Hyperawareness of changing environmental conditions creates an equally challenging and warranted affliction: *ecological grief*. Today there is a tremendous need to better understand the causes and consequences of shifting baseline syndrome if we are to make substantial efforts to prevent the further acceleration, and possibly even reverse this great loss of perspective.

~ ~ ~

As a child exploring the woodlands near home, I thought I was touching the wild. In a way I was, and in a way, I was not even close. Reflecting on these places, one day I decided to get a bird's eye view. The satellite image startled me. I was surprised to see that so much of the woodlands was literally missing and had been turned into field crops. But as a child I would get lost in those woods, eating blackberries and wood-sorrels, following wildlife tracks along the Black River. I thought those woods would last forever, or in the very least, cover much more ground than what the satellite image revealed to me. Little did I realize that even *then*, there was so much missing. But with a new understanding of Nature, it was still the wild. Not as wild as true wilderness of course, but the wild that remains forever interwoven into our modern reality. It continues to be a place where the *real* things are.

It is places like these that we need to fiercely cherish and protect forever. In time, perhaps, we will come to realize their great importance and maybe even give adjacent croplands back to Nature. I can at least hope for such enlightened reform.

It is in this woodland where I first discovered some of Nature's intrinsic truths. It is where a child would come to feel an unbreakable bond with her living, breathing world. It is where Pokey's remains were laid to rest to decompose and return to Nature. And it is where I truly learned how to love wild things—*real* things.

5

All Our Relations

While searching the forest floor for kindling, I venture up neighboring slopes far away from my newly built hearth. Stepping over dry pieces of wood that kiss the earth's surface. I am looking for naturally fallen twigs and branches that have not yet nestled into the earth. I've learned my lesson of not turning over earth-kissing logs and branches, for when upturned, entire dwellings of living beings are disturbed. Microcosms of living beings make their home in crevices of decaying wood: caterpillars, moths, beetles, spiders, lichen, fungi, and many more unseen beings. They are the beings and other living things less accounted for, less appreciated but no less important. Beings responsible for assisting the decomposition of wood and leaf litter in Nature's ongoing quest to create fertile soils. The knowledge of these hidden dwellings makes me very aware of the logs and rocks I choose for building my campfires. From the ground we walk upon, to the weeds we choose to pull, or plants we harvest, I try to be mindful of the living, breathing, unseen world that ultimately supports our own lives.

Early one Spring, I spent four days in the wilderness to find some much needed renewal. While hiking, I came upon the disturbing sight of a dead gray fox with what appeared to be a bullet hole in its head. The fox lay dead at the riverside just near the wilderness boundary. I had seen gray fox in this area before and although I knew the improbability, a part of me wondered if this could be the same one that I once had the great fortune of seeing up close. It didn't matter. I held the same respect for each wild being I ever saw. The sight of the dear, dead fox left a bitter ache in my heart as I continued my journey into the wilderness, for I knew this was *their* land more than it was ours.

Later I came upon an all too familiar sight, an overly impacted campsite. Looking around, I saw wounded trees in nearly every direction. Several axe marks could be seen in a large, still living Emory Oak and a small Juniper that grew closest to the fire ring. The limbs of other living tree beings were mindlessly ripped off, leaving behind ailing scars and gaping wounds seeping with sap. The rock-lined fire ring was bonfire sized. Despite being miles into the wilderness the unnecessarily large fire ring was littered with grilling grates and other man-made garbage. A folding chair carried this far into the woods lay forgotten beside the massive fire ring. This naturally giving space was being used by those with little wilderness awareness. By those who have little respect or honor for life and land. By those who live their lives disconnected from Nature. By those who do not realize what this Earth truly offers to them, and to us all.

An awareness that everything that makes up our living world ultimately contributes to our own well-being, nourishment, and life, doesn't seem all that farfetched a concept to grasp—yet modern behavior operates unyieldingly in contradiction to this knowing. In understanding and respecting our human-Nature connection, the path to deep balance reveals itself before us *and* within us. Once the realization of this relationship is made, it would take a great deal of effort to unsee it. While there are many wild communities of earth, plant, fungi, and animals that seem to exist as complexities of Nature, the overall connection to all that is remains simple. The awareness of our entangled connection with all else is known by some today as *kincentric ecology*, yet this awareness that all is kin is nothing new; it is an ancient knowing. This knowing is not limited to humans or human ancestry. It remains alive within and around us. It exists as Nature's unfolding of life-giving resources—the ripening of *kincentric awareness*.

A *de*colonization of human centrism could forge a path toward greater kincentric awareness, acknowledged by the First Peoples of the Earth. These Indigenous peoples lived with this acknowledgement intact for many millennia before modern civilization took root. The restoration of this ancient worldview requires a conscious response to the needs of our multi-fractured living world. It is evident as I write this book that we are living in an age of great imbalance, yet we have the agency to become a part of the whole of Nature on a journey that points us toward greater equilibrium.

Our relationship to our living Earth may ultimately depend upon our resistance to normalized and often culturally driven behaviors. What we now consider normalized conventional living is radically *abnormal* in the scope of humanity's history. Insatiable consumption and domination of resources are both atypical of our kind and immensely unsustainable, as they would be for many species beyond our own. Yet we willingly abide by these newly adopted rules of behavior set by dominant society, but the renunciation of these behaviors could clear away the pollution of such great unawareness. Indigenous peoples of First Nations recognized our great kinship with all else, and in doing so they acknowledged all things as having their own agency. The flowers, trees, animals, mountains, rivers and even rocks were considered other *peoples* . . . people who possessed individualized character and personalities and who contributed to the whole of Nature in their own way. They belonged in this world and were as much a part of all else as did humans.

As Indigenous American psychologist, Arthur W. Blume has asked, "If the rest of Creation [Nature] relies upon interdependence for health and well-being, why would human beings be any different? . . . Wellness is a function of the quality of our relationships with others." According to Indigenous psychology, human-centristic values so many live by today deny the reality of the dance of partnership in our interdependent existence with all else.

In society today, we generally regard other humans we cross paths with a degree of respect. We don't readily create conflict or lead with destructive behavior when we encounter members of our own kind. In our interactions with others, we have communally agreed that certain forms of behavior are either acceptable or not. Mostly, while running errands or simply carrying out our day-to-day lives, we meet and greet others courteously. Indigenous peoples believed this is the way *all peoples* (the plants, earth, animals, mountains, rivers and more) deserved to be regarded. It was paramount that this human-earth relationship remained cordial, peaceful and harmonious. If it did not, they may not receive the resources necessary for their survival that were so generously given.

Many people go into the mountains, but do not truly *see* the mountains. They do not come to know the mountains or forests they trek as part of themselves, only as places to visit, use and, unfortunately, abuse. By mindlessly plodding over entire ecosystems, the landscape surely wouldn't produce the same number of shared resources as generously as it did before we inflicted such disrespect in our relationship toward it. We see this today in many of our last remaining wild spaces, often littered with garbage and riddled with scars of abuse. Relationship-oriented living allows for the continual flow of natural abundance and reciprocity. But by living as *separatists*, natural abundance simply cannot be sustained.

Indigenous peoples ensured that their relations with all things remained honorable. *All our relations* is an indigenous-derived phrase and philosophy that reflects a world view of deep interconnectedness. It is an honorable message to live by. A reminder that we exist as a being of many, and that we ought to remain worthy, in our thoughts and actions, to be able to receive that which sustains us— that which is given from the non-human peoples that make up this Earth. The dance of reciprocity depends upon these principled relations. I once read how strange it is that we humans regard ourselves as human *beings.* No other living being is regarded in this way. Our language alone reveals a great chasm that attempts to epitomize our existence as most important of all. By cultural default, we resist the acknowledgement of all our relations.

As you go about your day, I urge you to ask yourself "Are *all my relations* [with all things] cordial, peaceful and harmonious?" When you see an ant cross your path, do you go out of your way to kill it for no good reason, or do you allow the ant-being it's space by walking around it or by stepping over it? There is a great difference between not seeing the ant at all while walking, versus having the awareness of the ant-being's presence and choosing to either kill it or not. Choosing to kill the ant-being is the biophobic response, which is not aligned with kincentric awareness. Whereas a conscious effort to spare the life of the ant-being aligns perfectly with the awareness of our great kinship. Of course, there are moments when we are not aware of what tiny beings cross our path; this self-evaluation is for those moments when we *are* aware.

The web of life is indeed sticky. When we lose an entire species to extinction, a thread is broken, and we lose resiliency. The great sadness I feel when I see wildlife or ecosystems die needlessly, is the tug and snapping of that thread. For the sake of all, we must learn to feel this connection in a deeper, individualized way. It is the bond vital for the sustainability of our life-giving Earth and ourselves.

Mother Kinship Bond

The sun had barely begun to rise when my mother gently wakes me to tell me she has something to show me. Excitedly she leads me quietly through the mostly darkened living room toward the back door. Still sleepy-eyed, I haven't the faintest idea of what it might be. As she slowly opens the east-facing door, I see a beautiful sight of a mama deer and her tiny fawn grazing on the lush green grass at the end of our yard. The blades of grass still glistening with dew, and the backdrop of field and woodlands paint the most enchanting picture of the dear doe and her fawn. Rays of light seep through the eastward forest trees, further intensifying the almost ethereal sight. In wonder, I watched as golden mist danced around the two as they continued to graze, unaware of our great admiration of them.

Imprinted upon me as one the most enchanting images of Nature I have ever seen, I can still *see* that image in great detail and intensity in my mind's eye. It wasn't anything exotic. We often saw deer where we lived, but somehow it remains one of the most breathtaking, memorable images of my earliest experiences of Nature. An experience for which I am forever grateful to my mother for waking me up that day, *way* too early, to share with me the beauty of Nature.

As crucial a mother's bond with her child is for her baby's survival, the same is true for the feeling of kinship with Nature. The earlier this bond is established the more likely that person will regard the Natural world with greater care. Without this bond, we will never care for or regard Nature as a part of ourselves. From their childhood, Indigenous peoples knew they were a part of Nature, and carried out their livelihoods accordingly.

We are the ones who must nurture and foster this kinship with the great Mother, our Earth, for she is already willing. By communing with Nature often, this relationship can be built. Just as connected as our mothers felt with us when we entered this world, knowing that we were once literally a part of her, we must also acknowledge this of our earthly Mother, knowing we remain a part of her. This Mother-kinship bond could not only change the world, it could save it.

Where They Belong

I often reflect on my early academic experiences in field biology and how scientific approaches often interfere with the natural flow of life. Our intellectual curiosity in many ways has turned into a form of exploitation of natural things, influencing natural behavior in collecting, categorizing, unnecessarily treading *onto* and probing *into* delicate ecosystems, over-handling of wildlife, and so forth. While the information we gather *is* tremendously valuable, much of our interference simply serves to meet our own fascination. We don't need science to tell us that we should not pollute our waters, pillage the earth, clear forests, or intrude excessively. Yet we still take it upon ourselves to do so. If we lived in full awareness of our connection with all else, wouldn't we inherently understand this?

The Indigenous person living by Nature's ruling force of waxing and waning resources understands that the tortoise belongs and is an important piece to all else. They do not take extraneous efforts to trap and collect countless specimens to measure and experiment with the animal to understand the tortoise's inherent place in Nature. Too often credited with much prestige, our intelligence is in many ways our ignorance to the interconnectivity of all things. While we certainly find ourselves in a time where science is extremely valuable in measuring the effects and progress of rewilding and restoration efforts, we find ourselves here also because of our own intrusion.

~ ~ ~

One summer while working on a remote desert research station, my colleagues and I came across a stunning Ring-necked snake. Deeply smitten by its beauty, the creature stole my heart and instantly became one of my new favorite species of snake. Brilliant colorations are rare in the desert so its contrast with an otherwise realm of subdued colors of camouflage gave the snake an exotic appeal. Worthy of its name: Regal Ring-necked Snake (*Diadophis punctatus regalis*), the snake was indeed *regal*. Nearly everyone who saw the snake was utterly delighted by its beauty.

Ring-necked snakes are thin, small, smooth snakes with drab gray to olive-gray dorsal (backside) coloration. Undersides range from brilliant yellow to orange with speckled black spots. The bright underbelly coloration turns bright reddish-orange as it makes its way towards the tail, terminating with the brightest of red-orange.

Disturbing these regal snakes causes them to flip over, coiling up their tails to reveal their brilliant undersides in defense. Since Ring-necked snakes have weak venom, exposing the bright underbelly is an attempt to trigger an instinctual response in potential predators, sounding the alarm of their bluff: "Watch out, I'm dangerous"! But to the field biologist, this display is an invitation to examine the creature's incredible beauty.

The species itself wasn't all that rare, but its phenotype was, at least for this particular study area. A phenotype is basically the observable characteristics or expressed physical traits of an organism. This can include things like varying shapes of body parts, markings, and coloration. Most Ring-necked snakes have a yellow-orange band around their necks just as the name suggests. This one did not. The snake was in fact a *ringless* Ring-neck snake. This piqued the leading biologist's interest, who then removed this snake from the area.

The following week I arrived at a lab to talk with a colleague and saw a newly acquired specimen sitting on a desk. At the time I didn't know that the Ring-necked snake had been removed from the research field area. I thought the snake had simply been released, as all studied wildlife generally were. The research station had one general rule: *No animal shall be killed* [within the station area] *that can be used for study.* Apparently, this no longer applied when a special phenotype was encountered. Obviously, this didn't sit well with me.

Annoyed and disgusted, I glanced at the unfortunate "specimen" as it hung half-coiled and lifeless in the jar of liquid chemicals. Since there were already older Ring-necked snake specimens, this seemed excessive.

I retreated into that lonely realm I have become all too familiar with in my life—no one else was concerned about this. I had no choice but to accept it. It is this practice in field biology that troubles me the most. I was a biologist, but this is not who I am. I *did* and *do* understand the importance of the practice and I admit how much I have enjoyed looking at displays of whole specimens. As a student researcher, I even proudly assisted in a project involved with describing a new species of a spiny reed frog discovered in the highly vulnerable Albertine Rift of the Democratic Republic of the Congo. My part in this worthwhile project involved recording anatomical measurements of the exotic tree frog specimens. To this day, I hold in high regard the evolutionary biologist and lab I then worked for, especially knowing how much they worked to document and preserve the exotic fauna through their research. The deep rainforests of the Congo wilds are treasure troves of biodiversity, and their work brought this knowledge to life by discovering and describing countless new species of frogs, lizards, snakes and more, giving the world more reason to value and protect these priceless habitats.

The study of biology, which appreciates diverse life, is a complicated field. While understanding the evolutionary linage of species provides us with invaluable data, we cannot ignore that we have arrived in a time of incredible biodiversity loss, and that we must tread more lightly than ever before. As a *do no harm,* or more accurately a *do not kill,* biologist, I believe it will be Nature's own agency that will steer us toward greater balance. We need only not to stand in her way.

In recent decades, there has been a growing resistance toward field sampling, but when conducted responsibly and purposefully, scientific collections have been foundational to measuring conservation efforts and deepening our understanding of species. However, collecting is in some ways becoming a thing of the past. In this age of quality photography and DNA sampling, physical specimens aren't always necessary for describing species nor to acknowledge its rediscovery, although in special circumstances, photographs and DNA samples aren't enough. With permits getting harder to come by, collecting has become a fine line to walk for many field biologists today. And while it is true that collecting biological specimens does not generally impact larger species communities and does contribute to ecological and conservation sciences, it is my personal choice not to take part in this practice. The true harm to species survival comes, not from field sampling, but from other modern forms of habitat loss and destruction that many field biologists would like to see humanity overcome. Yet there are cases of rogue scientists who have collected and killed our wild kin in excess. I often wonder just how much we have gained in understanding the evolutionary lineage of wildlife and have contributed to saving ecosystems through the practice of field sampling, but our collective curiosity continues. No matter where you stand, it probably would be wise to look at the importance of our own individual practices.

During my studies I met only one other person who shared my views, although they did not focus their energies on field biology. My colleagues were a mixed bag of conservationists, evolutionary geneticists, herpetologists, thrill-seeking hobbyists, and simple naturalists. One thing was certain, we all shared a deep admiration of wildlife and the Natural world.

Still, just as my love for my dear box turtle, Pokey, was misplaced in my actions of removing her from the wild, our intellect and scientific approaches seem to reduce our true sense of the greater story of life, in real time and with a sense of place. I was aware that many of my colleagues also collected native snakes, including venomous ones, to keep as pets. This, of course, also deeply disturbed me. And again, I felt alone. Because in many ways, I was.

Since encountering that beautiful Ring-necked snake, I have come across several more on casual outings. Loving each one I meet as much as I once loved my childhood friend, Nikki the garter snake, loving them *in* Nature, as part *of* Nature. For me, encountering animals on their Native ground is a most rewarding experience. It is where they remain whole and free as they breathe life into the surrounding landscape. It is where they belong.

The Way of Water

A long while ago, I took a solo retreat in the Mimbres Valley in southern New Mexico. I was staying in a hundred-year-old stone house overlooking a bone-dry tributary of the Mimbres River. The native piñon-juniper woodland was held secure by a shroud of unpolluted dark night skies and rich Native American history. A light rain draped over the land and distant thunderous songs rumbled through the air. The light drizzle barely moistened the earth but blessed the air with much appreciated humidity. While taking a meditative walk around the grounds one day, breathing in the rain-scented air, I witnessed something incredible. The rains had stopped the night before but left the day feeling refreshed. While walking the western property boundary I heard an unusual sound. It was a constant low *hissing* sound. It emanated from the north and was clearly natural in origin. I thought to myself, *could it really be*? I made my way back toward the area overlooking the tributary. Once the ravine came into full view again, I was dumbstruck by the awesome sight of a tumultuous wall of water making its way down the dry ravine. I watched in amazement as the water rushed through the paths of least resistance. Large limbs and other natural debris were carried with great force downstream. The remarkable sight left me slack-jawed as I realized this was the result of the accumulation of the previous day's rain. The tributary that originated from the Black Range mountains to the north came to life as the now fully saturated ravine flowed as if it never remembered being dry. It took days for the northern rains to fully saturate the watershed's subsoil before gathering enough water to spill out onto the surface, eventually giving way to the ravine below. I have witnessed flash floods before, but never anything like this. All the pieces of the puzzle were there for me to see, smell, hear and touch. The light drizzle of rain with darker clouds to the northern mountains revealed the origins of the impressive arrival of water. It was not raining the day I took that walk, but the inner workings of the Earth were brewing this release. It was as if a plug had been pulled from somewhere within the mountains.

The work I have been a part of in watershed restoration has taught me a lot about how water shapes and influences the land. And that without a blanket of life in the form of native vegetation, roots, and rich soils to hold the earth together, water becomes a destructive force. Tearing through the skin of the earth, bleeding through often human-inflicted wounds in the process called erosion. Water is both a destructive and life-giving force. Water carves mountains into impressive canyons and spires, breaking down the bones of the earth into obtainable nutrients and minerals, which in turn fuel and hydrate the bodies of all living things. Broken down earthen materials are transported and deposited into various nooks and paths of least resistance in Nature where they accumulate until new equilibriums are met, creating sediment traps where seeds of native plants may then sprout. The face of the earth is in constant transformation, often at unrecognizable scales. The Native ground . . . *earth itself*, is alive with a continuous ancient dance of shifting elements, and it is as dynamic as life itself.

~ ~ ~

We are drawn to water bodies. Rivers, waterfalls, springs, oceans, and lakes all hold great power over us. They remind us, even if only in a subconscious way, that we are all connected. They draw sighs from us, inspire us, and demand that we soften into the *being* that is closer to that of our true selves. The relaxing effects of being near water are often tangibly felt and rarely forgotten. In reflecting on this reality, my thoughts meander back to a dreamy river bend where I lose my *self* in life's song and dance; immersed and inspired, sensing deeply that indeed all water is connected through living beings, through life itself. Whether by clouds, glaciers, underground rivers or oceans, water reaches its tendrils out to us while the water within our bodies reaches out to the water that touches all. I find myself drawn to *that* river for reasons I do not fully understand. To touch its waters is like touching that which sees and knows all that is life, inspiring *me* to give and bring life. River waters have marked many memorable celebrations in my life—milestones that often hold only personal meanings, and of many wild meetings and greetings of Nature's creatures and *givings*— I will always feel honored to be close to and touch those waters, knowing we are never truly separate.

The nature of the river is deeply fascinating. Meandering rivers travel far and wide, reaching inland as much as possible, leaning deeply into the foothills of forests and grasslands. Not only does the meander itself have purpose, the meander *is* purpose. The wider the stretch of rounding inland, the more nourished the land. A river's sinuosity bequeaths fertility and inspires the land to continue to love and give birth, reciprocating stability and integrity.

I once read that being near water naturally inspires the creation of rituals. My own actions have confirmed this. For instance, I rarely pass up the opportunity to dive into the clear waters of alpine lakes while in the backcountry. Being on foot for days or weeks at a time, traversing wilderness, these immersions serve many purposes. When the weather is hot, they refresh the body and mind. When the grime of hard hiking covers my skin, they are cleansing, both literally and, do I dare say, spiritually. Why I feel so deeply drawn to touch these waters I don't fully understand, but I sense something profoundly instinctual tells me to do so. Despite their cold waters, I have immersed myself in many alpine lakes. Once I remember doing so while grey clouds loomed overhead. How could I deny those emerald waters so clear and icy cold? The walk for the rest of that afternoon left me in a calming state of relaxation. Perhaps I mistook the rise and fall of my blood pressure from the cold plunge for relaxation. Nevertheless, I have difficulty passing up the opportunity to dive into those alluring mountain waters. Rivers also draw me in this way. There is a deep cleansing effect of river-bathing, especially as the waters actively wash over one's whole self, there are little blessings on this Earth like it.

~ ~ ~

The sense of deep calm and relaxation that being in or near blue-green waters inspires has been studied extensively by neuroscience. All senses involved including touching, smelling, seeing, and tasting of water evoke calming effects. For millennia water has remained our most significant life sustaining resource. This may be in part why we experience feelings of *all is well*, when we are near bodies of water. Both observational studies and parents have witnessed babies' instinctual tendency to lick shiny objects or mirrors as an evolutionary response to reflective surfaces. In fact, adult humans remain attracted to shiny or reflective objects—think shiny new cars, diamonds, silver, and gold. This attraction may be linked to our need of water for survival. Our existence within the nearly 3.9 billion years since our first ancestor crawled out from primordial waters has ingrained within us knowledge of our most priceless resource. In this knowing, many of our modern human behaviors of extending our crazed attraction to, and surrounding ourselves with, worthless shiny objects in lieu of rich, life-giving environments, could be seen as wildly dysfunctional. Diamonds aren't a girl's (or human's) best friend; *it is water* that we seek to forever remain bonded to.

~ ~ ~

While part of an archaeological investigation, working as a student assistant, an anthropology professor told me that the Hopi do not pray for rain as other Indigenous cultures did, that instead they gave thanks to the clouds. That struck me, and since then I always try to give thanks to the clouds when they appear. I later learned that the Hopi believe we are all related to the clouds and that the clouds are in fact our ancestors and relatives. They believe that rains withhold from blessing the earth when we have lived disharmoniously. Whatever one may believe, it is an undeniable truth that our marriage with water is an everlasting one—a deeply intertwined relationship with the deepest evolutionary roots. It is remarkable to think that to touch the surface of any water here on earth, is to touch all of life. Water is the living umbilical cord that connects us to the rest of life and to our great mother.

Where We Are/Where We're Going

All wild animals, plants, fungi, mountains, forests, and oceans, have their own song, dance, and rhythm. Vibrations that are a part of the grandest orchestral piece we call *life* on Earth. Each song shares a story to anyone patient enough and willing enough to listen; stories that tell the most fascinating tales of Earth's history and ongoing saga. Even the cottonwood I rest against as I write these words has a story to share. The very limb upon which I am sitting lies horizontally nestled into the leaf-littered earth, seemingly half-dead, half alive. A part of its body still attached to the main trunk tells me it is of a wise old age. There's a large juniper growing within and around the massive fallen limb, which also tells me the limb fell many years ago. Tangled debris of smaller limbs and tired branches lie all around the cottonwood's base, telling stories of the many wind and snow storms the cottonwood has endured in its life. A hole in the underside of a smaller limb hovering high above me tells a story of its inhabitants. Perhaps a Nuthatch or a Flicker lives there, or maybe it is an abandoned Woodpecker hole.

The deer trail that I partially followed to get here tells me that wild animals often take refuge beneath the massive entanglement of limbs, branches and fallen leaves. The subtle depression in the earth surrounding this spot tells me this is a flood plain, where cottonwoods commonly grow, and the deep cut ravine nearby tells a story of a massive and sudden flood event. The Red-tailed Hawk I spotted in a neighboring cottonwood tells me this may also be a prime place to hunt small rodents. The hardened scat of coyote in the leaf litter near my feet tells a story of a coyote's visit. A trained tracker can become lost reading the impressions in the leaf litter. The cottonwood is so massive one could spend decades learning its story. It is truly an endless tale.

Nature's stories are written all around us. Yet we consistently ignore them as we've forgotten how to listen and to read them. I am still learning, and I think that is the point. I'll always be learning, and Nature will always be there to teach. Physiologically, wild animals and plants are *phenomenally* adapted, with an intrinsic knowing that they are intertwined with all else. No new sound, sight or scent is ignored. They are a part of the greater story told by this Earth. It is the common theme of *kinship*. In truly wild and free Nature, this is intrinsically understood. With this knowing, we too, can make our own true nature, second nature once again.

~ ~ ~

Whether we are fully aware, we come from Nature and we will someday return to her when our lives in our physical human forms are exhausted. Yet it is a wish of mine to remain feeling a part of Nature while I am still living and breathing, rather than living life as a bystander, until death brings us back together again. I wish to run with the grain of Nature as much as I can; to live a life I feel privileged to be living in this way. In this case there will never be a "returning to" since there was never a separation to begin with.

We not only need the wild, we need to also feel that we are a part of the wild. As long as we prefer to stay in the safety net of our *separatistic*-driven lives, following stories that are told *to* us rather than discovered and revealed *by* us through Nature, we will have to accept that we are the ones who will continue to cause harm to our wild cousins, our home, and to ourselves. Instead, let us strive toward reviving the resiliency we human animals all once shared in the understanding of our kinship to our greater ecology.

~ ~ ~

Near the end of 2018, we learned that Voyager II had entered interstellar space. I wondered about how far humans have come since that 1977 launch. During that time our sense of wonder and curiosity beyond Earth was, and remains, strong. Since then we have gained a better understanding of how incredibly unique Earth is, and yet we have grown so distant from her even as we remain her inhabitants. This led me to wonder, *how has our view of Earth changed since that launch?* We seem to ceaselessly ponder other worlds beyond our own, while we act with disregard for the Earth beneath our feet.

Voyager carried with it recordings of natural sounds and images of our beloved Earth upon a gold-plated record, which seems to suggest that humans hold great appreciation for the diversity of life. Yet as we continued to live as separatists, it seems that what we sent into the cosmos was a false portrait of ourselves. One in which all of our imperfections have been airbrushed away. We sent an empty promise. An image we cannot uphold. *Or*, did we perhaps send an image we believe is at the core of our true being? That we *do* truly honor and respect the diversity of life on our special blue Earth? And that somehow, we simply lost our way.

~ ~ ~

As I sat within that beautiful mess of tired fallen limbs, branches, and leaves beneath those wise old cottonwood trees, it was all that was needed for the inspiration to tell a part of Nature's story. Like kaleidoscopic wonder, Nature's layers revealed themselves to me from all around, as each layer carried me to the next, and to the next, in a never-ending story of stories told by our ancient Earth. Amid the great entangled mess, I was simply *wandering paint* on a canvas, bleeding into my surroundings, becoming a part of that story being told. A mere wavering leaf was all that I was, among the chorus of rattling leaves, inseparable from the wondrous story of life—a story in which we all play a part.

In many ways, modern humans have greatly severed their relationship with *wild*-ness and with Nature. And because of this, we are living in a continual state of deprivation by behaving separate from Nature. However as intertwined as we inherently are, this divorce can never truly be finalized. As long as we still require oxygen to breath and clean water to drink, we are bound to the mercy of this relationship. Today, humanity's ever dysfunctional and unloving relationship with Nature poisons our perspectives, as well as our literal home. Evidence of this can be found across nearly all landscapes.

One summer I worked along the Verde River in Arizona, conducting surveys of endangered and threatened bird species. On one occasion, an expert biologist came to share some insights he had gained in studying Northern Goshawks during his very productive career. We met in a forested area that had produced strong feelings in me. In fact, it struck my heart to the point where I had spoken about it to my colleagues. I felt that this forest had taken more than its fair share of unnecessary beatings. It was obvious that, historically, a much denser forest existed than what stood before me now. This is evident in most forests today, as many of North America's forests and rivers are experiencing the same demise. The visiting biologist of thirty-plus years' experience stood stunned and speechless while peering into the forest. Those accompanying him stood in silence as well, waiting for him to speak. After scanning the ground, the trees, and canopy he stood facing away from the others and just stared into the forest After a long-drawn-out silence he said, "This really saddens me . . ." He was speaking about the state of the forest, which I knew in my heart had a tenuous lifeline. Unequivocally he shared the feelings I had about the area. Despite hiking a distance into it, it was clear the forest had been over-thinned, cow-trodden, over-grazed—*beaten*. There was absolutely no understory left, and thus, no diversity where there otherwise ought to be. Just seeing an Abert's Squirrel stirred excitement.

The experience made me realize that we often don't know what healthy forests should look like. Because of the phenomenon of shifting baseline syndromes, how we are now used to seeing our forests, we fail to recognize the components that should make up a living, thriving forest.

Many government land management agencies also, and sometimes *especially*, misunderstand this, often leading largely uncoordinated and failed efforts to restore or protect habitat. Some use their "restorative" efforts as a guise to accommodate profit-oriented industries by clearing out ancient junipers, thus expanding or reopening allotments for grazing and logging. I've seen massive juniper clearing operations in Arizona that looked like bomb detonation sites in which entire juniper woodlands were decimated. The Bureau of Land Management agency claims these efforts are environmentally friendly calling them "vegetation treatment plans" and have called for the clearing of half a million acres of juniper forests throughout the West including Arizona, New Mexico, Nevada, Oregon,

Idaho, and the Idaho Owyhee Mountains. There is a long and tired misconception that Pinyon-Juniper woodlands *don't belong* in the West, despite many of the onsite Junipers being hundreds of years old. These so-called environmentally friendly efforts degrade habitat for a plethora of wildlife including the critically threatened Sage Grouse. The fact is that Pinyon-Juniper woodlands are being targeted to create more land for grazing cattle and many of these "treatments" are taking place on our public wildlands.

Large agricultural operations are recognized as one of the biggest ecological wrecking balls by wasting and misusing land and water resources, contributing to drier inland conditions nearly worldwide. This sector of business includes large food crops and feed growing operations utilizing poor, outdated farming practices that strip our land of valuable living soil, polluting remaining water sources, and releasing massive amounts of carbon in the process. Cattle grazing operations widely utilize national public land resources within and around our National Forests. These lands are deemed the lands of "many uses," which include logging, grazing, and recreation. Grass and other feed crops grown to feed cattle remain in operation to compensate for degrading landscape resources caused by free-roaming cattle. Many of these feed crops rely heavily on water diverted from natural sources of water from our rivers and lakes. All of these operations contribute to the hotter and drier world we are living in today. More accurately, our livable lands are becoming drier. East-coasters may find it hard to believe this, especially because they live in wetter and rainier regions. But this kind of massive land *mis*management is an issue that could eventually change the course of those same Eastern forests by contributing to overall hotter conditions.

As for public land (mis)management, Ecologist George Wuerthner sets the record straight by acknowledging "Within agriculture in the West, the thirstiest commodity is the cow." Not only do cows consume enormous amounts of water directly, but a massive amount of water is utilized for growing food for cattle when the land itself can no longer support them. In the style of cattle and public land management, cows are allowed onto lands to graze until the forestland's resources are essentially, and often critically, decimated. Land management agencies then move cattle grazing operations onto other allotments to graze. Often, previous allotments aren't given enough time to fully recover before reintroducing cattle. This leads to a domino effect of desertification, which many public land forests of the West are experiencing. These drier conditions increase the probabilities of wildfires, drought, and the acceleration of climate change.

Many of our Western forests today look like open parklands instead of diverse wild natural spaces. They are often easy to walk through with very little understory of vegetation. The understory is seen as nothing more than kindling, and so we do everything we can to remove as much of it as possible in a process called *thinning*. But forests, like Nature itself, evolved to rely upon its layers for resiliency. We are very determined to prevent forest fires today because of our widespread population. Now that humanity has established itself broadly across many landscapes, we often find ourselves in the way of natural occurrences like wildfires. The understory, which we are so adamantly thinning, actually helps forests maintain greater moisture to create healthier forests in the long run. Because healthier forests hold onto moisture and perspire, they also act as cloud seeders, helping to create rainfall.

In a scrambled mess to try to come up with Band-Aid solutions, we are inadvertently drying our forests and speeding up the process of desertification by over-thinning and clearing. We try to tame or prevent wildfires by changing the very nature of forests. Little do we know that we may be creating more crown fires and more kindling by over-thinning. Also, by removing wild natural windbreaks, thinning causes a tunneling effect for crosswinds to force fires farther into our forests. A rich and diverse forest, driven by its own agency, may prove to be more fire-resilient in the end. Therefore, you see more wildfires in the West than in denser Eastern forests. Eastern forests could someday face the same devastating challenges if efforts are not made to change these trends.

The drying effects of over-thinning are exacerbated by industries such as cattle grazing operations, which further destroy much of the natural understory. While it may seem counterintuitive, in the long run a healthy, dense forest has less potential to burn because of the higher moisture-retention potential in highly diverse multi-layered forests. Our forests in the West are indeed dry, although they may have not always been so, but over-thinning keeps them dry. Over-thinning prevents Nature from rebuilding her natural resiliency in the creation and maintenance of more plant and animal biodiversity. Eastern forests are more resilient overall because each layer of understory adds to the forest's ability to hold on to ground moisture. Increased vegetation not only helps to retain more soil moisture and promote more plant growth, it also increases atmospheric humidity. Conditions with low humidity, drought, and wind make the potential for fires more intense and more likely. Over-thinned forests expose whatever ground litter there is to more sun, which dries them out creating perfect kindling for fires. And because there is no understory, wind can channel its way through more easily. The only scenario in which thinning has a place is to *firewise* the space around your home to keep it safe from wildfires.

In healthy forests, natural wildfires tend to burn at lower intensities, spread much slower and are not apt to burn the massive amounts of acreage we see happening today. Also, wildfires are likely to be worse in forests that neighbor areas of high urbanization, and near degraded agricultural crops and grazing lands. Because of our over management and misuse of our forestlands and other neighboring natural lands and resources, wildfires today typically burn at moderate to high intensities that spread rapidly, burning tens of thousands of acres at a time. Forests that evolved alongside and even benefited from natural fires, tend to rejuvenate and recover well in *low*-intensity fires. They did not evolve to endure moderate to high intensity fires, certainly not at the frequencies we are seeing today.

Biodiversity for forest ecosystem health is the crucial element that can mitigate negative ecological disasters such as devastating wildfires. But our common practices are preventing natural biodiversity by clearcutting, overgrazing and over-thinning—efforts intended to mitigate wildfires actually perpetuated the Yellowstone fires of 1988, the Hayman fire of 2002 in Colorado, the Murphy Fire of 2007 in Idaho, and the Yosemite Rim Fire in 2013, where ultimately millions of acres had burned. Unfortunately, this trend continues as forest mismanagement continues. However, the consequences of over-thinning our forests in the West can be overcome and even reversed by reimagining the way we care for our forests and relearning what truly constitutes resilient forests. Of course, this is a delicate matter given how long these natural layers take to develop and thrive in the first place. The present risk is that our forests have become so vulnerable. They may not achieve their former richness, but while they are with us, they should be protected and, as much as possible, left to their own wild agency.

Recovery from intense fires is indeed a very slow process that only time dictates—but recovery is possible. Fires are an elemental player in healthy forest ecology, and we can rest assured that Nature is seeking to maintain equilibrium, even if we sometimes interfere with that process. Interestingly, I often think that wildfires, such as the ones we are experiencing currently, are not only appropriate but necessary. Our wildlands have suffered so much at the hand of human misdoings that our Earth is ready for renewal. Like the turning of steaming hot compost to enrich our soils, the Earth churns up her ground by setting them ablaze, making things hotter in the priming of new earth.

Having backpacked in many previously burned forests, I have recalled the signs of recovery. While baby ponderosas arise from the ashes to begin their new life journeys, they find they are often surrounded by newly established huckleberries, gooseberries, thimbleberries, and wild raspberries thriving in abundance. While risks of floods, erosion, and dangerous landslides keep people out of these newly burned areas, the newly established berries invite bears and other foraging wildlife back into these zones. The wildlife then take part in the process of recovery by giving back nutrients necessary for soil regeneration in a reciprocal dance of give and take. A dance in which modern humans are very often out of sync.

~ ~ ~

Over-trodden forests due to excessive cattle grazing, poor farming techniques and even things like excessive off-roading in delicate ecosystems are not the only ways our wildlands are becoming hotter and drier. Look around your city or neighborhood. What do you see that might be making things hotter and drier? The most obvious are emissions from excessive commuting in gas-powered cars and sprawling urbanization, but the construction of more buildings, roadways, sidewalks, idling engines, extreme rock landscaping, the unnecessary removal of native plants and trees, and even the continual use of air-conditioning all contribute to a higher heat index. Hotter is one thing, but hotter and *drier* races us toward a world incapable of sustaining life. Because, although trees and other plants may increase temperatures through natural greenhouse gas emissions, they help retain life-sustaining ground moisture while also creating more shaded areas and natural ground cover. We can survive a hotter world, but life would be seriously challenging in a hotter and *drier* world where fresh, unpolluted water is unavailable to us.

~ ~ ~

Having climbed so high upon the ladder of human-centrism, humanity today blindly walks about the Earth without recognizing that human life depends upon kincentristic relations with all else. Such distorted realities about our place in Nature keeps up blind to the natural order of things and contributes to the passive destruction that can only result from rising so high above our dear Earth in the over-admiration of the self. Unless humans can find their way back to their Great Mother and regain the wisdom of foresight, the future of our children and grandchildren will continue to face narrowing resiliency following the same path of self-destruction.

A Symbiotic Relationship

Just take it in is something I sometimes have to remind myself while exploring Nature. Although this usually comes natural to me, the trained biologist me often wants to identify and categorize. *What species of cicada . . . frog . . . beetle . . . plant is this*?" To justify this, I tell myself how important it is to do so (identify) and share it with others, thinking that if they know what is out there, they'll care more and opt to protect it. Other times, I simply want to know. This is how my analytical thinking gets away from me and I forget to just be a part of the dance of life unfolding around me.

A couple of summers ago, I spent five days in my favorite wilderness along the river. Enjoying the realness of Nature that surrounded me, I listened to the life-song of wildlife and observed how the sounds change throughout different parts of the day. In the early morning there is a chorus of competing frogs. After a while, a couple of Yellow-breasted Chats chime in here and there, then a Curved-billed thrasher "whip-whips" from the distance. Almost immediately as the morning's sunlight begins to flood the canyon where I am camped, the chorus of frogs cease until nightfall and other birds begin to take center stage. Past experiences of conducting bird surveys have trained my ears to be alert and aware of the various calls. I can't help but identify the sounds that reach my ears. As I listened to the birds, a spontaneous list developed: Common Yellow-throats, Goldfinches, Summer Tanagers, Bell's Vireo's, the ever-persistent, Yellow-breasted Chat and more. As I listened to the sound of passing time, I consciously had to remind myself not to get too caught up in this, yet I cannot stop. As I settled into my surroundings,

I began to subdue the rather ludicrous and satisfying compulsion for labeling.

A daily routine of activities developed almost naturally after arriving at the river's side. Before the sunrise and before making breakfast, the day began with a soak in a warm spring nearby followed by a refreshing dip in the cold river. While soaking, I noticed a beaver at work on the opposite bank from me. I watched as he swam and disappeared into a darkened den. I've seen him before. It was so nice to see he was still there. After my dip in the river, I returned to my camp. Throughout breakfast I continued to listen to changing sounds as the river's steady, gurgling waters declare its unceasing presence. While sipping some coffee, my eyes were drawn across a flood plain to an expressive stand of cottonwood and sycamores. The trees so tall, verdant, and majestic in appearance stand as many, but also as one. I imagined seeing flashes of rust-colored orangutans swinging high from branch to branch. Perhaps even lounging upon nests they are known for building; an image I had dreamt of seeing someday in distant jungles.

After breakfast and coffee came the usual chore of rinsing my eating utensils near the river. By this time the sun had peeked over the top of the eastern ridge just in time for mid-morning wanderings, which started off with a quiet sit beneath a large Goodding's Willow near a sharp bend of the river. As I peered into the deep waters, schools of tiny, minnow-sized fish darted around in geometric circles. I noticed at least two different types of these small fish. One was marked with bright coral-colored fins and the other with simple drab colorations. *I wonder what species they are?* I had done it again.

Snapping myself back to the present, I saw breathtaking appearances of large fish emerge from the water's secret depths. Around fifteen inches in length, the opal-like scales of the large fish shimmered briefly in the shallows with every magical reappearance. Mesmerized by these illusory forms, I watched on for several moments longer as they teased me. They were like delectable morsels of sweets for my eyes. At times, four at once would come into view, pleasing my nature-loving soul. I watched their graceful movements for as long as possible until they retreated to a place where I could no longer see them. I turned my attention toward a small snag of natural debris at the water's edge where a string of frog eggs hovered just beneath the water's surface. The natural debris of small drift logs, twigs and leaves where damselflies occasionally landed sheltered the bobbing eggs from becoming adrift downstream. Several aquatic flying insects continued carrying my attention onward and around to other delightful sights.

After receiving my fill of waterside wonders, the nearby woods summoned. I ventured around the next bend and plucked wild mint and tart sumac berries. While walking, I periodically relaxed comfortably under generous shade trees to read, write, or observe the unfolding intricacies of Nature. And sometimes I'd just wander about to . . . well, wander. Perhaps, I'd come across a snake or a beetle or whatever! It didn't matter. I allowed the mountains to decide. I had left my watch and phone behind because knowing the actual time was irrelevant. The sun indicated that it was close to noon and it was getting really hot, so I made my way back toward the river for a pre-lunch swim. My launching point was the very spot where earlier I had watched the large, shimmering fish swim in and out of view. It was perfect.

Splash! With a shallow dive, I was instantly cooled and revived. I felt a sense of renewal every time the river water washed over my body. After lunch I relaxed into reading, writing, or observing before the river called me back for another swim. In the afternoon, the canyon was filled with a chorus of cicada, an anthem of hot days, while turkey vultures and other hawks circled above, in and out of view. Occasionally I would hear the shrilly, sweet call of a Common black hawk nearby and scanned the skies, hoping to see this incredible bird.

My thoughts were mostly light and gentle, although at times heavier thoughts interrupted my tranquility. These dark thoughts were often evoked by the evidence of *human doings*—disregard   for the natural world in the form of garbage. Picking up garbage has been a practice of mine since childhood. When picking up garbage that has made its way into precious natural places, I like to imagine that it "feels good" to the Earth, as it would to an animal being groomed free of parasites. Being near the river, I felt that I had come home. My mind was calmer, thoughts clearer, awareness more keen, sleep more sound—and so I hoped to be able to reciprocate the benefit this place gave me as I plucked pieces of garbage from the Earth's body.

Many more times throughout my stay, I peered curiously into the river's water. That river was so precious to me … IS so precious to me. At one point before deciding to swim again, I saw a Spiny softshell turtle come to surface then descend out of view just as briefly as it appeared. Gasping in excitement I relished the aliveness of the river. While swimming I imagined burrows hidden in the banks where perhaps the turtles hid as I swam. The spot where I had seen strings of frog eggs just a day or two before was now bustling with tadpoles. The area was real, fertile, and alive.

~ ~ ~

Humans suffer a host of ailments as result of what I call the "domesticated diet." This diet consists of not only highly processed foods our bodies did not evolve to process, but also many unnatural interactions of under nurtured and under-fulfilled livelihoods which lead to an array of social, emotional, psychological, and physiological conditions. The domesticated human diet denies us the opportunity to experience being fully, well, *human*. The same is true for our domesticated four-legged and winged companions. Human beings were not designed to consume highly processed junk food and abide by junk cultural standards that we are led to believe are normal, and neither were our domesticated furry companions.

The healthcare industry has proven time and again a lack of awareness for whole-human nutrition. Our highly salted, sugary, and excessive animal protein diets do very little in keeping us healthy and out of the hospital. Same goes concerning our pet dogs and cats, whose food consists of overly processed meal and kibble. Cats for instance, are *obligate carnivores*. This means it is crucial for their health to obtain a diet high in animal protein and virtually no carbs—not much different from their wild cousins. Pet cats are notoriously inflicted with all kinds of medical conditions: diabetes, heart, kidney, liver, periodontal disease, and obesity. Cats hundreds of years ago didn't develop all these conditions, so why are these conditions now so prevalent?

Common cat food is highly processed junk food high in carbohydrates, devoid of natural digestive enzymes, augmented with countless fillers of corn, soy, and other unpronounceable ingredients, thus predisposing cats to an array of genetic disorders and diseases. These formulas are not even close to what our cats should be eating. Kidney disease, for example, is quite prevalent in cats and is a direct result of processed junk food and dry kibble. When a cat eats its natural prey, whether that is a rabbit, bird, or mouse, it devours a truly balanced diet of blood, raw meat, bones, organs, and partially digested fiber left in the prey's digestive tract. All of which provides the cat with complete nutrition and hydration. Many commercial cat foods fail to incorporate the proper meat-to-bone-to-organ-to-digestive enzyme ratios as precisely as nature provides in the prey animal. Cats are plagued by poor dental health because they are designed to eat the *whole* prey, bones and all. The bones of their prey keep their teeth healthy and clean. Misplaced love from pet parents and commercial pet food options help send our fuzzy companions to the vet and, sadly, often to their early deaths.

A different set of dietary criteria goes for our pet dogs, birds, and other animals. While cats remain nearly as wild, nutritionally speaking, as their wild cousins, the domestication in dogs has allowed for more variety. In the many thousands of years as our companions, dogs have grown more omnivorous than have their wild counterparts the wolves. Still, the pet industry fails to properly meet *their* complete dietary needs and they too encounter a variety of health issues, for many of the same reasons cats do. This radical misunderstanding about biologically adequate nutrition is for many quite costly and causes much unnecessary heartache.

Neither human doctors or veterinarians are sufficiently trained in nutrition and this may be by design. The healthcare industry *depends* upon the modern ailments we so readily inflict upon ourselves, and our beloved pets. This is the reason veterinarian clinics are as jampacked with pet clients as hospitals are with humans.

Raw, no-grain, whole-prey diets are being embraced in the pet industry, but there is still a pet *industry*, and industry seeks profit. A growing awareness among pet owners who are beginning to see the light are taking it upon themselves to offer their pets species-appropriate diets. An awareness of proper human nutrition is on the rise as well, recognizing shady healthcare practices, false health food claims, and junk food lobbyism.

The domestication process itself has essentially backed us into a corner. In the process of domestication, we've created highly demanding food crop and animal needs, and are forever at their mercy. Meeting the nutritional, physical, healthcare, and social needs of the 'domesticated' takes its toll and is incredibly costly. And mostly, we fail to meet these needs sustainably and appropriately. Monoculture crops require precise care and tending to meet profit-worthy yields. Vet, hospital, and therapy bills plus many other newly acquired modern needs scream at us, requiring a great portion of our time, money, and attention.

Nutritionally, western diets consist of far too much animal protein and far too little fiber. We are the exact opposites of our feline friends. Proper human ratio of fiber intake is drastically higher. In fact, we get so little fiber in our diets that we experience a host of gastrointestinal disorders. Most people don't seem to fully understand that what goes in affects what comes out. The fascinating fact is that human poop is mostly made up of bacteria, not old food. That is a good thing. But for our bodies to produce proper poop formation, we must consume fiber, and lots of it. Fiber is what our beneficial gut bacteria thrives upon; without it we experience toxic buildup that leads to constipation and other less than ideal gastrointestinal issues. Most western diets are so low in fiber and so high in animal protein that our bodies fail to run smoothly. Yet by evolutionary design, when given proper nutrition our bodies are magnificent biological machines that depend upon symbiosis with microorganisms.

It is also true that in the case of meeting proper social, physical, and psychological interactions with the world around us, the fully integrated human being is a stunning display of symbiotic relationships.

~ ~ ~

We always had pets growing up. My mother could rarely turn away an animal in need. She was a natural caregiver for both humans and animals. I will always remember one of the most precious gifts from my mother when I was around the age of eight. One day when I got home from school, my mother told me there was a surprise waiting for me in my room. I didn't know what to expect. When I opened the door, my jaw dropped as *I* dropped to my knees to meet face to face with the most exquisite cat I had ever seen. My heart made an instant connection with the two-year-old Siamese cat named Harley. From that day, Harley and I were forever bonded.

Every day after school, my greatest joy was to greet his sweet face. We traveled together, walked the yard together, slept together. He became such a part of me that I couldn't sleep without him. I remember one night frantically looking all over for him. It made my knees shake, not knowing where he might have run off to this late in the night. Then I found him, curled up on one of the dining room chairs. I gently picked him up and carried him to my bedroom where he happily curled up next to me and drifted back to sleep.

When Harley was around six years old, he developed feline leukemia. The symptoms weren't yet obvious, but he was sick. After two more full years of companionship, his health took a turn for the worst. I found myself at the vet's clinic with my dad, having to make one of the hardest decisions of my life up until that point. Afterward the doctor came out to tell me, "You must have given him *a lot* of love, because honestly, when I last saw him [two years prior], I didn't think he was going to live much longer." I was around fourteen years old and devastated. For many more years, Harley visited me in my dreams, and at random times I could smell the scent of his nape in the air. I still miss that boy, but our connection is undeniable. And while Harley was incredibly special to me, I have continued to love other pets as deeply. Some with unshakable bonds that their passing left me desperately trying to piece together the broken pieces of my heart.

Recently my most precious companion of twelve years, my Siamese cat Persia, suddenly became ill after a life of vibrant health. My deepest intention in her care was to keep her healthy and free from pain. The new healthcare journey turned into a difficult, wild ride from hope to desperation, beginning with the first vet's seemingly hopeful diagnosis of a very treatable condition, to a quick downturn of her health, which led to visits to the emergency vet, which *then* led to many unnecessary diagnostic tests and veterinary neglect that caused her condition to deteriorate. I was beside myself.

When we can no longer provide our beloved furry companions with safety and comfort our hearts shatter and we become lost in despair. Never did I imagine how losing her would make me feel so utterly incomplete. The depth of my grief was almost too much to bear.

The loss of my beautiful companion highlighted the absolute love I had for her, which she had always returned in ways only a pet and their human companion could know. That love, as many who have felt it would say, is a love like no other. Like many pets, Persia lived a life of sheer purity. I will remain forever grateful to have known such a spirit, and for the many joyful years she brought to my life.

"How lucky am I to have something that makes saying goodbye so hard." - Winnie The Pooh.

~ ~ ~

The domestication process of earth, plants and animals has in many ways dissolved the innate sense of our great symbiosis with all. Through domestication we often treat the Earth and her inhabitants as simple commodities rather than extensions of ourselves. However, the innate sense of our great symbiosis still lives, revealing something else about us, and may be why we feel so deeply connected to our pets. Truly, they are "totems" to that distant past, highlighting the deep inner knowing of our symbiotic relationship with all other species, grounding us in the ancient knowing of our connection to Nature. In losing them we become disoriented in our sense of place in our ever-disconnected modern world. We tend to love our pets so intensely because they are the ones who keep our truest kincentric selves alive.

It is at dawn when one catches the loveliest rays of light and life. In early summer months I take delight in the still-open blooms of evening-primrose on early morning, barefoot walks. Just as I take notice, their blooms seem to shrivel and fold right before my eyes as they fall into a daytime slumber. Enjoying the clarity of dawn, my attention is intensified by the lingering crispness of the night-cooled air. It is a time when one can experience the often-unnoticed sights and sounds of Nature. I have often wondered why noises tend to *sound* so different during this space of time and have learned that sounds travel farther in cooler air. This is the reason one has greater hearing acuity in the early morning hours. Howling coyotes, hooting owls and cooing Mourning doves set the perfect mood for this sliver of time in space. While the sun sits still beneath the horizon, cool air allows the morning songs to reach my ears with a purity that can only be understood when experienced. I delight in dusk and nighttime treasures also. One can catch the evening-primrose's bloom just before dawn as well as after dusk beneath a dark sky of stars. Its flower ranges from white to hues of yellows and pinks. With eyes fully adjusted, ambient starlight gives the bloom a fluorescent-like glow, a phenomenon quite fitting of its nickname, *Moon Flower*. The nightly bloom pairs with the activity of bats and moths. Nighttime insects drawn to its blooms in turn invite the bats to a feast in the nightscape's dance of life—a beautiful co-evolved dance of night-blooming flowers and night pollinators. Other night-blooming lovelies include the Sacred Datura, Four o'clocks, yucca and many species of cacti, all of which release their alluring scents for a chance to rendezvous with their nighttime pollinating counterparts. During the night, the loveliest acts of life carry on, ushering life forward to new days ahead, as we lay in unconscious slumber.

While camping in a favorite wilderness, my partner and I were awakened in the middle of the night by the call of a Mexican Spotted Owl in the ponderosas above us. *Hoo... hoo-hoo...Hooooo!* We were delighted, as Mexican Spotted Owls remain critically threatened. We were in the owl's perfect niche—an old-growth forest near a robust riparian system. I have been fortunate to survey these unique birds in my work and was well aware of our great fortune to hear one in one of my favorite wild places. Unfortunately, Mexican Spotted Owls are experiencing a trend of decreasing population. They are poor adaptors to the onslaught of drastic changes occurring in so many of our wild forests. They have been in direct conflict with logging, cattle grazing and developers for many decades. I felt both relieved and honored as their call lulled me back to sleep. The deep, dark, and lovely ancient forests would not be the same without the presence of these unique birds.

Life is equally, if not *more* active in the darkness of days. It is remarkable how much life-song and dance we miss being diurnal beings. During the hottest times of the year, and in many parts of the United States, an unmistakable sound roars through the trees. An ear-piercing roar that defines the particular "just right" conditions for one insect's delight. After the first rains of the "dog-days" of summer, this thunderous song marks the emergence of *cicadas*.

When the perfect amount of heat and moisture combine to re-saturate the native ground and stir them from their subterranean chambers, the cicadas begin a new part of their life's journey; a journey toward complete physical transformation and a chance to pass along the continuation of their unique legacy. Often erroneously referred to as locusts, a type of grasshopper, cicadas belong to a completely different Order of insects (Homoptera), which undergo incomplete metamorphosis, skipping the pupal and larval stages altogether. Instead, they hatch as nymphs, which look a lot like termites. In the beginning of their radical life cycle, immature cicada nymphs fall from the tree from which they hatch, then burrow into the ground where they will inhabit a subterranean existence feeding on the sap of roots until their first and final emergence. Depending upon the species they will remain underground anywhere from 2-17 years.

The unique and incredibly punctual life cycles of cicadas have intrigued naturalists for ages. Their unusual journeys have fascinated me since early childhood. As I grew to learn more, I fell more in love with this natural oddity. As a child, I collected countless dead cicadas and cicada *exuviae*, the shed exoskeleton left behind after molting from their immature forms called *imagoes*. The tendency for cicadas to emerge in great numbers is one reason for their longstanding multi-generational success. While fully transformed, adults fly and crawl among the trees seeking a mate. In doing so they are easy prey for multiple critters including raccoons, rodents, cicada killer wasps, many birds and more.

For as long as I had loved cicadas, I had never witnessed their nightly emergence. Then one night in late July, I was sitting under the trees in the yard when I noticed a rustling in the old leave litter. Like a taut spring suddenly freed, I sprang toward it. I had been hearing cicadas in the nearby trees that night and was I sure it was a newly emerged cicada. It was! Overwhelmed by the thought of being able to witness an emergence I waited patiently for the next one. When another finally made its appearance, I had to restrain my excitement. I watched with admiration as the predestined-to-be-transformed individual fulfilled its arboreal journey upward, holding my breath each time it reached meticulously with its hooked forelegs for a new foothold in the variegated tree bark. It continued upward until it found a branch it was satisfied with to hook on to for the last part of its journey as an imago. The entire process from emergence to the final transformation of unfolding its bright green wings was remarkable. I watched the seemingly unreal, yet oh so real, transformation as the cicada periodically shook its pliable wings into full expansion. The newly expressed wingspan stiffened, completing the transformation. From emergence to full transformation took roughly two hours. We often find the close-to-home wildlife mundane, yet the process of the cicada's unique transformation rivaled the 'exotic' that so many tend to hold in higher esteem. It was an incredibly fascinating experience, and it took place right outside my home.

~ ~ ~

When awakening in wilderness I can feel the subtle drop in temperature at sunrise; the crispness of the morning that marks a new day in the woods. It's a welcoming sensation, Earth's early morning pep-talk: *"Up-an'-at-'em. Many wonders await you this new day!"* It's an aspect of being in wild nature I love perhaps most of all. A kind of letting go of conventional time, allowing our own inner clocks and cues of Nature to lead us through our day, experiencing the loveliness of extraordinary freedom from the ball and chain of ticking clocks of measured time—the untethered primal freedom experienced by our ancestors. When I camped alongside that river I love so dearly, I could *hear* time passing in life-song. I needed no help from an alarm clock to alert me, the dawn's chorus of frogs and insects perfectly sufficed. Nor do I need a clock to tell me when I should eat, for my stomach will do so. Through a greater piece of time, the cicada's thunderous song marks the warm days of summer. And as I write these words, the crowing calls of new male white-wing doves mark the beginning of spring. The expression of time is merely a dance with Nature's song. A dance of life-song and a rhythm to live by.

Niches

Our dear old planet hosts an amazing array of exceptional relationships. Beyond my back yard, Broadleaf Milkweed grow in nothing but bare, sandy earth. I have seen more insects than I can count visit these milkweeds, including many species of ants, flies, tarantula hawks, an array of beetles, bees, caterpillars, butterflies and so many more still unknown by me. Each time my dog and I go out for a walk, I stop by the unassuming milkweeds to see who might visiting. I can hardly believe just how many different insects I can find snuggled up inside and around the milkweed flowers and leaves. Losing count, I have decided that I will sometime try to document them more methodically to pacify my own curiosity. Although the milkweed plants themselves are few, the secret is out among the insects of the milkweeds' highly prized nectar. Growing in nearly pure sandy earth, which is their preferred substrate, these plants are indeed a precious resource. Our most majestic of pollinators rely heavily on milkweeds. When most people think of the butterfly-milkweed relationship, they often think of the Monarch, although these plants support more life than we know. In the western United States, milkweeds have been targeted to protect livestock. The same toxic glycosides that Monarch butterflies depend upon for survival, are in fact toxic to cattle. Therefore, diligent efforts are made to eradicate as many milkweeds as possible on lands used for cattle grazing. What I love most about the Broadleaf Milkweed is that it thrives in hot, nutritionally depleted sandy soils often associated with the desert. They act as oases for multiple beneficial insect species in places where resources are lacking. For this, the Broadleaf Milkweed ranks high on my list of precious plant lifeforms.

In life's unceasing will to thrive, the life dance between species and ecosystems can be witnessed everywhere. Life is a strong force. If you live in the humid south, you may find it difficult to keep life from growing in corners of your very home in the form of mold. Life always seems to find a way. In some deserts, photosynthetic cyanobacteria will even grow on the underside of marble or granite rocks. These microbes can thrive on the minimal light that these semi-translucent rocks permit. We know there are countless examples of life thriving in the most "inhospitable" corners of nature. As our world becomes drier and pollution of all kinds increase, our planet is indeed becoming more of an extreme place for life to thrive. But *extremophiles* (microorganisms that thrive in conditions of extreme temperature, acidity, alkalinity, or chemical concentrations) and other well adapted plant and animal life will exist and continue to find a way to thrive no matter what environmental hurdles get thrown at them. As far as we are concerned, we are always living at the discretion of Nature itself, not the other way around. Nature's journey toward equilibrium is endless, a journey that will exist with or without us.

Chernobyl is a modern example of life flourishing in a placed deemed uninhabitable, at least for humans. Wildlife that have taken refuge there seem to be thriving in abundance without humans in their way. Although the effects of such high radiation on the future of these plants and animals are still debatable, it may very well be that wildlife inhabiting these forests don't live long enough for mutations to take hold and develop into cancerous tumors.

Perhaps over time, the plants and animals there will reach a new resiliency. The returning of plant and wildlife in Chernobyl is something we should note—it tells us what Nature can do when humans step aside. As for the people who are making their way back to this radioactive zone to live, and for the approximately 150-300 who never left, they live in a growing, biodiverse forest in what is considered the most polluted place on the planet.

While the radioactive exclusion zone itself isn't exactly an ecological niche in and of itself, it is a space with extremely special circumstances. A niche is the role plant and animal species play in the natural world. Sometimes these roles take place between two or more different species or environments. Species that have evolved abilities to thrive under an array of different conditions and make use of a variety of resources are referred to as *niche generalists*. The set of wide range resources and conditions a generalist uses is called its *fundamental niche*. Koalas are *niche specialists* relying solely on the leaves of the eucalyptus tree for sustenance. Koalas also live within the eucalyptus tree because this is their only food source. The smaller the niche of a plant or animal the more vulnerable the species to external influences, including human activity. Koalas and Monarch butterflies are exceptionally vulnerable to human impact, just as many other specialized plant and animal species are.

In the wilds of Asia, several species of frogs have found one of the most enchanting of places as part of their niche—elephant footsteps. As elephants march their way through the jungles, their footsteps leave behind large depressions in the earth. After a decent rain these depressions fill with water, attracting various species of aquatic frogs. As perfect mating grounds, these pools bustle with frog song and are likely where tadpoles begin their life's journey. It is quite possible that if we were to lose these elephants to extinction, several frog species could soon follow. The life dance between elephants and frogs is a stunning relationship that reveals how the inner workings of Nature operate in quite unexpected and enchanting ways. For me, the story of frogs in elephant footsteps inspires a true sense that in natural order, *every* aspect of nature belongs just as it is. I will never forget reading about the relationship between the elephant and frog—it truly is a *wild* form of kinship.

The niche of our ancient ancestors was once just as *wild*, before becoming vastly domesticated by modernity. However, what we have already discussed and what we'll discuss next, reveals that in the grander scheme of it all, our human evolved niche is still pretty wild.

6

Our Primal Nest

A Killdeer Story

A couple of summers ago a pair of killdeer had established their nest near my home. Nearly every day since their arrival, I remained diligently aware of their activity. I could hear their high-pitched calls even from inside my small home. They called to one another every time one sitting parent was ready to switch egg-sitting duties. Watching this behavior from my patio was incredible as it became as consistent as clockwork. Curious, I calculated the frequency they would trade off, which was about every thirty minutes. There is a retention pond on the property adjacent to us that I can see in the distance and every time a killdeer parent switched off from the nest, they'd almost always fly toward that pond. I knew it was time for a switch when I heard a particular call. Soon after some initial calling from the sitting parent, a reply could be heard in the distance. Then, as always, the off-duty parent made an appearance. It was spectacular to watch!

Killdeer egg incubation is usually around 28 days, and we were expecting them any time. We had gone on a six-day backpacking trip and wondered if we would miss the chance to see the hatchlings. We had grown accustomed to their presence, and I felt honored to be able to watch this process take place from home. When we returned from our trip, I was delighted to see they were still around! Later that evening, watching from the kitchen window, I recognized a change in their behavior. I grabbed my camera before heading to the patio to confirm, and it was just as I had suspected . . . they had hatched! Through the lens of my camera, I could see a tiny, puff-ball killdeer hatchling with wiggly long legs. At first, I could only spot the one baby, then I spotted another two. Four eggs had been laid so I wondered about the fourth baby. The other two didn't seem as precocious as the first hatchling who wandered about more sure of himself. The others stayed closer to the nest, venturing out only a short distance from time to time. The parents seemed flustered—unsure of whether to walk about with their young or continue to sit at the nest. After all, they had been habitually trading out nest-sitting duties for about a month and seemed devoted to continue doing so.

However, the hatchlings seemed restless, torn between the comfort of huddling under mom or dad and their curiosity to explore their new world. This made mom and dad very uneasy. It was amusing to watch the new parents try as hard as they could to keep their babies in the nest. At one point the sitting parent grabbed a little wandering one by its foot and dragged the baby back into the nest. It was very comical and made me laugh! The sun was setting, and I knew I'd have to wait until morning to know if the fourth egg had hatched.

They were the first thing I thought of when I awoke the next day. I felt I knew, but I had to be sure . . . as expected, they had all left. The fourth egg *had* hatched. I looked at the nest site and could barely see the mottled eggshell fragments. They were really gone, off to face their new lives. New wonders and new dangers. I was beyond grateful to have observed this dedicated pair trade off nesting duties over the course of nearly four weeks. They worked so diligently through the blistering hot June days, the ever-threatening presence of ravens, and even stray cats. We had watched on as they faced every potential danger to their nest and newly hatched babies with fierce protectiveness, tirelessly utilizing the *broken wing display* (a distraction that ground-nesting birds use to keep potential predators away from their nests; the bird hobbles about as if injured, attempting to lure a predator away from the nest).

It felt as though they had become family. I was deeply saddened not to hear their sweet calls and exchanges any longer. I felt as if a hole were left in my soul. I imagined running off with those little ones, excited to face their new lives. Although I felt honored to have played a part in keeping them safe from traffic, I still missed them.

Species Typicality

Typical animal behavior is sensible and straightforward—a wild animal does not try to be something they are not. Animals can teach us a lot about how to be fully integrated human beings. The bird that watches fervently over its eggs or nestlings does not shirk those duties, handing over the care of their young ones to another to care for, because they can't. It would spell disaster for their species if they did. Their species didn't evolve to abandon their nesting duties, and neither did we.

Consider the maternal behavior of cats. Mother cats lick their kittens not only for cleanliness. The seemingly obsessive licking habit also plays a crucial role in their kitten's neural development. A mother cat's licking stimulates the neural wiring that promotes keen motor skills necessary for survival. Without this form of stimulation kittens may not develop the agility needed to respond to their environment as adults.

Similarly, touch for a human infant is just as crucial for healthy human neurological development. Simply picking up a baby from the crib to be held for a few moments here and there is not enough. Babies in this crucial window of development need nearly constant stimulating touch. If this form of stimulation is not met in babyhood, it may be difficult for these babies to adapt properly to environmental stimuli as adults, creating lifelong psychological afflictions such as anxiety and obsessive compulsiveness. At varying degrees, distressed babies become distressed adults.

The brains of children who have been left to prolonged crying have shown dissolved synaptic connections, leaving the child to be mentally, neurologically, or even physically underdeveloped. This happens because excessive cortisol during critical stages of neurological development causes shrinkage of the hippocampus.

It may be surprising to learn that babies in many culturally indigenous societies don't usually cry, at least not nearly as spontaneously and routinely as babies in modern societies do. Indigenously raised babies are often more emotionally and physically secure as more of their immediate survival needs, both physical and psychological, are typically met in a timely fashion. This is a result of being raised in a more human species-normal environment where their needs are fulfilled more readily by their mothers and other members of society.

Generally, unlike in western cultures, the attention of mothers in culturally indigenous societies is not so easily diverted from their young. Instead of being distracted by so many modern societal fabrications, indigenous mothers have more healthy social time, not just with their young but with other members of their society. Each member in a small band society has a contributing role to play, which includes caregiving of babies and mothers. Indigenous peoples don't regard babies as burdens as do many modern people today, unless there is great scarcity of resources that would create an unsustainable environment. Indigenous mothers live in a way that makes them better able to anticipate their baby's needs before the baby becomes unnecessarily distressed. The human animal evolved to be able to care for babies in this way.

All of this is part of the greater evolved developmental niche or our "Evolved Nest," a concept and term coined and researched extensively by Darcia Narvaez Ph.D., a Professor of Psychology Emerita at the University of Notre Dame. Narvaez's studies reveal how early experiences in development impact social and moral characters in today's children and adults. By integrating clinical neurobiological, developmental, and educational sciences her research has uncovered how species-typical behavior in humans contributes to overall human development.

Human babies require an environment of exceptional nurturing and continued sense of security beyond the physical womb. This external womb plays a part in the Evolved Nest. Narvaez points out that today's society follows a "culture over biology" approach to raising babies. This promotes behaviors that align with society and modern culture, rather than following species-typical biological behaviors, such as extended breastfeeding, near constant touch, and co-sleeping. Today many might think of such displays as excessive parenting and absurd, when in fact these are the components that have been our way for 99 percent of human history. The abnormality of modern caregiving is generally not realized as such in greater society, as these behaviors become more ritualized by dominant culture. The research of the Evolved Nest simply shines light on our evolved nature of fundamental human caregiving.

Narvaez stresses that "By not understanding babies and their needs we are creating species-atypical human beings," which one could surmise leads to a society populated by under-cared-for, anxious and often amoral adults with deeply unconscious resentments. Often such repressed adults themselves walk into a clouded path of childrearing led only by conventional examples of caregiving, which creates a cascade effect of species-abnormal behaviors. In many ways, our modern world has created unfeeling substitutions to aid many of us on that obscure path, a further manifestation of humanity's most recent "un-nestedness." Baby monitors, rockers, bouncers, play cribs and other dysfunctionally-related childcare tools and contraptions are not natural, although they are now normalized. Instead of relying on unnecessary substitutions, indigenous mothers utilize an almost intuitive sense in which they are more attuned to the needs of their young. Instinctively utilizing species-normal behaviors to ensure the wellbeing of babies has been a model for success millions of years in the making. We evolved to be cared for and give care in this way.

Today, mothers simply are not able to practice these abilities as their time is consistently divided and allocated toward other constraints such as working forty-hour work weeks, modern obligations, and the heavy reliance on a capitalistic-centered society rather than a nested-centered society. It is not that we don't know how to care for our young, because we instinctively and intuitively do; it's that modern society as we know it encourages against our naturally evolved caregiving capabilities to the point that we instead operate atypically to better fit into what society expects of us.

Meanwhile, wild animals carry out their nesting duties fully—a tendency fueled by instinctive behaviors that have ensured long-term species survival. It would be considered dysfunctional behavior for the killdeer to abandon their eggs for longer than is necessary, and it would spell disaster for their species. Other animals have different methods of keeping their young safe through due diligence and evolved strategies. Mother deer, for instance, will stray away from their young fawn to keep from luring predators to their young. Mother deer typically leave their young in areas with thick vegetation to better ensure their safety and may often leave their fawns for long periods of times during both day and night. Since the mothers must often browse for food to produce milk for their young, they take advantage of as much grazing time as they can, while returning to feed their fawn periodically. This method also prevents their fawn from becoming too weak from needlessly following its mother, which could also make them easy prey. While this may seem like risky behavior, mother deer abandonment isn't abandonment at all. It is simply an evolved method of deer caregiving . . . the deer's *primal nest.*

Regarded as deeply affectionate and diligent caregivers, cougar mothers remain tucked away in their dens for up to ten days after giving birth. In a form of motherly communication, she will also purr constantly for the duration of those first ten days, establishing an unbreakable bond with her kittens. This bonding, secured by their mother's presence, is crucial as kittens are born completely helpless and blind, opening their eyes after around one week. The mother will eventually leave her young in the den to hunt, sometimes staying away from her kittens for days at a time. Securely hidden, the vulnerable kittens depend on her return to survive. If the mother cannot return or is killed, the kittens will not survive. The mother may relocate her kittens into different dens if she senses a location is no longer safe. Kittens remain in the den while their mother hunts until they are around six weeks old. They then begin exploring alongside their mother and will remain with her until they are approximately 18 months old. The period between leaving the den and 18 months of age is crucial for the development of critical hunting skills achieved through lots of social play. Cougars generally are only social when caring for their young. They revert to their lives as solitary animals after their kittens are able to be on their own.

Unlike cougars and deer, human babies evolved to stay close to their mothers or held by other members in our band almost constantly. Moments of abandonment tend to induce great stress in human babies. Because of this, babies cry when physical needs, such as warm touch, are not being met. It is not normal for a baby to be left crying, but it is normal for the baby to respond by crying when his or her needs are not being met. Conversely, cougar kittens evolved to accept their mother's absence when the mother is hunting. Excessive crying spells would make kittens vulnerable to predators, therefore they did not evolve this way. In humans, as stated before, neurobiological studies reveal just how crucial touch is for both baby and mother. Although we really don't need neurological scans to tell us this is true, do we?

We can think of touch as a form of early communication. Since touch between mother and child has been found to activate somatosensory and socio-affective areas in the brain, we know the touch component is crucial for processing early life sensory perception. This means that babies will recognize themselves as "me" or "self" and the mother as "another," with the mother's touch indicating "me" and the baby's touch indicating "other." This sense of self-awareness is significantly important for early human brain development. Without this processing, a child may develop a lack of belonging and harbor feelings of deep abandonment.

Grounded by our evolutionary development, the Evolved Nest is also believed to mold not only our neurological and physical development, but human moral development as well. Maxwell Maltz once said, "It is not the child who is taught about love, but the child who is shown love who then grows into a loving human being." Although not in so many words, it was indeed our primal nest to which he was ultimately referring. Lack of care early in development has manifested in today's children and adults in a myriad of ways. I tend to think of a most pointed example as a springboard into just how far off base *un-nestedness* can steer humanity. The example that comes to my mind is Harry Harlow. The fact that Harry Harlow (known for his cruel experimentations of maternal-separation and social isolation on rhesus monkeys) created such disturbing experiments substantiates the fact that he himself may have been sorely *un-nested*. The fact that he had to prove the obvious: that maternal abandonment would result in neurological, mental, and physical disturbances in both mother and infant, is wholly absurd. This kind of deviant, unsympathetic behavior in the form of such disturbing experimentation attests to the consequences of not having had basic human needs met. Harlow is an extreme example of how *un-nestedness* can lead to amoral adult behavior. It is what happens when our human intelligence turns us into robotic reductionists—unfeeling *care* leading to unfeeling humans.

~ ~ ~

The primal nest, as I will refer to it, isn't just for babyhood; it extends well into adolescence and adulthood. It begins with the care of the mother-to-be and in infancy. It can be reassuring for many who have had a lack of care early in life that it can be psychologically rectified in early adulthood. Yet how much better it is for a child to start life with the proper care early in his or her development. For tens of thousands of years, we lived in small bands where the components of this nest were fulfilled throughout an individual's lifetime. The human species-typical Evolved Nest for healthy infancy, childhood, and ultimately adulthood involves nine recognized components comprised by Narvaez as: (1) Positive low-stress perinatal experiences whereby the mother-to-be experiences a low stress pregnancy, no separation of baby and mother at birth, and no unnecessary painful procedures. Today, systemic medical practices are tailored toward forgoing natural processes for convenience, which impacts critical periods of development for the women and their babies. (2) On-request extended breastfeeding is especially important, since human breastmilk is quite thin compared to other mammals. Babies need lots of it to meet their developmental needs. (3) Positive motions and touch like rocking and baby-carrying. (4) A positive and supportive social climate. (5) Free play. (6) Multiple caregivers other than just mom (these are called allomothers). (7) Responsive social relationships for healthy brain development. (8) Nature connection; a sense of relationship with the environment. (9) Healing practices, such as routines carried out to care for illness, wounds, and emotional distresses.

These components make up the most complete guide for natural human caregiving—components that have proven to be a successful and integral part our species and ancestors for hundreds of millennia. When intact these components foster a life-lasting sense of belonging that carries on positively into adolescence and adulthood, and into social structures made up of fully developed human beings capable of dealing with life's challenges. The giant chasm between contemporary wisdom and indigenous wisdom highlights the fallacy of normalized behavior versus truly normal human behavior; an ever-growing contrast fueled by our great disassociation with Nature and with our own reality.

It is amazing how extensive and extraordinary Narvaez's work is, yet it simply reveals a very ordinary part of who we are. Understanding Nature in this way allows us to better recognize the patterns of true normalcy. In the case of the human primal nest, our intrinsic traits are our allies. It is the language of Nature that tells us how to fully embrace the whole human animal experience. Our true nature is being revealed to us all the time. To fully embrace it, we must simply pay attention to our basic needs.

In my conversation with Darcia Narvaez about her research, it became clear that Indigenous wisdom aligns more with who we are as humans. Wisdom that has been our way for hundreds of thousands of years. It is what holds our primal nest together, gives us the recognition of our interconnectedness and gives us the confidence to trust our intuitive senses.

Egalitarian societies such as the San Bushmen are prime examples of this secure and fully developed human social net, which is met by Nature's guiding force of deep instinct. The San Bushmen are the world's most successful, humble, and resourceful humans, thriving for many millennia in a desert deemed inhospitable! They did so by abiding in natural order and living simply. The Bushmen of the Kalahari represent perhaps most accurately human species-typical behavior of child rearing, care, and nesting. By engaging in these instinctual and biologically driven behaviors the whole band benefits, from motherhood and infancy into adolescence and adulthood.

It begins with caring for the young. Kung women typically experience their first menstruation around 16 years of age and give birth to their first child between 19 and 20 years of age. Mothers practice babywearing, whereby large pieces of leather or cloth are used to put the baby in a sling that is tied around the mother's body. Babies are typically carried closely to their mothers, often making skin-to-skin contact. Studies have revealed that babywearing is deeply therapeutic for both mother and child, contributing to a greater bond of intimacy. The constant close physical contact has been shown to increase oxytocin levels in the mother, keeping postpartum depression at bay and allowing her to be a more adequate caregiver. Also, these babies are generally healthier and calmer because more of their primal needs for survival are met more readily. When the baby is worn closely, mothers can better anticipate the baby's need to nurse before the baby becomes unnecessarily distressed. This provides a tremendous sense of security for the baby as well.

Signals between mother and child are continually being communicated to the point where mothers soon begin to intuitively anticipate their child's needs with great accuracy. The method of babywearing proves equally beneficial for the health and well-being of both the babies and the mothers, as no feelings of stress are induced by moments of abandonment. Equally so, just as babywearing can improve maternal bonding, paternal bonds can also be fostered and strengthened in fathers who practice babywearing. This near constant touch has neurological benefits as well, stimulating neural-motor and muscle development in infants, similar to kittens being licked by their mothers. Since the baby goes wherever mama goes, the child's social development is fostered every time the mother interacts with others. In addition, babywearing keeps the mother's arms free to carry out other necessary tasks. It's an all-around win-win practice.

Previously mentioned, the endless benefits of babywearing and primal nesting are believed to be the reason why in so many indigenous societies, babies typically don't cry. This is the sense of security that keeping baby close invokes. This contrasts tremendously with babyhood in western societies, whereby caregiving is often portrayed and carried out as an exhaustive, stress-inducing endeavor. Modern society encourages mothers to adopt the use of multiple cleverly marketed contraptions to hold, carry or rock their babies for them in the form of baby bouncers, rockers, play pens and strollers—all of which offer no human-bonding warmth or anticipatory motherly intuitiveness. Thus, by the time a mother realizes her baby's needs, the baby is well into a crying spell, which is difficult to stop. Mother and baby are both stressed by this time.

This is certainly not intended to shame modern mothers, but to point to the radically atypical ways modern society has officially and widely adopted. More so, modern mothers lack the support to be able to carry out their more typical mothering capacities fully. Modern mothers are not allowed by societal norms to be true mothers. I witnessed this at an airport when I saw the designated breastfeeding stations designed to keep breastfeeding mothers out of the eye of the public. A mother who senses that her baby needs a feeding shortly after arriving at the airport may have to wait in line with a crying infant until she can scramble about to find a "suitable" spot to breastfeed in private. This is incredibly stressful for both the mother and the child and is certainly not ideal for crucial human development.

Within indigenous societies, mothers tend to breastfeed for 3-5 years. While many people would think this is an absurd amount of time, it has been shown to be the most typical range because human babies are born underdeveloped in comparison to many other mammals. This may also promote a more sustainable fertility rate, which would be considered by modern economically driven standards as quite low. Breastfeeding for 3 to 5 years tends to abate back-to-back pregnancies, with typically a 4-5 year spacing between children.

It was not until the advent of agriculture that *Homo sapiens* diverged from extended breastfeeding. As we began domesticating plants and animals for food, we precariously began experimenting with the milk of other species of mammals to supplement our own. Babies were also offered starchy porridges earlier in their development. While normally extended breastfeeding could have helped suppress fertility, ending breastfeeding earlier meant women began having more babies, thus fueling the incongruous growth we often associate with the agricultural revolution. A demand for even more earth to be toiled over and worked to compensate for that growth became inevitable.

~ ~ ~

Regarded as the First Peoples, the San Bushmen who are believed to have descended from the first inhabitants of what is now Botswana, have maintained many remarkable traits typical of human behavior. These characteristics have given them the foothold necessary to appoint them as the planet's most ancient Indigenous society alive today. It is a great misfortune that this first nation is now struggling to maintain independence from continuing governmental dictatorship, displacement, and discrimination brought on by humanity's renunciation of our connection to the earth. The San's original hunter-gatherer way of life now remains our world's most accurate representation of species-typical human behavior. The San's tremendous uniqueness lies in their long-standing ability to maintain a cohesive natural way of life despite world-wide modern westernization, and their extraordinary resistance to adopting modern fallacies.

Again, modern humans live on a substantially less varied diet compared to nomadic hunter-gatherers. The San consume berries, fruits, nuts, tubers, and other plant material (a diet typical of all human ancestors), as well as up to 108 species of insects. Subsisting alongside the ebb and flow of natural seasons, the San simply accepted that there will be periods of less food as well as periods with greater abundance. They did not resort to hoarding nor did they waste their energies on long-term sustenance. They simply understood the ebb and flow of the land's resources, whereas modern humans trapped by vulnerable industrialized agriculture often resort to excessive hoarding of food, along with absurd over-nourishment, not necessarily in a healthy way. While the San do rejoice in discovering an abundance of food sources, they did not excessively manipulate Nature to serve them as post-agricultural humans do. They simply made do and moved on. By living this way, concern for depletion of resources by the human hand is essentially absent.

The San also possess unique intuitive hunting strategies that have been successful for tens of thousands of years.

While foraging is a major part of their way of life, the aspect of hunting completes their legacy. Hunting is not something they just *do*— hunting is a part of who they *are*. The San regard the act of tracking an animal as dancing with Nature. In fact, the word *dance* in the Kalahari Bushmen language, *!XO*, also means to revere or *oneness*. Despite their small stature, they have successfully hunted as their ancestors had before them with time-honored tracking techniques. While tracking, a deep relationship is formed between themselves and the animal they are pursuing. Masters of reading Nature's language, windswept sand and insects guide them by keeping a sense of time. The San can sense the state and character of an animal not only by its tracks but by reading the signs in weather. For the San, the experience of tracking is carried out in a moving meditation. Maintained by an intimate relationship with the land and its creatures, attention to detail and a deep connection with the environment provide the San with worthy nourishment. Many of their techniques utilized while hunting are sensory.

The San's specialty in reading animal behavior is not an ability unique to San Peoples. Any healthy able-bodied human could learn to be as intuitive and aware. These abilities arise naturally when one spends time in a natural environment. The muscles of intuitive senses must be used with some form of regularity, or they will simply waste away. Believed widely as a lost art, these skills can certainly be restored.

Today, there are few truly intuitive and connected hunters. Most modern hunters do not fathom the taking of a life as do the indigenous hunters who understand the true sacrifice of life to give life. Many modern hunters thrill in the sport of killing "dangerous animals" and in boasting about their trophies. A modern hunter once told me how much he enjoyed the tradition of taming the wild earth through hunting, as his grandparents did. This sentiment is worlds away from the Bushmen's take-only-when-needed model of respectful hunting. Of course, modern hunters who carry themselves with much more grace and gratitude could surely exist.

Gratitude and humility are natural traits present in indigenously intuitive hunting skills. In societies like the San, arrogant behavior is seen as distasteful and is usually shunned immediately as it arises, especially so in hunting scenarios but in other dealings too. This is an effect of the San's fiercely egalitarian society. Unimpeded by modern reductionistic thinking, the San experience the animal they are hunting as an ongoing dance with all else where humility naturally must lead. Their bond with the earth and her creatures transcends scientific empirical thinking. San Bushmen utilize intuitive senses and ancient skills to aid them on their hunts that modern hunters can only dream of possessing. Our contemporary approach to life has caused us to lose sight of the greater collective in which we are inseparable and to which we owe our lives.

~ ~ ~

In contrast to the original, free roaming way of life of the San Peoples, governments and agriculture have since set up residences across vast ancestral lands, causing the Bushmen to recede into the confines of civility. And while many San would like to maintain rights to hunting and gathering, established governments do not recognize hunting and gathering as an adequate form of subsistence. San people now risk being fined for poaching or trespassing and have to navigate their way through ever-decreasing ancestral lands fragmented by farming to forage and hunt. Agricultural strong holding has reduced their ancestral lands so significantly that the lands are experiencing a tremendous loss in biodiversity, which make hunting and foraging a nearly impossible way of self-subsisting. Subjected to colonization, agricultural and governmental ruling, our earth's last hunter-gatherer peoples have been forced into the unsustainable world of endless progress and economic growth. Many of their lives today have been reduced to puppeteering for tourists, government handouts and violence driven by a newly acquired dependency on modern life. For newer generations of San their pre-historic nomadic lives are fast becoming a forgotten memory.

The San's resistance to acquiesce to modern ways has been their greatest strength and a testament to their exceptional uniqueness. Learning that the San peoples, and others like them, are losing their way of life feels like a sharp blow to my own innermost sense of human belonging. The losing of our first, and last, ancestral peoples may very well redefine our own humanity. If Indigenous peoples are allowed to thrive, they will remain the sinew that ties us to our true humanity. But if they must struggle to survive, our humanity will find itself confused and disoriented as the last tethering thread that binds us withers away from the elements of modernity. It now falls on the rest of us to mend the broken threads that keep us bound to our true nature before we lose our way forever.

Thriving Human Beings

Studies suggest that when we commune with Nature regularly, our minds and bodies relax into an almost meditative state where we begin to feel a sense of kinship. Why would that be? Why would simply listening to, observing, or sitting with Nature foster a sense of connection, or even a deeply rooted knowing? Many times, this sense just *feels* right and good. One feels *at home,* as though we are reconnecting to something our species knows is true—an innate knowing we are trying to remember that has slipped from our present memories.

Both Dr. Ian Frampton's and Dr. Narvaez's research reveal that we are still our ancestors trying to make sense of this modern world. The confusion our brains experience when living in *dead,* urbanized, unfeeling environments and the consequential behaviors are a result of our recent un-nestedness and deprivation of Nature. The confusion and distress responses that appear in Frampton's brain scans of people deprived of natural environments represent our species' instinctual response to something we do not fully understand. As would any other animal, human beings behave abnormally when their basic needs aren't being met. Deprivation of a species-normal environment and habitat results in wildly deviant behavior. This has been witnessed in captive zoo animals. The behavior of many captive animals has been reported to deviate radically from the behavior of their wild counterparts when their needs aren't being fully met. While in captivity, many animals develop unusual tics and many other obsessive or compulsive behaviors. Elephants may sway compulsively from side to side. Birds may begin to rip out their feathers and large predators may pace endlessly from one end of their enclosures to the other. I've seen these behaviors, and it is difficult to witness. In fact, to think that one is gaining a sense of how these animals behave in the wild by observing them in captivity is sorely misguided. In captivity, the animals cease to fully exist as they are meant to because many elements are missing. Humans and non-human animals cannot fully exist without their species-nurturing environment. Any animal will become distressed when deprived of the type of environment it evolved to inhabit. Whether we recognize this about ourselves, in many ways humans today are found living behind the bars of modern captivity. The knowledge of how atypical environments can radically shift species-normal behavior points us toward questions about our own capacity to thrive as human beings.

What makes up a truly thriving human being?

The primal nest concept in which all species including humans are a part was mentioned earlier. The components that make up the human *evolved nest* are both incredibly simple and complex. In many ways the complexity comes from our intellectual ability to break down each critical component. Unfortunately, this is where we currently stand in our own state of humanity. The human nest's simplicity, on the other hand, comes from the instinctual nurturing of stable conditions over multiple generations . . . far from where we are today.

We know now that the most critical stage of our moral and physical development begins in infancy. If there is but one thing we can do to truly change the world, it is to prioritize the care of our young. It is the deeply cared for, fully secure children who grow into fully aware, caring and connected human beings. They would in turn be the ones to usher into this world new generations of nested ones as a fully aware people who know their place as part of Nature.

Since typical models of infant care have already been established, let's turn now toward the care of toddlers and young children. One of the components of our species primal nest is *free play*, sometimes referred to as self-directed play. The instinct of play in our species is a strong one. Adequate play is essential nourishment for all growing children. Just as kittens and cubs must play to develop hunting skills, the evolutionary function of play in humans contributes to the development of life-sustaining skills. In contrast to the primal human nest component of constant holding, touch, and mother-baby play, self-directed play is where the child be wild!

To better understand the evolutionary importance of play, it is important to differentiate between play and self-directed free play. Self-directed play allows the child to play uninhibited on their own terms without any interference or restrictions from adults. This form of play is crucial for psychological, emotional, and physical development. But restricted play, bound by ruling parameters such as those in sports or other games where external coaching and directing is involved, can lead to a rise in anxiety. With classroom curriculums looming over a modern child's head, there are more than enough adult-directed activities in this child's life. Free play allows a child to be a child. The deprivation of a child's free play has contributed to problems of self-control, attention, anxiety, and depression.

Upon reflection, my childhood was filled to the brim with uninhibited and unstructured play and discovery. This liberation is how I came to learn about the sweetness of wood sorrels, the beauty of the natural world, and how I grew to feel inextricably connected to that living world. For the Bushmen as well as many other hunter-gatherer societies, it is considered very important to allow children to play freely as this is how children acquire life-long skills. According to psychologist researcher Peter Gray, the freedom to play has continually declined since the 1950's. This has led to greater psychological problems in children. Gray states: "We are living in an age that might be thought of as a 'play deprivation experiment.'" With increased digital entertainment and learning tools plus more paranoia and distrust of others, fewer children are playing freely outdoors than ever before.

Our earliest ancestors did not stress as much as modern mothers do when letting a child play freely. It was considered natural for children to explore their environments on their own terms. This is crucial to building a child's problem-solving skills, creativity, coordination and much, much more. The natural tendency to protect young ones has overstepped the boundaries of evolved play. This tendency to intrude and control the activities of children has become the way of modern parenting. We've forgotten how to play. Yet by understanding the evolutionary importance of play we might begin to rethink how we raise and educate children. Self-directed play may even hold greater importance than classroom learning. Evolutionarily this makes sense. Basically, free play is our primal education system.

Free play allows children to find and develop connections to their own sense of themselves—much like how I learned about my love for Nature through simple exploration in the woods. It teaches children how to make thoughtful decisions through problem solving and exerting self-control. It allows children to develop relationships with others by learning to make friends. Perhaps most important, free play makes children happy, keeping anxiety and depression at bay. All the above help to build better connected adult human beings.

Kids who are allowed an abundance of free play with fully intact "nesting" in their early years tend to grow up to be cooperative and kind, instead of overly competitive—the kind of competitiveness we see prominently in today's modern societies. This uncooperative competitiveness can come from being under-nurtured. The under-nurtured fall victim to feelings of incompleteness, continually searching for affection, love, and acceptance, which often manifests as a competitive unwillingness to work well with others.

While self-directed play in most environments is great for our overall human development, unrestricted play in the outdoors reigns supreme and is fundamental to our species. With adequate physical exercise, exposure to the sun and fresh air, the outdoors provides incredible health benefits. It is where children are more likely to gain lessons from taking risks, forcing them to make thoughtful assessments and develop critical thinking skills. As naturally inquisitive beings, play also helps children build intuitive senses by encouraging attention to details. Most important, being outdoors helps children develop an appreciation of the living natural world. When communing in nature, we recognize that we are a part of the greater earth.

The name of the evolutionary game is instinct: meeting basic human needs. The nest ensures that our evolutionary basic needs from infancy to adulthood are met. For children, play is an essential basic need. And for children and adults alike, feeling cared for, having a sense of belonging and purpose is essential. Although not all, many women feel a deep, basic need for mothering a child. Specific needs may vary from individual to individual, but they all stem from our basic evolutionary needs that make up a part of our individual development. As renowned historian and author Yuval Harari has said, "We are still animals and our physical, emotional and cognitive abilities are still shaped by our DNA." We are not exempt from biological laws.

~ ~ ~

Nature operates by using simple signs, a language of subtleties to which organisms respond in their environment. We, too, have been players in this great dialogue. *Being* a part of Nature helps us home in on these often-under-appreciated skills.

A keen mother senses her baby's needs by clueing in on subtle displays in the baby's behavior. Most animals respond to the subtleties in their environment, just as human beings once did so well. We paid attention to the subtle signs and language of Nature as deeply as the wild species, living by instinct still do. These abilities are a part of our species evolutionary make up. It is our species-normal behavior that has kept us in equilibrium with our natural surroundings for many millennia.

The same driving forces that ultimately erode our literal earth, erode our sense of self and our sense of belonging. When we fail to nurture our own as part of all else, we create a world of broken people. When all our needs are met it is easier to feel a part of everything else. When the threat of abandonment by one's own surroundings or caregivers is absent, we trust in our natural environment, which seems to present itself as all-nurturing and abundant. The *self* disappears upon realizing this deep kinship between oneself and one's surroundings. Recognizing and respecting our human-earth connections is our true nature. We needn't return to the Savanna to become thriving human beings. By simply restoring the expression of our species-normal behavior, whether that is engaging in the components of our primal nest or reorienting toward the natural world and practicing fine-tuning our awareness to the many connections Nature makes apparent to us, we come that much closer to realizing our true place as human beings.

Thriving human beings exist only as a cumulation of living by species-normal behaviors, unspoiled by the world of senseless progress and growth. Abiding by natural evolutionary-driven laws include communing with nature often, living within that once fully intact evolved developmental niche or primal nest, taking resources only, when necessary, a willingness to foster our ability to "read" the language of Nature, the feeling of having a reciprocal relationship-orientated relationship with Nature, and a willingness to rekindle lost or forgotten natural ways of knowing and sensing. For most of humanity's existence, humans thrived as naturally cooperative beings capable of deep companionship. By occupying our evolved species-typical niche, we can return to a state of thriving, rather than a state of trying.

Our Elders

Accumulated knowledge about the inner workings of the real world is what eventually blooms into wisdom. In today's world, meaningless distractions keep us from acquiring what our ancestors learned about the world and the ways of Nature for millennia. Many of us in the recent world haven't even experienced a culture that honors and respects its elderly. It is a world in which "high tech" is ruling our lives and *real-life* knowledge of the world is deteriorating alongside our own abilities to be sociable, kind, and generous. While it is true that the distractions of new technologies since the beginning of the industrial and scientific revolution have dampened our inborn abilities to acquire personal insights and real-world experience, the total disregard for elders in many westernized societies has also in many ways dampened our sense of human wellness. Ageism is a new form of deeply compromising discrimination; a prejudice that has fueled an ever-growing disconnect between ourselves and our living ancestors.

Discrimination and distraction seem to have contributed to diminishing the wisdom of our elders so prevalent in modern cultures. Instead of sharing their real-world insights, some of our elders are now caught up in the technological vortex themselves, spending their time staring into digital screens just as younger generations do. Yet many elders still choose to resist the use of these technologies. It is not only a lack of their knowledge of the use of these often-unnecessary technologies that drive this, but their own observations and insights of how disconnected and less sociable people have become as a result. Indeed, many of these technologies are radically life-changing, but not necessarily in a good way.

The existence of ageism itself reveals to a great lack of wisdom. Judging the elderly by their resistance or inability to utilize constantly evolving technologies is deeply dehumanizing. It may even be that these people are the wisest among us. Perhaps we should heed their resistance as a warning. Our dominant westernized culture not only dehumanizes our elders, but all of humanity. By not heeding the advice of our elders we deny the betterment of ourselves by not learning from historical experiences. We repeat history instead of leading our lives with wisdom.

In Greece, older members of society are believed to possess great wisdom by the knowledge imparted to them throughout their long lives. Older people in Greece are shown respect by being served first at each meal. When they speak, people listen to what they have to say instead of disregarding their input. The term 'Old man' is a term of endearment and an honorable title, not a demeaning one.

In Japan, Respect for the Aged Day (Keiro No Hi), is a publicly celebrated holiday that honors its elderly population for their contributions to society. The holiday elevates the elderly by celebrating their wisdom as well as their longevity.

Each of the Native American nations possess their own traditions in respecting the aging and elders. In most Native American cultures, it is expected of elders to pass down their many life experiences and wisdom to younger generations.

In most Westernized societies however, the practice of honoring and respecting our elders has fallen away as these societies tend to follow a youth-oriented culture only. This conventional way of dehumanizing our elders reveals our human brokenness. Following a youth-oriented instead of a human-oriented culture demeans our own humanity as we try to navigate our way through our rapidly changing world. By not listening to our wise elders, we lose our wise elders.

But why should we listen to our elders? Why should we be concerned with losing our wise elders? When I wonder if we have over-glorified the knowledge of native First Peoples, I think about my own realizations while in Nature that seemed to spontaneously reveal themselves to me. I think about the awesomeness of the sudden, and sometimes not-so-sudden, awareness. I think of how each mysterious bend in a trail drew me curiously onward, further into the wilds with a strong wish to know more about everything that crossed my path. These feelings lead me to believe strongly that the knowledge our ancestors must have possessed, having spent their lives fully immersed in Nature, was very great indeed.

Earlier in this book, we talked about how bioregionalism is one of the most basic reasons we needed our wise elders. Listening to what our wise elders had to say about valuable life-lessons, resources and skills prehistorically contributed to our long-standing survival. While egocentrically lost in our newly acquired distractions, we find ourselves less inclined to pass on knowledge to others or listen to the wise peoples that are still with us. As more and more people (even older members of society) are continually targeted by distracting technologies, we risk losing once invaluable trans-generational and inter-familial wisdom.

In the oral transmission of knowledge, storytelling was the tool in remembering important details. Also, because we lived in small, tight bands, wise elders were always available to us, passing on knowledge and information necessary for the time at hand. When we abandon this way of passing on information, the knowledge we seek becomes lost in our overly complicated compilation of digital information. In oral transmission of information, knowledge is sacred. This sacred knowledge is held near and dear to one's heart as a lifeline to one's own survival. The knowledge continues to live on each time it is passed on to others. It is a sacred tool. We have increased our risk of losing this knowledge by writing it down instead of retaining it through stories as our ancestors did. Unless people have the willingness to learn crucial information, they will never learn it. It requires a great deal more interest and work to seek written knowledge in a library, or even our World Wide Web than to have been told stories that one will never forget.

Just as Nature itself is created and nurtured from the bottom-up and from the top-down, humans also require this nurturing; from the bottom-up in the raising and caring for babies, and from the top-down in the sharing of wisdom from our elders. As part of our primal nest, this meets our millions of years in the making of biologic basic needs, completing the picture of who we really are as humans.

7

An Unnatural Relationship

Raking Leaves

Raking leaves to be placed into giant plastic bags and hauled away as garbage where they ultimately end up in landfills makes no more sense than green golf courses in the desert. In the forests and other wild places, the slow decay of fallen leaves provides vital nutrients and habitat for many soil-enriching invertebrates and microorganisms—life-giving organisms that rely on the detritus (dead plant and animal material) as food. The byproducts produced by these organisms in turn sustain life of other plants and animals, all the way up the food chain. The blanketing of leaves that fall season after season is crucial for thriving habitats. Today's *normalized* orders laid down by civilization tell us that raking leaves is necessary. It has certainly become a normal practice to rake the leaves in your yard, but the practice of removing blankets of leaf litter is not at all normal for Nature.

Deciduous trees evolved to drop their leaves when the leaves no longer provide them with photosynthesized nutrition. When the leaves have done their job, they drop to the earth. Leaf "litter" protects soils from erosion, enriching and building the soil year after year. Leaves also act as a natural mulch that helps the soil retain moisture longer and protects delicate tree roots from extreme temperatures. Many animals benefit from fallen leaves; birds are often seen scratching around leafy ground in search of insects and grubs. The only reason we rake the leaves today is to keep our tailored green lawns showcased and to abide by social norms. This is what "good-looking" neighborhoods should look like.

The economically driven world is simply a belief system we all buy into, both literally and figuratively. Society tells us that we must rake the leaves, so we then have stores filled with all kinds of yard maintenance tools for us to purchase. Instead, we could let the leaves fall and watch as the natural world around us flourishes. I know this isn't practical, or even acceptable in many culturally tailored neighborhoods, nor would it be safe for wandering wildlife who might be inclined to scavenge in and around leaf litter. The point is this—many things we do are not *naturally* normal and are often downright backward. Invite an aboriginal forest dweller into suburbia and they would be beyond perplexed at the sight of people raking their leaves simply to throw them out as garbage.

Seeking to understand the dance and language of Nature is the only way we can really understand the nature of Nature. The *language* of trees dropping their leaves is understood more clearly when one looks for what lies beneath those leaves.

If our ancient ancestors were to see several wild kin of various species lying dead all about, they would naturally think something was seriously wrong and might even feel threatened themselves. It would be a sight too unusual to ignore. Yet today, dead animals along our highways and roads are as normalized as the roads themselves. Many of us pass on by without thinking much of it. Owls, foxes, armadillos, coyotes, ravens, skunks, raccoons, turtles, deer, snakes, and more are killed on roadways every day. Yet we consider this normal.

When I was a young girl, my father and I would drive along a two-lane desert highway to visit my grandmother on the weekends. The hour and a half drives were always an enjoyable experience. I admired the vastness of the desert and scanned the landscape, curious about what might be living out there. Occasionally I'd have the great fortune to see jackrabbits, cottontails, mule deer, hawks, turkey vultures or other fun critters along the way. Each drive was the same, yet different.

There was relatively little traffic then, and at times it seemed as though we were the only ones out there. Sometimes we would have to drive back home at night, and the stars always seemed to shine more brilliantly. Lightning storms were spectacular, as the expanse of the desert allowed us to witness the lightning strikes as they flashed across the night sky in an awesome display. Profiles of distant mountain ranges would come to life with far-off illuminating strikes. I remember imagining what animals might be wandering the desert's nightscape as I peered into the darkness, prepared to see the unexpected with every illumination.

Our drives made me realize just how destructive our presence was. Each time we approached roadkill, I turned away and delivered a silent *prayer* that went something like this: *"I am so sorry. This is because of us . . . without us, you* [the creature] *would not have died in such an untimely and unfair way. Please forgive us."* The words fail to convey the powerful emotion I felt at the time, yet it was always deep and sincere and reflected the great respect I had for these living beings. I didn't have a name for the source to which I was praying, nor did I come from a religious background. I sensed I was speaking directly to what Tom Brown calls "the spirit-that-moves-through-all-things," Nature itself. At least that was what I felt in my heart. The secret prayer became a ritual at every road-killed animal I saw. Never did I tell anyone I did this. Nor did I feel a need to. It was just something I did. The sight of an animal killed by traffic seemed so unfair, but what sent shivers of sadness through my body seemed to elude everyone else's consciousness. I didn't understand why this was accepted as part of normal life. In my young heart, I just knew it wasn't meant to be this way.

Still today, variations of this secret, silent prayer come to my mind at the sight of my fallen wild kin. I believe it is little things like this that create one's own sense of spirituality, and mine has always been deeply intertwined with my love for the natural world. It makes sense that our ancient ancestors might have adopted earth-based forms of spirituality as a people living closely intertwined with the natural world in their day-to-day lives.

It doesn't matter to me whether they are rabbits, foxes, or turkey vultures I see lying dead on the side of the road, in my heart their untimely deaths in this way feel shamefully discordant with the laws of Nature—that they didn't live to fulfill their niche of being a part of the whole of Nature. We humans are the variable that causes this great imbalance. Even as a child it made sense to me that the creatures who lived there contributed to the very existence of the desert I admired so much.

Ecologists recognize how roadkill inevitably shifts animal behavior by drawing ravens, vultures and other scavenging animals to the roadside, which further increases road-killed animals. The estimated *one million* animals that are passively killed every day by cars reveals disturbing major ecological disruption. While it may be easy to think that the loss of wildlife due to traffic is simply accidental and something society just accepts, there are ways roadkill can be reduced and even avoided. *Wildlife corridors*, such as specially designed culverts, natural bridges, and wildlife-friendly fencing, when placed in areas where roadkill is particularly prevalent, have proven to greatly reduce our impact on native wildlife. Only in realizing our interdependency with all life will we be persuaded to implement such solutions. In creating wildlife corridors alone, we could prevent a substantial biodiversity loss instead of driving millions of wildlife to their deaths every year. Wildlife corridors may even *save* money by reducing injuries and property damage. They could be considered beautiful natural assets that cities and towns could showcase, and could provide meaningful jobs. It is estimated that when wildlife corridors are placed in high incident zones, they could potentially reduce vehicle-animal collisions by up to 97%.

Vehicular collisions with our wild kin are not the only reason that animals are dying in alarming numbers every year. In addition to those killed by traffic, our wild kin are also being targeted intentionally through killing contests and the Wildlife Services agency, contributing to staggering biodiversity loss.

Killing contests are competitions in which contestants are awarded prizes based on the number of animals killed in various categories. Animals targeted by these killing contests include prairie dogs, mountain lions, foxes, coyotes, marmots, bobcats, raccoons, and other animals the participants deem *dangerous pests* and *vermin* that they are "helping" to eliminate. With a large percentage of the animals being carnivorous creatures, killing contest participants are willfully targeting many of our most important predators whose losses cause major ecological instability.

The killing of animals by Wildlife Services are by employees of federal wildlife management agencies as an effort to favor domesticated livestock over our indigenous wildlife in response to concerned ranchers and other private interests. Known for targeting our most important predators and other keystone species, Wildlife Services account for hundreds of thousands of our wild kin being killed every year.

Ecologists now recognize what many of our ancient ancestors always knew—that in the absence of our indigenous wildlife, ecological degradation is sure to follow. The ecology upon which our own lives depend becomes compromised. By losing our wild kin, we are losing a part of ourselves.

That same desert highway of my childhood has since been expanded into four lanes and the traffic has more than doubled. Movement is life, and all wildlife, including humans, must move to acquire resources necessary for survival. With increased habitat fragmentation by human actions, we have hindered this very natural process of life. Millions of our wild kin are being killed every year for simply wandering outside of boundaries we humans have set for them. But we must never forget that *we* are also tucked into the greater wilderness in Nature.

When Carl Sagan first laid eyes upon that pale blue dot, our dear planet Earth, he was deeply humbled by the realization that human-conceived boundaries of nations and countries never really existed at all. The same is ultimately true for boundaries of Nature versus non-Nature. We live upon *one* wild Earth. The modern human's exaggerated sense of importance is ludicrous and nonsensical, for in human against human there is not one higher than the other. Neither is there for man against ape or ant. It is only a blur where Earth ends, and humankind and all living beings begin. No such boundaries exist.

"Ever since the Cognitive Revolution, Sapiens have been living in a dual reality. On the one hand, the objective reality of rivers, trees and lions; and on the other hand the imagined reality of gods, nations and corporations. As time went by, the imagined reality became ever more powerful, so that today the very survival of rivers, trees and lions depends on the grace of imagined entities such as the United States and Google." ~ Yuval Noah Harari

If investigating what lies beneath fallen leaves reveals how much we fail to understand about Nature, what truths then lie beneath our modern lives? The lives we are led to believe is our only way. The true essence of what makes a human being *human* is not often found as plainly in the civilized world. And yet, in some ways it exists blatantly obvious if only by the sheer absence of that true nature, that the sense of wanting to belong is shared by us all.

It is undeniable that civilization has fueled many unintended consequences. As the popular proverb goes: "The road to hell is [often] paved with good intentions." The disorientation that comes from our modern lives can be curbed simply with a reorientation toward simpler ways of living and by recognizing the natural world as our ally, not something we would want to undermine or dominate.

Civilization is quintessentially based on fictional realities. As Yuval Noah Harari says: "The real success of our species is that we alone can talk about things that don't exist at all." (Such as money, politics, and corporations). The worth of all agreed-upon realities that make up modern life, pales in comparison to the true realities that naturally enfold us. Cities, pavement, and other modern technologies are all dead things. In Nature all things, including so-called non-living things such as rocks, exist dynamically in life-giving processes. Ever-changing alongside other elements they exist *animately* to uphold life. Modern realities are only shadows, existing because we say they do. The living elements that will someday, long after we are gone, weather away the physical forms of these dead things are what is truly real.

When in the city, I often feel alien as civilization presses upon our minds what is expected of us to be good, responsible, and acceptable citizens. The one thing that has remained consistently apparent to me, even as kid, is that humans need something more—a returning to wholeness, they desperately needed *Nature*.

The illusory notion that wild Nature only exists beyond the boundaries of civilization is the reason most of the land we know today is withering away in some form, succumbing to accelerated degradation and decomposition, ultimately becoming ever more primed to nourish the Earth that will exist after our time. The limited view of linearism ignores the *whole of Nature*. Natural reality is an endless circle of birth, death, and rebirth. Even wild places that have been severely impacted by unnatural human-doings, when left to their own agency begin the unstoppable process of regeneration, recovery, and repair. In failing to live in awareness of our own connection to that process, we simply get in the way of this life-giving progression.

In many ways modern humans live distorted realities living as separatists, even in withholding our dead from returning to the earth. We selfishly hold onto human life by embalming the dead and purchasing ridiculously decorative and impenetrable caskets. Our bodies belong to the earth, yet even in death we exist as separatists, lying dead and ungiving to the cyclical process of life and Nature.

On Naming

Once while conducting bird surveys, I heard the unmistakable sweet call of a black hawk emanating from somewhere beyond the canopy. I soon spotted a juvenile black hawk perched high above in a massive cottonwood. I listened as the young hawk responded to its squawking parent in the sky.

For a few years after this experience, the sight and sound of the common black hawk starred prominently in my life. It was a simple matter of right place and right time-ness. On another occasion while backpacking I again heard that sweet familiar call. Scanning the sky, I spotted the black hawk circling beyond its nest in a towering ponderosa. I then heard a separate call emanating from within its nest. Excited at the prospect of seeing a nestling, I climbed the steep mountainside as far as I could by following along a faint deer trail, thickly ladened with native shrubbery and rolling scree underfoot. Once I was nearly parallel to the nest, I could see the flying black hawk's mate on sitting duty. While no nestling could be seen, being able to see the nesting parent from this point of view made the arduous climb worth it. It was exhilarating to be so high up in the forest canopy in an eco-zone that so few humans have a chance to connect with; the arboreal realm belongs to tree and sky beings.

There is always great joy in witnessing wild animal families in Nature—a feeling of certain *completeness*. As we continue to seek wholeness in our own lives, being able to witness wild *bondings* in Nature feels deeply satisfying.

When the common black hawk flew into my life, I knew very little about the species. All I knew was that their range was considered quite limited, which made their appearances even more special. I took it upon myself to learn more about their kind and browsed field guides and the internet.

As we all know, utilizing the world-wide digital library of information can result in a plethora of unexpected results. I am always caught off guard when using the internet to research some aspect of Nature. When I simply searched "black hawk," the first result was a military utility helicopter, not a bird. The prioritization of information in the digital world points toward our disconnect with our living world. When looking for information about real aspects of Nature, be sure to clarify whether what you are searching for is a plant, animal, person, etcetera. Examples of convoluted terms include *mustang* (a car); *jaguar* (a luxury car); *impala* (a car); *apple* (a tech company). The names of living indigenous peoples are also undermined. Searching the name *Apache* results in a military aircraft or *Winnebago*, a recreational vehicle. It is heartbreakingly interesting that the names of many of these modern entities that are causing harm to our world were inspired by Natural living things.

Perhaps one of the most disturbing examples has taken the name of our most precious, biologically diverse rainforest, *Amazon.* That name now symbolizes a globalized online marketplace whose patrons help send billionaires on joyrides into space. Ironically, that company directly contributes to the loss of the real, living, breathing Amazon, and other precious ecosystems in selling and distributing merchandise to consumers worldwide. In recent years it has contributed dramatically to accelerate climate change. In 2018, it was estimated that Amazon the company released 44.4 million metric tons of carbon dioxide into our atmosphere, a carbon footprint greater than that of Switzerland. Between mining and processing and utilizing and transporting raw materials to produce cheap merchandise, many of which are single-use products designed around convenience and disposability, it is easy to see how the company contributes massively to climate change and to habitat destruction.

We live in a world that has prioritized the non-living over natural, living things. Our modern tendencies, albeit unconsciously, are to banish from our memories and from our existence these *living* entities to whom we owe so much. Seeing clearly our radical disassociation from Nature in this way is a reminder that I must return to the *real* world wide web for answers.

~ ~ ~

Many Native traditions partook in elaborate and thoughtful naming traditions in which they turned to Nature for inspiration and insight, carefully deciding on names that reflected the spirit and character of the individual. Often these included names of animals paired with an action word such as *sitting, dancing, running, stalking,* etc. An example would be something like "Jumping Badger," the name originally given to Sitting Bull, the Hunkpapa Lakota leader remembered for his courageous efforts to unite and lead Sioux peoples in a resistance to domination. When reflected upon, the name "Sitting Bull" certainly signifies his great stubborn resistance to dominating forces.

Sometimes names were chosen to align with expectations parents or elders might have of a young person, or to possibly inspire and instill honorable qualities. Indigenous peoples believed that the animals originally taught human beings how to live harmoniously alongside the natural world. Many animals were revered and respected for embodying certain extraordinary traits and characteristics. Native people also assigned certain qualities to different wild animals. In certain traditions the Eagle may represent love, the Beaver wisdom, the Wolf, humility, and so on.

When paired with honor and respect, the spirit of these animals was carried on through a person's livelihood. Like Nature, the names of Native peoples were dynamic and could change over time to better represent a person's accomplishments or experiences. Naming traditions were the sinew that bound our ancestors to wild Nature, representing an intrinsic knowing that we are forever united with our living, natural world. Such traditions honor the fact that we owe our lives to those who walked, crawled, or flew across this world before us. I will continue to honor the living black hawk, *the bird,* as a part of the living, breathing web of life we share. In honoring the living, breathing things who still exist or have existed before our own times, we acknowledge our true reality.

Of Butterflies and Men

Modern consumerism may be normalized but it isn't at all natural. Imagine carrying everything you owned on your back. Intellectually we realize the absurdity of this. Nevertheless, we can't seem to divorce ourselves from our modern consumeristic tendencies. That fact alone proves it to be a less fulfilling aspect of humanity, since there always seems to be more that we want or think we want. There never seems to be enough. As minimalist and change-maker Joshua Fields Millburn has said, "We are spending money we don't have, to buy things we don't need, to impress people we don't even know (or don't even like)."

It has been observed that people considered to be the least affluent in the world display an ability to be happier with less, as they are often more capable of finding joy in little things. Regarding this phenomenon, some may argue there is little choice in the matter, and while that may be true, what harm comes from enjoying life to the fullest no matter how few possessions one has?

Similarly, many anthropologists agree that pre-agricultural hunter-gatherers could be considered the *original* affluent societies. It's easy to see how this could be true. In a realm free from modern dualism, capitalism and consumerism, there would be less grasping for a more prosperous future and less need to reach beyond meeting immediate needs and joys. It would be a life devoid of domineering material and monetary wealth while also experiencing far fewer infectious diseases and more diverse, biologically appropriate diets. Although most in post-agricultural societies labor less in the fields for their food, they spend much more of their time working for a livable wage to *pay* for their food. This mode of living has major consequences for the well-being of human lives as well as for non-human life. As modern history unfolds, and the declining life-giving resources are becoming more and more poisoned, humans living in the modern world will ultimately become the new impoverished.

Comparatively, ancestral peoples supported the health of societal members by being actively involved in the care of both mothers and young ones within their communities, thus allowing space for the primal nest by promoting societal cohesion and stability. There were no corporate jobs, therefore no need for institutions of childcare. The mother, alongside other members of the band, took part in raising the young rather than sending them away to be cared for by strangers. This contributed to more self-actualized, psychologically and physiologically balanced human beings. Children benefited from playing freely with children of all ages and since they were not subjugated to separation from the whole of society, were well balanced and better cared for overall. Also, there were no healthcare institutions. Instead, some members of the society possessed knowledge of plants and foods that were beneficial for healing. Alongside a more varied diet this may have promoted greater overall health and general well-being. These are all aspects *typical* of our species. Today many of these components have been abandoned to follow species-*atypical* behaviors shaped by the modern world. We must now question what is truly normal.

~ ~ ~

In my childhood home, a calendar of endangered species hung on the kitchen wall near the back doorway. I can recall my fascination with every creature as I peered at the photos of each month. Throughout the year I passed that calendar more times than I could know as I sprung outside to play. One mid-spring while walking about the yard, I noticed a large, sage-green winged being dancing around my mother's flowerbed. I thought I had seen it before. *It's a Luna Moth!* After getting as many glimpses of the remarkable creature as I could before it flew away, I ran indoors to see if what I thought was true. It was! One of the months in the calendar was dedicated to the endangered Luna Moth. Sheer gladness filled my heart as I ran back outside and waited near the garden, hoping it would return. It never did, but I will never forget seeing that Luna Moth dance upon my mother's flowers.

The Luna Moth may look like a butterfly, but it is a type of silk moth. Moths differ from butterflies in that they tend to hold their wings outstretched while resting, whereas butterflies tend to fold their wings. Although moths and butterflies differ in many ways, the caterpillars of both share one thing in common: they eat *a lot*. The menu of the Luna Moth caterpillar is made up of the foliage of hickories, alder, persimmon, walnuts, sumacs and more. Some caterpillars of *butterflies* eat so much they can grow 1,000 times their weight. As adults, Luna Moths no longer have mouth parts and no longer need to eat. They also only live for around a week. Their job as fully transformed adults is to find a mate and reproduce. Luna Moths are an important food source for owls, bats, and the rarely seen nocturnal whippoorwill.

Butterflies differ from Luna Moths by playing a crucial role in pollination. Butterflies also have reduced mouth parts but retain a functional part called a proboscis. They still consume food, but instead of eating nearly a thousand times their body weight in foliage, they sip nectar from the flowers.

Although the life of the caterpillar may seem incredibly destructive, it is preparing for a life of not only giving back, but of reversing the damage it has caused in its underdeveloped state. The reciprocal dance of caterpillars and butterflies and of life itself is a uniquely sustainable relationship. In an interview with author Sailesh Rao, we discussed the role of human behavior in the current ongoing ecological destruction. Sailesh works to promote a new story of human nature. To adapt to the current ecological changes we are facing, humans must make a conscientious effort to live in a new alignment with our ever-changing living world. In his most noteworthy approach, Sailesh Rao uses the analogy of the caterpillar and butterfly to describe where we currently stand at this point in human history, suggesting that we are nearing the end of our own destructive caterpillar stage, and that we must now occupy the state of the butterfly by giving back and restoring the damage we have caused. Even the Luna Moth gives back. Although they do not play a prominent role in pollination, they become the food source for another prominent pollinator—bats. We too must find *our* way to give back.

Nature is made up of countless reciprocal relationships whereby each species involved provides a benefit for the other in a remarkable dance called ecological mutualism. The overall fitness and chances for survival of these individual species is increased by this partnership. Humans today will have to choose whether to make a conscientious decision to participate in such a partnership with the Earth.

While the idea of steering away from outsourced manufacturing and global marketism is a noble idea, domestic manufacturing is only a partial solution to our crisis of destruction over consumption. Never have we successfully been able to use technology to mend ecological crises, at least not on a broader scale. We cannot simply manufacture our way out of the mess we are in. Utilizing resources regionally and locally is also only part of the solution. Conscientiously consuming *less* of everything overall is our answer. A thriving human being is one who can find contentment in meeting his or her basic needs. By learning to live with less, one may even find they have more freedom in their lives—freedom from hoarding stuff we do not need and from the ever-dehumanizing marketeering.

"We are living in difficult times where we are simultaneously distressed, distracted and confused. We are conditioned to blame ourselves or "them." But the problem is systemic, a system that is set up contrary to natural laws of the earth, of human development, and of nurturing children. To realign ourselves, we must let go of junk food, junk teachings and junk ideas." ~ Darcia Narvaez, PhD.

While our oldest ancestors lived and died in a world dictated by natural order, so many living in the world today struggle to eke out a decent livable wage, forever stricken with hopes of "American dream-ness," seeking a simple break from economic hardship. Some live dependent on the fantasy of a delayed economic return, attempting to achieve a status that is better-than-what-is-present in our current lives. Yet our most resilient ancestors had little choice but to *live in the present*. The hunter-gatherers' were able to resist illogically-perceived dysfunctional lifestyles we see normalized today. Our modern way of living in the eyes of these rare ancestral archetypes would make little sense since there is little material wealth maintained within typical egalitarian societies. We have been led to believe that dominant culture knows best, and while culture does seem to dominate the roles and actions we live by, when we look beneath the leaves fallen from the tree of modernity, we find key fundamentals are missing.

Perhaps we struggle so much in this modern life because this is not who we really are, which is something I deeply believe.

If we humans were freed from the so-called necessities of our atypical lives in modern society, the healthier our own species could certainly be. At the heart of the matter, we all know that the healthier *we* are the healthier the world we live in will be. The amount of plastic waste produced by the management of disease alone is an ironic example: plastic breaks down into micro (and even *nano*) particles reentering our water supply where it then continues to cause various diseases and conditions. Staying healthy and avoiding disease in the first place could help us to prevent this kind of waste, yet the waste created by our modern world *contributes* to disease. We find ourselves caught in another seemingly endless cycle, spiraling out of control.

Our modern ways have not only made us less healthy emotionally, mentally, and physiologically; modern life has made us *busier* than ever before. Our newly acquired busyness is one way that modern humans like to show off our importance. Saying one is *"so busy"* often indicates a sense of value and self-worth. We wear our busyness as an honorable badge as we fulfill what we believe is expected of us. This obsession with productivity comes with many consequences. The busier we become lost in the distraction and confusion of fast-paced modern obsessions, the less likely we are to care not only for ourselves, but for those around us as well. The busier we are, the more unreliable we become to others, and even to ourselves by not meeting our most basic psychological and health needs. Most of our time is spent fulfilling the requirements tied to modern life's expectations. Our calendars are filled to the brim with modern minutiae of often stress-inducing, societal obligations. We daily find ourselves carrying out a variety of menial tasks, many of which lack any intrinsic value or contribute to our sense of wellbeing.

We *all* suffer from this completely dysfunctional psychological badge of honor. We live in a world where we long for freedom. From debt, from the 40-hour-plus work weeks away from our loved ones and the homes we must work so hard to afford, from excessive digitization. Freedom from these things can, at least partially, be acquired by living a simpler existence. This is often perceived as a radical alternative by those who live according to conventional standards. Our busy lives leave little room for introspection, self-care, self-improvement, or other self-fulfilling projects while we work approximately an average of 2,080 hours a year just to get by. Don't all beings deserve a right to an adequate life? In today's world one must *earn* their living as well as their freedom, while our ancient ancestors lived freely. No gimmicky, money handling middlemen required.

When one is allowed the space, time, and freedom to care for their basic needs there is greater opportunity to develop the moral character and disposition to be available to care for others in a better way. It seems that the busier we modern humans become, the more selfish we become. Yet learning to live with less and make do with what is more readily and sustainably available to us, puts us on that path toward increased freedom. Donning the *busy badge* not only leaves us more stressed and under-cared for, it also makes us less able and willing to participate in other more meaningful and selfless efforts. The person busy with modern distractions easily ignores the littered roadways, increased noise, light, and air pollution because when you have the absolute need to keep busy, you don't have the time or mind-space to take notice and care enough about litter or other social or environmental issues affecting us all. In our busyness we develop a blindness to the aspects in our lives that hold *real* meaning and purpose.

Modern humans now have little time in their lives to get to know their authentic selves; a limitation that keeps us from understanding our true place in Nature. The way knowledge flows has shifted so dramatically that people take no thought of its abnormality. Knowledge is meant to be taught, but *higher* learning is now limited to tuition-based institutions or at the mercy of one's own willingness to learn. However, many find themselves so stressed with the pace of life, it leaves little time to self-educate and learn anything new, like the true nature of ourselves and of Nature.

Independent research has been a hobby of mine since childhood in which my fascination with the natural world was the driving force. There were no "wise elders" who could share with me the unspoken language of Nature beyond books, field guides and documentaries.

For many Indigenous societies, knowledge is an honorable, sacred thing meant to be passed on. This contributed to the survival of our earliest human ancestors. The moment we accepted the fallacy that the transmission of knowledge requires an exchange of funds instead of being generously given, is the moment in time we turned our backs on building resilience in our species. The withholding of knowledge made us vulnerable, and as the modern world expanded, the wise ones who possessed great ancestral knowledge were eventually shunned and forbidden to share the old ways. These old ways became regarded as threatening, for the knowledge of the old ways allowed for too much freedom, too much independence—ideals that modern society does not support. And in a world where expanding concepts of capitalism and ownership began making its way across all frontiers, knowledge of freedom needed to be kept at bay.

Our modern world seems to be deprived of wise elders, those ancestors who ushered new generations into resilient, independent livelihoods by nurturing and passing on knowledge. These wise elders shared far more than sustainable foraging and hunting skills. Beyond the usefulness of plants and the animals, they shared what they knew about the nature of reality. They also believed that with every generation, the spirit of Nature lives on . . . if those they taught were willing to continue sharing their wisdom with others.

~ ~ ~

Our saving grace at this present time in history is to seriously rethink many aspects of our modern lives that prevent us from realizing our own true nature. Here are a few that we humans can afford to be free of:

Freedom from meaningless and often harmful work environments: This includes incessant productivity of ecologically harmful products and services so often associated with our daily lives. Our actions and the thoughts behind our actions as well as how we choose to live our lives are directly influenced by the "ideals" that corporations feed us to dominant culture. Instead, the work in which we so often participate directly serves the interests of corporations, not the needs of the people. Freedom from work that does not serve our needs for health and overall wellbeing is a concept misconstrued by modern conditioning as frivolous or lazy. One must "earn a living" measured primarily by monetary means, whereby people are valued more for their monetary worth than their human worth. We find that the modern obsession with work often exists at the expense of indigenous ideologies, our greater ecology, and therefore at the expense of our own wellbeing.

Freedom from shame to be fully human: Care of our families and care of ourselves today is in direct contrast with how corporations and governments feel we should be caring for our families. Lack of societal support of species-normal care of our babies, mothers and families is another deeply dysfunctional reality of the modern times. Airport breastfeeding stations mentioned before is an example of this. Shaming mothers into isolation to care for and feed their babies points toward our shattered humanity. When following the laws of Nature, such as a mother caring for her baby, is regarded as inappropriate, we have certainly lost our way.

Freedom from the dominant-culture-knows-best model: This may seem like a bit of a cliché, yet it remains a relevant issue. Freedom from the compulsions of senseless conformity is quite the challenge in today's world. When I was an undergraduate, a professor of mine asked a question referencing a modern pop star relevant to that time. When I responded that I didn't know who he was talking about, he berated me and said, *"How do you not know who they are? It's pop culture!"* This was something I had little interest in. I wasn't totally surprised by the response since I had learned to deal with pop culture-oriented friends and acquaintances. Mostly this has been easy to navigate, although I do find it fascinating that so many are caught up in the unrealistic world of fame. Certainly, any parent would regard their child perfect just as they are without encouraging them to emulate the overly plasticized famous. But young minds become carried away with the unrealistic ideals of pop culture figures because of the unrelenting digital outlets we carry in our pockets. But pop culture isn't our main issue—it is dominant culture, *period*. When our dominant culture says, "be true to yourself," (so long as it fits within the parameters of acceptable norms), we find ourselves in a box with deviant humans behaving as freely as society allows. While it is inspiring that overall, people are becoming more accepting of others, there is still a host of things dominant culture tells us is best that could not be further from the truth.

For instance, the use of single-use plastics is widely accepted yet it causes tremendous harm to our planet and so in turn to ourselves. Dominant culture tells us breastfeeding in public areas is unacceptable, or that wrinkles, scars, and imperfections are things to hide. These are our true states of being, and for our own wellbeing, we must accept them with compassion and understanding.

Freedom from the choice-lessness of an earth- and human-harming grid: In a world with incredible resources, we still fail to give people a chance to live more meaningful, healthful lives, and instead force them to live by unsustainable standards. I live in a large but underpopulated county and in recent years, one small town situated about 10 miles from the main town celebrated the incoming of a new store. The town is a small and struggling community without a local grocery store. Many members of the community strive to find work and many more people lack the resources for a personal vehicle. While a local transport shuttle exists, many people opt for catching a ride with a family member, riding a bike, or walking the long highway into town, ten miles each way. The pandemic caused discontinuation of the shuttle services, so people find themselves particularly strapped. The much-celebrated store was a dollar store, built just two miles away from the village center. There is growing evidence that dollar stores target struggling communities, leading to further economic distress. They do so by making it nearly impossible for more suitable and beneficial grocers to claim the same location. Dollar stores are essentially junk food stores. Most do not sell any fresh fruits or vegetables, forcing struggling communities to eat only what is immediately available to them: processed junk foods and drinks. Dollar store corporations continue to get wealthy as members of communities with little choice continue to become addicted to unhealthy, nutritionally poor food choices. County ordinances could be implemented to prevent dollar stores from targeting our communities and preying on the poor— ordinances that would encourage full-service grocery stores to take root instead. Our socio-economic divides stretch far and wide, and when one delves deeper into the unsustainable inner workings of such divides, one finds it is incredibly inhumane.

Freedom from disinformation, relentless social media, and the endless digitization of our lives: When his students were underperforming in their studies, philosophy professor Ron Srigley challenged them to give up their smart phones for one week, believing that mobile technology was to blame. (After he had asked the students why they thought the entire class had performed badly on a test, their reluctant explanations revealed they were overly distracted and had trouble focusing on their assignments.) As an experiment he offered extra credit for students who were willing to even try to give up their devices. If they agreed, they would give him custody of their phones for nine days. About a third of the class took on the challenge in desperation to turn around their failing status. Srigley noticed some immediate effects. At first the students felt frustrated and disoriented, but what they wrote about their experience was nearly consistent across all participants. For one thing, they noted how rude it felt when someone they were talking to would use their devices in the middle of a conversation, admitting that they themselves did this. Another student noted how much people avoided eye contact, reaching for their device before eye contact could be established, seemingly avoiding all interactions with people they did not know. Some students missed keeping in nearly constant communication with their families, although noted that their face-to-face interactions with family members felt more present. Others admitted they were able to pay better attention and thus felt more productive. They also noted how much they loved having fewer interruptions, and one student said, "I didn't feel bad not answering phone calls because there were none to ignore." Having not missed the incessant interruptions, when having his phone returned to him after conclusion of the experiment, he ultimately gave it up for good.

Some students revealed that they became more fearful without their smart devices. They were filled with anxiety over what they would do if they were attacked, kidnapped or had an emergency. Srigley pointed out this revealed that students generally "perceived the world to be a very dangerous place," despite that the city in which they were living had one of the lowest crime rates. In the avoidance of dealing with strangers, smart phone users generally learn to mistrust people they do not know. Whereas in a time not too long ago, interactions with people we did not know was part of normal life.

A growing number of people are rejecting their devices to embrace a more meaningful existence and a way to maintain better mental health, including *zoomers* (Generation Z's). The decision to renounce their smart devices stems from a host of personal reasons from mood improvement to better productivity. Neuro-scientific studies are showing that addiction to smart phones is causing imbalances in the brain leading to more depression, anxiety and even fatigue. Time in quarantine has revealed a particularly alarming reality of how these technologies rule our lives. While the technology has allowed us to stay connected, it has done so by being inextricably and overly attached to us as our basic attire. With fewer defined work-life boundaries, the technology used to carry out many of our jobs now follows us everywhere we go. It's no wonder people are experiencing more stress than ever. Being on-call all the time, for everyone, everywhere, is the intrusiveness people are now seeking to be free of.

In efforts to take back their minds and true sense of worth, those making the decision to ditch their smart devices are still in the minority, although they are part of a rapidly growing movement and "dumb" phone sales are seeing a rise in recent years. This points toward a desire to turn away from the near constant source of online entertainment, needless scrolling, predatory algorithms, and obligatory availability. A hopeful prediction is that more people will abandon public online social networks to opt for smaller, more localized community networks where they can engage with real people.

Many people wanting to ditch their smartphones are met with work and societal pressures to stay forever bound to these technologies that have been masterfully woven into the folds of every aspect of our lives, including work. This has been associated with greater anxieties and frustrations where home versus work lives blend, leaving little free time for oneself and needs. We remain caught up in the pervasive world of digital networking.

Renowned historian, Yuval Noah Harari once said it was indisputable that thanks to social media, we are now more connected than ever, but not in a harmonious way. As modern humans remain swept away by everlasting gossipy dialogues about other people and their lives as portrayed in the digital world, online social platforms impede our own true humanity by revealing our most obvious modern social disjuncture. Then how, one might ask, do these digital trappings help to harmonize our lives or adequately facilitate our need to be sociable creatures?

Dr. Narvaez's work on human development reveals that better *nested* people have more moral depth, are more secure, less anxious, more able to deal with adversity or contrast, and less fearful overall. When you mix relentless social media platforms with under-nested adults you are left with a menagerie of fitful banter, threatening dialogue, and disinformation. This *out-of-touch-with-reality-ness* can be nipped in the bud with better child nestedness and curbed by regular access to Nature, more meaningful social time, understanding one's own humanness better, and a willingness to lessen our interactions with life-interrupting technologies. By recognizing true human needs versus fulfillment prescribed by marketeering we can gain a better sense of freedom for ourselves and our families. The freedom from endless digitization may seem an impossibility in today's digital-revering world, but do we really need intuitive smart technologies everywhere we go? When applied purposefully, seductive technologies could convince anyone that they are "needed," as they certainly can prove themselves to be extremely beneficial. But most intuitive technologies are simple marketing strategies that target peoples' minds, time, and vulnerabilities, as well as their wallets.

When I think about how our lives have been overturned by smart technologies, I recall the freedom my siblings and I were so fortunate to experience as children, exploring our neighborhoods and woodlands. My mother allowed us incredible freedom to explore and play unimpeded. To this day I can't imagine my life without having had this experience. It taught me to trust my own instincts, evaluate risks, come to know myself well, and allowed me to build a relationship with the Natural world. We didn't need cell phones to track our whereabouts. Of course, our mother may have worried about us, because that's what mothers do, but not to the point of denying us this very natural instinct of exploration. Many children of today aren't so lucky. With technology driving helicopter parenting, children are taught to fear the real world of Nature and other people by taking refuge in technological outlets instead. By denying an integral part of what it means to be a human child—the freedom to explore their surroundings, the building of lifelong skills of interacting with others and with the natural environment—these human attributes are quickly becoming extinct.

Freedom from big brother in space: Last Fall, while working a remote restoration project, I was ambling through the darkened desert toward my tent when a strange, unearthly sight of maybe a dozen stringed *stars* zipped across the night sky. Shaking off my disbelief, I looked again. The string of lights disappeared briefly then mysteriously re-emerged, only to again fade away. I could hardly comprehend what I had seen. Later I learned the startling answer: *satellites*.

Elon Musk's constellation of tens of thousands of satellites in low Earth orbit called *Starlink* are now *scribbled* over our universally shared natural constellations. Increasingly known to outshine our naturally existing stars, the satellite's brightness has been met with criticism throughout the astronomical community over concerns that both the brightness and radio wavelengths interfere severely with scientific and recreational observation. Scientific observers and naturalists alike now must contend with another form of litter that pollutes our night sky visibility from Earth. Despite SpaceX's efforts to reduce the satellites reflectivity, their brightness levels remain an intrusive annoyance.

A major intent for creating and casting tens of thousands of low orbit satellites into space is to provide world-wide satellite internet connectivity. Ventures into wilderness now can be experienced with incessant notifications, online shopping. and texting. With *big brother* in your pocket, the many irritating intrusions of everyday life can now follow you no matter where you go. In a time when our devices have become our vices, there will soon be no escape from the constant lure of market targeting. SpaceX may claim to "gift" the globe with greater connectivity, but what they are really doing is encouraging the need for constant internet connectivity. This means more screen time and ad-space, where browsing consumers have in turn become products of the industry. The seduction of these technologies provides the perfect platforms for marketeering ad-space. More time-consuming ads will not assist people living in underserved areas in creating enriched lives. It has become clear that living in over-abundance, as we do in Western nations, is our most modern form of poverty, and digital marketeering promotes this. With less time spent outdoors and more time spent staring into glaring screens, humanity is losing touch with reality.

The intrusion of total global connectivity would also prevent us from finding true solitude and unconfined recreation in our last wild spaces. As technologies follow people into the wilderness, more and more outstanding opportunities will be missed, such as the opportunities to experience wild Nature fully present without the intrusion of smart devices. The need for internet connectivity has its place, but the wild isn't it.

~ ~ ~

I find that I am continually adding to this list, but I've opted for a few worthy points that could aid us greatly in a quest to be liberated from modern delusions and confusion. We may find it hard to believe, as it is becoming ever more difficult, but we *do* have choices. By voting with our choices and actions, we can curb this trend. This could foster a society that makes these choices easier to pursue by putting health and well-being first, both of people *and* planet, with the understanding that they share the same basic needs. It sounds like a tall order, yet we've managed to already do the seemingly impossible—we have created *false realities* that capture the masses.

Opting against continuously being tethered to smart technology is a challenge, but it can help us. There are many things one can do to limit the intrusion of *big brother*, the soon to be widely used Starlink. You can enjoy the freedom of leaving your phone at home or utilize airplane mode more regularly. Embrace your ability to navigate and learn about your world without tethered connectivity. I do this regularly—Nature offers insights into the living world that programmers couldn't even dream of. Many of these wonders are to be *experienced*. There is nothing like experiencing even the briefest of wild encounters. While utilizing your senses to witness the interactions of Nature's various parts, you are hearing, seeing, and experiencing true reality. This sense of wonder can never be replicated on a display screen, no matter how advanced the technology of virtual reality might be. These moments are yours and yours alone. They involve all our senses. They are gifts of being fully alive and present. They stay within your heart as true knowings and are moments where perhaps wisdom begins to blossom. These experiences are the *realness* of Nature. They do not manipulate you, steal your worthiness, nor your time like digital ads are created to do. I encourage us all to discover this true sense of freedom that wild Nature has given us. I promise you, *that* is a life worthy of living.

~ ~ ~

Everything goes back to those first moments in life of making connections with Nature and your world in a positive way. This is what sets a trajectory of conscious awareness of our greater ecological kinship. But if modern humans remain victims of dysfunctional and distorted realities, whereby a mother struggles to bond with her baby because she lacks communal and societal support; or if we are at the mercy of corporations and social media to direct our actions and desires; and as long as we fail to embrace resiliency in our knowledge of kinship, we will continue to forge a path toward destructive human behavior.

The bond between our Mother Earth and ourselves must be established as early as possible and maintained as a central part of who we are and what our lives and livelihoods represent. This connection isn't a mystical thing, it is natural. The risk of becoming deeply entangled with modern constraints can be greatly reduced the earlier these connections are made. If these positive connections are made, one would naturally live more in accordance with what is beneficial to all, rather than only what is beneficial to you, or to nagging corporations.

Psychologists believe the earlier and more strongly we bond with our mothers, the better off we become—psychologically, physically, emotionally, and so on. The same is true of bonding with our earthly mother. The research by Dr. Narvaez reveals that these connections are key to fostering better moral character; something she believes is more our default, true state of being. Greater morality tends to foster greater understanding, and greater understanding is necessary to foster more sensitivity for the needs of others. Extending this understanding toward other beings with which we share this world could reorient an otherwise destructive trajectory into a more sustainable one for all.

We are the only species on Earth who can investigate and make sense of our evolutionary past. As new information comes to light and continues to paint a broader picture of that past, one would think such evidence would bring about a sense of humility of our place here on this earth as simply *one* of several human species that have existed before us. Instead, we carry an air of competitive top *dogness*. But as intelligent as we are, we can't fathom how long other species of pre-historic humans have existed. If superiority is measured in timespan, then one of our closest relatives, *Homo erectus*, certainly appears more superior given how long they have walked this Earth—two million years! Given the archeological evidence, the debate continues over what drove *Homo erectus* to extinction. Some suggest they succumbed to extinction only after being outcompeted by other human species (very likely *Homo sapiens*), while other evidence points to climate change. We *Homo sapiens*, however, have only been around for a mere 250,000 years or so.

Given the current series of self-inflicted crises on our hands, a long-standing future seems almost inconceivable.

Perhaps if we free ourselves from the chains of disillusionment so associated with modern living, the chains that have accelerated ecological instability, a simple reorientation toward pre-historic human species-typicality that has worked for us and for our ancestors for millennia may at least give us a fighting chance.

It all goes back to biology and to Nature. The biology of Nature dictates the optimal range of behaviors for flourishing the way humans were meant to thrive based on our biological, neurological, and psychological needs for survival. Feeling ecologically connected is part of our species-typical biology. To cultivate balance in our relationship to Nature, we must recognize our inseparability to all. The presence of our ever-growing anxieties makes sense. There is a deep knowing that we are losing that which inherently sustains us. Not only are we losing our home, we are losing aspects of ourselves by perceiving Nature *outside* of ourselves. All organisms need an environment in which to thrive—without the environment the organism would cease to exist. *Are we ceasing to exist well before our time?*

8

Equilibrium

Within each dynamic layer of the Earth there are systems continually working toward achieving the state of homeostasis. The gradual readjusting in response to changing environments is hardly noticeable to most of us relatively short-lived beings. Because the quest for equilibrium is never complete, we can only get small glimpses into what a new homeostatic balance would look like. Many times, we humans interfere with this process by continually interjecting new variables, causing environments to continually readjust. Take a burned forest for example: A totally burned forest may never be a full-fledged forest again, at least not in our lifetime, no matter how hard we might try to make it so. An old-growth forest requires hundreds to thousands of years or more to create and develop its multiple layers. However, if we allow the burned forest adequate space by eliminating unnatural pressures such as further habitat destruction by means of over-management of its resources and other forms of abuse, given enough time to recover it can become a beautiful grassland while we are still around to enjoy it. Forests are no doubt our most precious of ecosystems, but grasslands also have great ecological importance. This recovery is a small part of the Earth's finding and maintaining equilibrium.

In each of the Earth's layers are systems made up of even more systems and layers that are on a continual journey toward natural equilibrium. Each system within a system is a regulatory system of another, and ultimately of the whole. Even humans and communities of organisms are a part of these regulatory systems. Nature regulates the state of our own existence in unexpected ways.

Some data suggests that the brains of human embryos may be altered during early development in response to hormonal changes in pregnant women during periods of great environmental stress. While scientists are still trying to understand the effects these changes have on our species, some evidence suggests they could contribute to an array of conditions including gender dysphoria and even obesity.

Potential gestational stressors that are of great significance are chemicals in our environment, specifically endocrine(hormone)-disrupting chemicals. Today, many if not most household and selfcare products including, but certainly not limited to, lotions, perfumes, makeup, shampoos, body washes and even commonly prescribed medications and electronics can expose us to endocrine-disrupting chemicals.

As an example, beauty salons expose consumers and workers to hazardous chemicals that have been linked to health conditions such as cancer, hormone disorders, respiratory and neurological problems. Concerns for consumers and salon workers include higher rates of birth defects and miscarriages. According to the National

Network on Environments and Women's Health, salon workers were also twice as likely to experience postpartum hemorrhaging and the intubation of their newborn babies.

Research also suggests that air pollutants can alter fetal chromosomes, leading to a host of disabilities. Infants born to mothers regularly exposed to high levels of air pollution associated with urban environment have a significantly greater risk of developing chromosomal abnormalities than those exposed to cleaner air during their pregnancies. These same pollutants also increase the chances of obesity and cancers developing in adulthood of those born to mothers exposed to these chemicals during pregnancy. Environments filled with these dangerous chemicals can lead to the alteration of fetal brains, ultimately interfering with gene activity and even influence fertility.

Both female and male reproductive health are influenced by these chemicals. According to leading scholar of reproductive health Shanna Swan, from 1973 to 2011 sperm counts on average in Western countries have declined by 59 percent. Following those projections, sperm counts could reach zero by 2045, threatening human survival.

While scientists are still trying to explain the connections to environmental toxins, we do know is that the biology of our species is responding to these chemicals in a myriad of ways. Ultimately, there seems to be a integral system in place for Nature to self-regulate by preventing future pregnancies in response to potentially more harmful environments. An effect that may benefit Nature as a whole.

Although environments differ from region to region with some people being more exposed to stressors than others, trends of *post-natal* developmental outcomes are on the rise. Perhaps these epigenetic changes may be sounding the alarm for our species' long-term survival. It isn't difficult to acknowledge that a less polluted environment is warranted, or that both men and women trying to conceive, and of course pregnant women, should be given the utmost care in a safe and healthy environment. The point is, our biology is working *for* us, not against us. It is remarkable to think of ourselves as a part of these greater regulatory systems, whether we are aware it is happening to us and whether we like the outcome of being part of such a system, we will remain forever at the mercy of Nature's quest to find and maintain homeostasis.

Nature's Layers

The morning was crisp and chilling. My partner and I left for the trail just after sunrise. After reaching the trailhead, I contemplated whether to wear my jacket or leave it behind and bear the coolness. In spite of the freezing nighttime temperatures, I knew the day would eventually warm sufficiently and I wouldn't need it. Experience has taught me that the extra layer could soon become an annoyance since hiking creates its own warmth. But far too often I've ignored my own reasoning and paid the price of discomfort. I kept it on and onward we went.

The trail's topography is typical, yet lovely, meandering through a diverse landscape of native flora, gradually rising and falling in elevation as it did so. I enjoyed looking at the often-ignored natural intricacies in the equally lovely and diverse understory. The *Big Tree* we were hoping to greet again lives within pinyon-juniper woodlands, just outside the Chihuahuan desert. As I walked along, gratefully aware of the morning's calm and natural peace, I heard something and said, "Sounds like a small waterfall." Seeking the source, we found a small ravine lined with diversely weathered rock outcroppings. The trail crossed a small creek that to my surprise was flowing. Not far from this crossing was a small but unique waterfall. Hiking down to its base, we found whimsical shrubbery crystalized with ice where the splashes of the waterfall met the ground. While admiring the iced vegetation, I could feel the nipping coolness of the earth, reminding me it is still winter, and at that moment I was glad I kept my jacket.

The trail continued across the landscape, encircled by distant mountain views. Forested ridgelines formed the wilderness to the north, which appeared ever so enticing. The views of these mountains expanded as the trail passed through an open meadow grassland. The wooded edges of the meadow were alive with scrub jays who bounced about the pinyons and junipers. Catching a glimpse of their vibrantly blue bodies in the sun is always captivating, no matter how common they are.

There are three signs along the trail to the Big Tree, and according to one of them we were only a tenth of a mile away at this point. As always, I peered across the canopies to see if I could spot it. *Not yet.* Anticipation builds when one is to meet with such an ancient living giant. Whether first time or last, it is always a wondrous experience. Soon the Big Tree came into view. Its massive trunk and towering canopy is impossible to miss. Standing back about 60 feet or so is the only way to photograph the tree in its entirety, which never does Nature's beauty justice anyway.

Lying down at the base of the tree, I looked up its enormous trunk and tried my best to capture its grandiosity, but its wide canopy escaped the lens of my camera. With the canopy spanning over me I could see natural signs of wear and tear. A few large branches appeared to be missing. Its ancient status made me wonder how much the Big Tree has endured. Lightning strikes? Cruel humans? Sickness or disease? I also wondered how many animals had sat upon those branches. I imagined everything from ringtail cats to coatimundi, golden eagles to mountain lions. Did they know this was the biggest tree in the area? Did they understand its significance? Its *magnificence*? Probably not. But I like to think there is a kind of awareness that crosses the barrier of species. The tree appeared to be in incredible condition. No discernible destructive carvings. No bullet holes, from what I could tell anyway. Sadly, large trees like this often show signs of abuse by humans including being pelted by bullets. The Big Tree appeared to have been treated with respect, as should be, despite the trail being heavily traveled. These rarities hold key to longevity in the wild. They are champions of the wild—true survivalists.

The Big Tree is an alligator juniper (*Juniperus deppaena*) and is the second largest alligator juniper in the nation. (The largest ranked alligator juniper in the nation is in Prescott,

Arizona). However, this large juniper tree is approximately 63 feet tall with a diameter of 70.2 inches, and circumference of 18 feet 4 inches. Its crown spread is approximately 62 feet. Its age is estimated to be 800 to 1,000 years. Although its size is a rarity, its species is quite common in the region. Alligator junipers are most easily distinguishable by their unique, checkered bark pattern, which resembles alligator hide. These plants have a limited range, found only within the Southwestern United States throughout New Mexico, Arizona, Texas, and in parts of Mexico as far as Oaxaca. It is of the largest of juniper species in the Southwest and serves as an important plant for wildlife. Its powdery-blue colored berries are eaten by multiple bird and mammal species, including humans. When picked at just the right time, they make a sweet snack on the go. The plant provides valuable habitat for wildlife at nearly all stages of life. Their large size offers shade and shelter for elk, deer, and several other animals.

A creek runs near the Big Tree where a downed cottonwood trunk creates a natural bridge. As I explored the area dense with scrub oak, I found that the space abounds with richness—thick leaf litter, decaying wind-fallen branches, mosses, and fungi, all signs of a healthy forest. Mesmerized by the brilliant green mossy mats at my feet, I dropped down to examine its earthly intricacies more closely and was completely charmed by the micro-world's natural whimsy. These mossy mats were in fact, *cryptobiotic crusts*, made up of multiple organisms including lichen, mosses, fungi and more. Cryptobiotic crusts are often found in dry areas, such as this place, where harsh conditions prevent abundant vascular plant life. They are also incredibly special. The community of organisms that make up these crusts depend upon the micro-climate and conditions to form soil stabilizing structures that retain moisture and prevent erosion. They can be hundreds and even thousands of years old. I was careful as I walked about them! Trailing alongside the creek, I found mossy trunks and branches and was tickled by the fact that mosses really do (for the most part) grow on the north side of trees.

We spotted a set of elk tracks as we made our own route back. Trying to imagine just how tall the majestic creature was, I walked along its steps with honor and amusement. The tracks led us near a mature ponderosa pine—another long-lived being. Ponderosa pines can live up to 400 years. Seemingly the only ponderosa for miles, we stopped to marvel at its loveliness and leaned into it to smell its unique, sweet aroma. The chemical responsible for the vanilla-like scent is found within the resin that when warmed by the sun emits the sweet odor. Near the ponderosa we spotted some black bear scat, full of seeds. Another treasure I wasn't expecting to find. I was grateful for the liveliness of this place and was happy to be there. Enroute back to the trailhead, leaving the Big Tree behind, we stopped one last time to catch a glimpse of the tips of its canopy and said goodbye. For me, leaving areas like this are bittersweet, as though walking away from loved ones.

As on many outings, Nature's layers revealed themselves to me as a striving existence toward completeness. On that short hike to the big juniper, Nature's layers from the thick leaf litter to the seed-ladened bear scat, to decaying branches and ancient cryptobiota, all played a part in the continuation of neighboring layers: the bear's digestive system, priming seeds for future germination; decaying branches and leaf litter acting to protect the sub-soil from the harsh sun before someday becoming the soil itself with the aid of lichens, fungi and mosses; and the lone ponderosa also contributes in its own way.

I spend a lot of time in ponderosa-dominated forests where I like to examine the bark of the ponderosas, intricate patterns of sandwiched layers. Occasionally I lean into their cinnamon-colored trunks to smell that unique, sweet aroma. The ponderosas reveal how their own layers provide incredible resiliency for their species. The ponderosa's unique shedding bark is a perfect example of the selflessness of Nature. As the ponderosa grows, the puzzle-shaped pieces of its bark flake off and land at its base, creating natural mulch. With the aid of many unseen living beings, this natural mulch continues to break down, protecting and eventually contributing to the forest's substrate. The ponderosa bark's jigsaw puzzle-shaped layers also act as a protective environmental barrier for the great tree-being by protecting the tree from intense sun, weather, and low-intensity fires. Its resin is made up of various terpenes, the volatile oils responsible for the ponderosa's vanilla-like aroma. These active compounds also act as the tree's biochemical defenses against disease. The ponderosa's inbuilt layers keep the species partially fire-resistant and incredibly resilient; the same qualities that apply in various ecosystems. When Nature's layers are allowed to function naturally, entire ecosystems are better able to resist damage from fires, disease, and other invasive threats.

~ ~ ~

Nature's layers aren't always straightforward. They exist as interacting components of natural order. There are four main layers or *spheres* that make up our living Earth: the lithosphere, hydrosphere, atmosphere, and biosphere:

<u>The Lithosphere:</u> Without the lithosphere, there would be no mantle, rocks, soil, cryptobiotic crust or even life. There would be no planet Earth. Without soil and minerals there would be no plants, algae, or fungi. Without plants and algae there would be no breathable air, and so on. This should be obvious, yet humankind continues to live in ways that seem to ignore these realities of our living world. The pulse of the earth can be found in each of these components. The lithosphere's pulse includes shifting tectonic plates, mineralization, and even earthquakes. We often think of things like rocks and minerals as non-living, yet the lithosphere is incredibly dynamic. The earth's crust breathes and consumes. Rocks, for instance, can uptake massive amounts of carbon dioxide from our atmosphere. Rocks are also homes to billions of microorganisms. There are many processes of the lithosphere still waiting to be discovered. Rocks can even grow. The microbial life that exists within the tiniest pores and crevices of rocks have been known to turn carbon dioxide into carbonate minerals, forming more rock through a process called biomineralization, as well as through geochemical

processes. The building of living bone in a body by cells called osteoblasts is also referred to as biomineralization. The *geologic* process of biomineralization, by-products of rock-dwelling microorganisms, build the bones of the earth . . . rocks. The Earth's crust is certainly not dead.

<u>The Hydrosphere:</u> The hydrosphere's pulse can be found in meandering rivers, melting glaciers, ocean eddies and aerosols that swirl about driven by atmospheric currents. We owe a lot to this layer. Oceans are one of our largest carbon sinks in the world, sequestering carbon at its deepest, darkest depths. And just like the lithosphere, we are still learning more about the hydrospheric processes. Sylvia Earle, the greatest living marine biologist/oceanographer alive, says that we should be thanking the ocean with every breath we take. *Because without it we wouldn't have breathable air.*

<u>The Atmosphere:</u> To protect our atmosphere we must make great strides in abandoning our dependence upon fossil fuels. Not just reduce the use of fossil fuels but find a way to cut it out of our system and support efforts to do so This is arguably our most important priority right now. By eliminating our dependence on fossil fuels, we protect not only the atmosphere, but the hydrosphere, lithosphere and ultimately, the biosphere.

<u>The Biosphere:</u> This is possibly the most troubled layer of the Earth, and as a biologist is where most of my focus is directed. With habitat loss, species endangerment, and

looming extinction, we earth-ruling humans have our hands full. The health of the lithosphere, hydrosphere, and atmosphere breathes life into the biosphere—the layer of Earth's lifeforms, and into our very own breath. Our existence relies on codependence. To thrive, all these layers and the layers within *those* layers, must remain healthy, as global regulatory interactions among these main layers contribute to climate stability—the integral components that contribute to our own human habitat.

Ask yourself how these layers affect your existence. The answer is this: we could not, *would not* exist if any of these components of Nature were missing.

We cannot progress to a wholesome and healthy existence if we continue mining ceaselessly into the earth for precious minerals. Industrial operations such as mining, seem to give no thought to impending consequences, leaving behind toxic voids in our Earth that have the devastating potential of seeping into ground waters.

Modern lifestyles that continually pollute the atmosphere with carbon dioxide and other natural ecosystems with consumer waste is indefensible and must be stopped.

It is imperative to stress that we cannot simply *buy* our way out of unsustainability. Products sold as "sustainable" or "earth-friendly" may soothe the consumer's conscience, but too often products with these labels are still harmfully impactful and one of the most twisted of all modern lies. Fabricated by the "imaginary order," *greenwashing* is a practice executed by product manufacturers to ease the minds and hearts of consumers by leading them to believe that they are doing their part by buying products that are labeled "environmentally friendly."

My deep passion for the wellbeing of the creatures of the Earth, *creatures of the biosphere,* does not blind me to the other layers and components of Nature. Geologists, for instance, surely recognize the connection between the lithosphere and the biosphere. Just as oceanographers recognize connections between the hydrosphere, atmosphere, and biosphere.

Those fortunate enough to have spent their childhoods immersed in wild Nature, or those who happen to pay special attention to the inner workings of natural order also learn to recognize these integral components. Intellectually, many people certainly can acknowledge the incredible beauty in natural order, but oftentimes it is the *naturalist,* the forever curious and wondrous child of the earth, who tends to perceive these truths more clearly.

Pandemia

It is certainly without question that modern consumerism has in many ways led us to many vulnerabilities, some in obvious ways, and some in unexpected and crucial ways. After a massive outbreak, such as a pandemic, one country may be inclined to point a finger toward another, yet many nations worldwide may have easily, and equally, been to blame. Some of our most risky practices involve massive animal agriculture and engaging in exotic animal trades.

Many countries, including the most civilized of western countries such as the United States, practice holding massive numbers of live animals, domestic or wild, in unfavorable conditions. And in attempts to understand the mode of disease-causing agents better, many countries research various pathogens in our world's virology laboratories.

As an example of a mode of susceptibility, it has been known for many decades that mass domestic farming operating under unfavorable conditions can raise an outbreak threat just as any exotic wet market might. Many countries raise and slaughter meat (chicken, beef, or pork) in massive numbers and in conditions that are essentially no different than wet markets. There is a reason many of these industries operate behind closed doors and with heightened security. *This isn't the life for any living sentient being to live.* While you might not see an outbreak originate from backyard chickens, massive chicken, beef, and pork farms are often grappling with undesirable pathogens that can pose a threat to other species, including ourselves. This doesn't necessarily mean that specific pandemics evolved quite this way, but it certainly points to the many modes of outbreak possibilities.

Mass domestic farming, wet markets, and the popular wildlife trade risk the potential emergence of novel zoonotic pathogens that can be transmitted between animals and humans, possibly leading to epidemics. Expert epidemiologists believe we are entering a "pandemic era" simply because of the precarious nature of these operations and our massive global market—again illustrating our incredible interconnectedness.

Melting glaciers could also expose us to potentially dangerous pathogens. Recently, in 15,000-year-old ice in western China researchers discovered 33 different viruses; only four of those viruses had been previously identified. While these particular viruses do not seem to pose a threat to humans, we still know very little about how newly uncovered strains of bacteria and viruses will respond to our rapidly changing climate.

While epidemics are increasing in frequency, we not only live in a world threatened by zoonotic pathogens, but chemicals, diabetes, obesity, and other health concerns plague us. We find ourselves caught in disease-ridden whirlpools in this modern world of affluence.

As far as the human-caused unleashing of dangerous pathogens, it is time we seriously re-evaluate many of our industry practices, including animal husbandry. Harboring many animals together is not normal for Nature, yet the emergence of potentially harmful pathogens *is* a natural response to the harboring of multiple animals. Thus, Nature is executing her role perfectly of continually seeking equilibrium.

Understanding the significant role viruses, including coronaviruses, play as naturally occurring entities in Nature has become pivotal. While several species of coronaviruses *do* reside in bats, many coronaviruses are also found in pigs, cats, birds, rodents, dogs, chickens, and other animals. Unfortunately, outbreaks of viruses such as SARS and SARS-Co-V2, which can cause COVID-19, have led to the demonization of much wildlife—specifically bats. Bats are natural carriers of coronaviruses. In fact, coronaviruses have evolved alongside bats for millions of years, much like the millions of strains of harmless bacteria, fungi and viruses that live within and on our own bodies. All animals, including ourselves, are carriers of viruses, but most of these viruses are harmless, existing as a natural part of an animal's microbiome. It is interesting that many of the coronaviruses that have been discovered pose little or no threat whatsoever to humans. But while some coronaviruses are still unknown to us, it is best not to go poking around in the habitats of bats.

We need bats as much as we need birds and bees. Bat species occupy nearly the entire globe, accounting for 20% of *all* global mammal population. Bats deserve a great deal more respect and praise from us, as they possess a myriad of unique qualities that directly influence human lives. For one thing, there are over 500 species of plants known to rely on bats for pollination. In fact, without bats, we would no longer have basic crops like bananas, mangoes, and cocoa. A fascinating balance between pollinators ensures that flowers of all types become pollinated. While bees pollinate the bright daytime blooming flowers, bats pollinate nocturnally blooming flowers, for which no suitable alternative pollinators exist. Important crops also rely on bats as natural pest control. Without them, farmers would have to utilize more chemical pest control alternatives that can be incredibly harmful to both wildlife and humans. Loss of crops alone would cost farmers an estimated $3.7 billion per year in agricultural losses. Fruit-eating bats play a crucial role in seed dispersal across wide ranges of forests. It is estimated that 50% of old growth forests depend upon bats for ecosystem balance and health. The loss of bats would be a devastating blow to the overall stability of global biodiversity and food security.

~ ~ ~

Despite what so many captivating articles might say, viruses do not *lurk* as villains in the dark. They simply exist as part of Nature. While they *are* opportunistic, they are not out to get us. It is only when conditions prove favorable for viruses and other pathogens to spillover (jump from non-human animal hosts to human hosts) do they become a threat to us. Corralling live animals of multiple species (that might never have crossed paths in the wild) in unnatural environments, or venturing into highly potential viral territories, creates the perfect condition for possible spillover events to occur.

Species-specific microbes rarely cause harm within the communities of one's own species, but intrusive behavior such as mass-farming, mining, plowing, and clearing of forests can potentially cause certain species-specific microbes to jump from one species to another.

According to epidemiologist and virus hunter Peter Daszak, more than a million people are infected with unknown coronaviruses every year. This has been confirmed by testing communities for coronavirus antibodies. With every infection, the virus has an opportunity to spread into denser populations.

While many may not want to be reminded, it is in fact modern affluence that has allowed SARS-CoV-2 (that can lead to COVID-19) to spread so widely and rapidly. Much of what we consider normal in modern life such as shopping, dining out, flying, are all examples of the affluence modernity has granted us, in which we willfully participate. Without thought of our over-abundant lives, we create our own misfortune. In times like these one is perhaps too enraptured, too comfortable to ask themselves, *Is all of this worth it?*

We have ventured far beyond simple satisfaction in meeting our basic needs. Rather than wading comfortably in the waters of contentment we've pushed the boundaries of voracious consumption. We are indeed the perfect host for such virulent hitchhikers.

~ ~ ~

Epidemics reveal most pointedly our undeniable kinship with our living world. The need for developing new vaccines requires tapping into valuable, non-renewable natural resources, possibly decimating many wild animal species in the process. Populations of horseshoe crabs, sharks and other species have all been targeted for their unique hematological (blood) properties that scientists use to formulate safe vaccines for humans. The disruption of these beings inevitably causes ecological disruption for not only their species but other species who rely on them. Since we are a part of all else, this in turn harms *us*, furthering ecological instability.

Although it is a practice that *I* do not wish to be a part of, I am. We *all* are. Make no mistake, vaccines are one of our greatest modern achievements. Vaccinations have proven time and again to be incredibly effective at curbing infectious disease, yet the unfortunate truth is that nearly all vaccines utilize animals for their unique properties and as trial subjects. Although due to purification processes the final vaccine products often do not contain many of the animal products used to create them, wild and domesticated animals are nearly always used in initial vaccination development.

The horseshoe crab (*Limulus polyphemus*) is one of those animals. A living fossil that has existed for over 400 million years, the horseshoe crab has become an unfortunate target because their unique blue blood has been found to contain an endotoxin considered vital for vaccine development. Pharmaceutical companies perform an estimated 70 million endotoxin tests a year using this prized blue blood. And given the current urgency for new vaccines, the already threatened horseshoe crab population has faced massive capture. Millions of crabs are subjected to bloodletting by injecting needles into their hearts. After the blood is collected, the horseshoe crabs are supposedly released back into the ocean where they will either recover or die. An estimated 10-15% of these crabs will die and many more will fail to return to their mating grounds. In certain regions horseshoe crab populations have fallen by an astounding 90% in the last 15 years.

The eggs of horseshoe crabs provide food for a plethora of marine wildlife, including birds. The Red Knot is one of those birds. The already threatened Red Knot relies on horseshoe crab eggs to fuel their 9,000-mile annual migration journeys from South America to the Canadian Arctic each spring. The Red Knot could not survive without healthy populations of horseshoe crabs.

Additionally, sharks are targeted not for the harvesting of their blood, but for their livers, which contain *squalene*, an oily substance containing unique immunologic molecules. Although squalene is argued to be an unnecessary component for vaccine production, experimentations continue at the expense of shark populations. If we pay close attention, we will find that any resource we extract for our own use, whether considered living or not, is ultimately connected to another.

Since the beginning of the scientific revolution, animals have been a part of the development of many of our modern innovations and necessities including medicines, chemotherapies, safe blood transfusions and more—things you and I, dear reader, have benefited from. It is also how we have successfully traveled to the moon, and how we will eventually go to Mars. Tortoises, mice, frogs, fish, dogs, monkeys, apes and even spiders have been sent into outer space on *our* behalf. Personally, I feel uncomfortable that in the age of massive biodiversity loss we still find the need to tap into shared natural resources and to exploit our living kin. My wish is to avoid the need to develop new vaccines altogether. To avoid the need for future vaccines, the goal should be to avoid spillover events and epidemics in the first place. When there is ecological imbalance, Nature always finds a way to reorient herself onto the path toward homeostasis, no matter at what scale and no matter if we are a part of that equation or not.

As I write this, the current pandemic has taken away a part of what it means to be human, since humans are social creatures. Being social is another "vitamin," another part of the evolved niche of humans. No matter how small a social circle might be, even if with only one other person, our being social tends to contribute to a better quality of health and life. Gatherings and many other social events are currently a danger to us. Touching, hugging, kissing and handshaking are all social aspects we must learn to live without, at least for now.

What part have we played in this? The current pandemic is a result of our unnatural relationship with Nature, regardless of origin specifics. If we maintain a senseless global market, uncaring economic growth, and our sense of kinship to our living world remains neglected and ignored, the emergence of infectious diseases and the need for new vaccines are here to stay. However, by acknowledging this we can choose to be part of a new, thriving reality. The health of our wild kin, our environment and our own fellow human beings relies on all of us. When humans cooperate, we can do amazing things . . . or we can do terrible things. Collective actions can put the threat of highly transmittable viruses to rest, which would be a testament to our intelligence. Future outbreaks could be prevented by doing what we humans have been known to do best—work together. If together we can discover the initial cause of spillovers, we can then realize our kinship to all else across the sticky web of life.

The lineage of all species can be traced back to a single common ancestor; a single-celled entity regarded today as the Last Universal Common Ancestor, or *LUCA*. Believed to have lived around 4 billion years ago, the simple prokaryote known as LUCA, most likely a primitive form of archaea, endured extreme environments—environments in which no complex organism would have been able to survive. An impressive feat of survival for a tiny single-celled microbe with unprotected genetic material. The thermophilic (heat-loving) single-celled organism likely existed in deep underground hydrothermal vents rich with hydrogen gas, carbon dioxide, sulfur, and iron for millions of years. The teeny microbe waited in suspended animation until eventually the changing environmental conditions pressured the little microbe to transform into an early form of complex life, granting all life as we know it. A radical, 4-billion-year-old legacy.

The deeply fascinating world of microbes is made up of bacteria, protozoa, archaea, fungi, bacteriophages, and viruses. (Viruses are technically not biological living entities or "organisms," but that will be covered later). While germs can cause infections, not all microbes are germs, and not all infections caused by microorganisms are harmful. Microbes are a necessary component for the existence of complex life. In fact, from the atmosphere to the ocean depths and everything in between, microbial life dominates the world's biome.

Data suggesting human fetuses are exposed to bacteria and other microbes prior to birth refutes the age-old idea that the womb is a completely sterile environment. A diverse microbiome exists within uterine amniotic fluid and tissues. Although this microbiome could be considered beneficial for the child's heath, the most crucial stage of inoculation of the fetus occurs in the birth canal, which ensures complete inoculation of a baby's gut microbiome.

Recent studies have discovered a link between cesarean section-delivered babies and long-term chronic health problems such as allergies, asthma, and other autoimmune disorders. Although lifesaving in true emergencies, some of these costly procedures are unnecessary. As an example, medically induced labor can lead to weakening or undetectable heart beats in unborn babies. Naturally, this is a frightening situation when c-sections are often performed.

Babies delivered by C-section are also more prone to harmful infections than those delivered vaginally. This makes sense given how cesarean sections bypass the inoculation of beneficial, immune system-building bacteria within the birth canal. This "seeding" of trillions of beneficial microbes occurs when your mother passes on the microbiome that will become a part of your immune system for life. After the colonization of those first microbes, bacteria find their way into the gastrointestinal system, establishing and stabilizing your immune system. Although considered a crucial stage in immunological development, this process of inoculation continues beyond the birth canal through skin-to-skin contact and breastfeeding. The various microbes a child is exposed to contributes to the diversity of their own microbiome, including handling of the baby by other members of family and friends, as well as exposure to natural environments.

Just as our planet's ecosystems thrive best when made up of a diversity of life, the same is true for our individual microbiomes. No ecosystem is exactly like another; no human microbiota is like another. A diverse forest thrives, as does a diverse ocean, but they do not constitute the same diversity of lifeforms. Our bodies are the same. In fact, all complex living things, including humans are essentially *super-organisms* with more microbial DNA in our bodies than even human cells. It is *diversity* that maintains our planet's and our species' resiliency.

Studies have revealed that modern Hadza hunter-gatherers of Tanzania have greater gut microbial diversity than modern urban dwelling humans, indicating that our ancestors' more robust microbiome attributed to the hunter-gatherer lifestyle promoted a more diverse microbiome. The Hadza's microbiome was also found to host bacteria better suited for digesting and extracting fibrous plant material, allowing for greater nutrient uptake.

The impressive microbiotic biodiversity in the Hadza points toward the inadequate diet of modern humans. Dietary fiber is necessary to feed our gut's microbiome, yet most of our modern diets do not contain nearly as much as that of our ancestors. This has led to a loss in gut biota diversity in humans, suggesting that simply adding substantially more fiber into our diets can promote greater diversity of beneficial microbes in our guts. The studies also revealed that on a regular basis, the Hadza eat about *ten times* more fiber than Americans do. That is a lot.

Not only do our guts host trillions of beneficial bacteria, but our entire body is covered in microbes. From the inside out we are hosts to more than 100 trillion microbial hitchhikers, ten times more than the number of human cells in our bodies. Despite humans being made up of trillions of microbiota in the form of bacteria, fungi, archaea and even viruses, researchers have found that the overall number of that microbial life is decreasing. This startling loss is due to modern life—antibiotic use, excessive hygienic care, poor diet, and lifestyle.

While most microorganisms that exist in our world are generally harmless and often beneficial, *pathogenic* (disease-causing) microorganisms, including certain zoonotic viruses and bacteria have the potential to cause disease in multi-cellular beings such as plants and animals. Poor gut health can make fighting these infections incredibly difficult and potentially deadly. We can promote superior gut health by preventing intrusive and often unnecessary procedures at birth, increasing regular exposure to other natural sources of microbial sources such as spending time in Nature, reducing the need for antibiotics by eating a high fiber diet, and maintaining a healthy, active lifestyle. It usually isn't until we experience severe digestive complications that we begin to truly appreciate the microbes living inside of us.

Our gastrointestinal tracts are truly fascinating aspects of our anatomy. Equipped with five times as many neurons than there are in the spinal cord, the gut is sometimes referred to as our *second brain*. Our guts and our brains communicate constantly, influencing each other's biochemical signaling known as the gut-brain axis. While we still have a lot to learn about the connection between healthy gut microbiomes and the function of gut neurons, we know they are invariably linked. Gut neurons play an important role in digestive, hormonal, immune, and metabolic regulation, as well as our psychological health by regulating emotions through serotonin production. Stomach pain can be an indicator of depression and anxiety, as well as poor gut health. Studies of people with a less diverse microbiome, perhaps from antibiotic overuse or poor diet, experienced more inflammation, anxiety, and tended to become stressed more easily.

Decreased microbiome diversity and gastrointestinal distresses have been linked with autism, as have Cesarean sections, with a 21 percent higher risk of autism than vaginal births. This would make sense given that the mother's birth canal is known to provide the child with a proper microbiome, supporting the health of growing children well into adulthood.

Gut microbiota is so intriguingly complex that remarkably, *keystone* strains of gut bacteria have even been discovered in healthy guts—that is, strains whose roles are as pivotal as the roles of beavers, wolves, and bees in their environment as keystone *animal* species. Keystone species are essential for thriving ecosystems. It only makes sense that as complex as the microbiome is, the ecological make-up of the human gastrointestinal tract would be comprised of its own set of keystone species of microbes. In Nature outside of the body, different species of animals impact the overall ecosystem in different ways. *Microbiotic* interactions within diverse communities of microbes would undoubtedly help to facilitate healthy digestive processes. Equally so, these interactions would also result in competition for resources present in the gut, influencing population dynamics of gut microbes. That means there would also be a certain number of species or strains that would be foundational to the overall structure of microbiotic communities in stabilizing ecological conditions for other strains, thus allowing different strains of bacteria to be able to continue to carry out communal life processes within a stable gut ecosystem. This fountain of stable conditions would promote vital biodiversity. It is truly remarkable that similar processes occur within nearly every layer in Nature, from the inside out, from below and from above—processes Nature has found to promote and maintain equilibrium for diversity of life, from even *within* life itself.

~ ~ ~

It has been established that life would essentially cease to exist without diverse microbiomes, so let's delve into greater detail concerning our latest attention-grabber— viruses. Measuring between 20 and 400 manometers, many times smaller than living human and bacterial cells, viruses are the smallest of microbes. Viruses require living host cells in which to deliver its RNA or DNA; the host cell then replicates, leading to a potentially deadly viral infection.

Viral infections can be tricky. Not only is there potential for these replicated viruses to make a person very ill, but research also shows that respiratory viral infections can severely alter healthy gut microbiomes. It can also become extremely difficult to reestablish a healthy microbiome after becoming ill with a viral infection. And because viruses are so small, they have many opportunities to hide within the body. The Epstein-Barr Virus is known for hiding undetected in the body for years. These viruses remain latent until the immune system becomes compromised, then a host of debilitating symptoms can manifest.

Viruses are microbes that pre-date complex life. They are not villains. They simply exist as part of Nature. By biological definitions for life, viruses are non-living entities. You may remember from a biology class that there are seven main characteristics of all living things: 1) have different levels of organization, 2) use energy, 3) grow, 4) have the ability to reproduce, 5) respond to their environment, 6) adapt to their environment, 7) have the ability to maintain homeostasis. Although the lines between dead and living viruses become somewhat blurred when a virus acquires the ability to replicate, most viruses fail to meet all these criteria for life.

In natural existing ecosystems, bacteria and viruses take part in a dance that is responsible for nutrient recycling. Viruses and bacteria that occur naturally within soils and freshwater systems work together to enhance the rate of decomposition, which in turn produces simple inorganic components such as carbon dioxide, nitrogen, and phosphorus. This interaction involves the bacteria's becoming infected with viruses that cause the bacteria to consume other bacteria until they essentially burst through a process called lysis. The bacteria then release many more bacterial cells infected by the virus, as well as many crucial nutrients that continue to support the ecosystem's food web. These freshwater viral-bacterial interactions are found to be a crucial link in the carbon cycle between terrestrial and atmospheric regulation, making this a truly *wild* example of how not all viral infections produce negative outcomes.

Many viruses also function as part of our gut's diverse microbiome, or what some microbiologists refer to as *virome*. Just as it would be impossible for us to wipe out every existing bacterium, the same is true of viruses. If we could even manage to do so, life would cease to exist. Viruses and other microbes exist as checks and balances, with certain viruses existing as part of our microbiome and others evolving into pathogenic strains alongside changing environmental conditions in an innate drive to maintain equilibrium. And while viruses aren't technically alive to begin with, they still exist as part of the matrix that supports life. This knowledge supports the original belief that all things in Nature belong. In the right time and under the right conditions, given our ever-changing environmental circumstances, everything, including viruses, have a role to play.

We are inseparable from the wild forces of Nature, and as such, we are *wildly* connected to weather and climate. In Ross Calvin's book, *Sky Determines*, he points out that the sky "determines" our fate, but not in any mystical sense. If there are no clouds, there is no rain—it is as simple as that. If this persists long enough, there will be drought; and if there is drought, crops and ecosystems inevitably suffer. We are then forced to adjust by using water wisely, for we are uncertain when the sky will determine when the rains will come again. What we do here on this Earth influences weather patterns and climate. We have been influencers of climate since the beginning of time, as have all other living beings. Yet in a relatively short period of time, modern humans have influenced, and continue to influence, the climate in more drastic ways than other beings have. We are as intertwined with our Earth's weather patterns and climate as we are with our living wild kin. What power our great kinship brings!

We will have to adapt to the new and rapid environmental changes, just as our ancestors and our wild kin have been doing since life on this earth began. As they did, we will either flourish or perish in the process. In adjusting, we find balance in the natural order of things. Something we know for certain is that there are ways in which Nature unfolds into reality, and then there are ways in which it is *thwarted* into reality. There is enough evidence to suggest that as a species we have been taking too much, too quickly. If we can create such a negative influence on our climate, as we evidently have in recent times, then why can't we have an equally opposite effect if we reverse how we choose to carry out our lives? Reversing the trend of taking too much, consuming too much is all it might take to make our way back to a more balanced world. We may not be around to see what is truly possible, but this knowledge can give us a sense of what we are capable of—that we can do what is best for the sake of our own descendants, our wild kin, and our wild home.

Our Keystones

In a power-seeking quest to learn as much as we could as enlightened observers, we began dissecting every aspect of Nature until we could no longer clearly see the assemblage of her moving parts. Context becomes lost in this way of seeking knowledge. Nature is, after all, comprised of a network of systems called ecosystems. Networks within networks. In learning to see the components of Nature as living systems, we resist becoming destructive reductionists. Reductionism assumes individual components of Nature are more important than the relationship between the components. Behavioral ecologist Stephen Harding suggests that the objectivity of reductionistic thinking hinders our ability to see fully functioning networks as a whole. The dance of life, earth, sky, water, mountains, oceans, and atmosphere is the *terrabiota* that lives and breathes through a diversity of individual lifeforms on this wild sphere we call Earth.

Our modern way of life continues to disrupt naturally functioning systems before learning to understand them as a functioning whole. In doing so we have caused entire systems to malfunction—effects that can be witnessed in the form of erosion, habitat degradation, species invasiveness, desertification, more frequent raging wildfires, extreme weather patterns and more. This is what happens when humans try to manipulate and control nature. We lose balance. Nature has extraordinary ways of organizing itself, in which life depends on various interactions of plant and animal species. This is ecology.

Ecology is built and maintained both from the *bottom up* and from the *top down*. Which is of greater importance, top to bottom or bottom to top, depends upon the different effects each species has over the greater ecosystem. While balance between the two is important, some species do hold greater importance in the survival of ecosystems and to the overall survival of life.

The starfish experiment of biologist Robert Paine revealed definitively the importance of keystone species. The discovery began with the observation of starfish in tide pools. Robert Paine began experimenting by removing a single component from individual tide pools to see what effects might follow. In his experiment he removed the predator component, the Ochre starfish (*Pisaster ochraceus*). The removal of the predator starfish caused detrimental effects to the remaining species communities within the tide pool. His experiment revealed that the removal of a single predator could disrupt the abundance, diversity, and distribution of resources to other organisms in the shared ecosystem. Paine had assumed that by removing the starfish, the prey species would thrive more abundantly. Instead, the opposite occurred. The other species within the tide began to multiply uncontrollably and the tide pool sickened with unhealthy organisms. He realized the species within the tide pool depended upon the predator to thrive. This led to one of the most important discoveries in the science of ecology; "keystone species."

Removing the predators leads to the degeneration of systems. This degeneration is a phenomenon known in biology as *downgrading*. Today, signs of downgrading are evident nearly worldwide, and the solution is simple:

Remove the keystones and the living world deteriorates. *Return* the keystones and the living world flourishes.

One of the world's most notable conservation efforts, which astounded biologists everywhere, occurred in Yellowstone National Park after the reintroduction of gray wolves. From the rebalancing of deer, elk, buffalo, beaver, and bird populations to the natural restoration of rivers, wolves play an almost sacred role in the maintenance of healthy ecosystems. We owe our lives to the wolves and to other keystone species who supported the diverse forests that our ancient ancestors thrived in.

Essentially, predators chase prey animals into stronger communities by driving natural selection. As revealed in Paine's experiment, unchecked by predators, prey numbers increase as fitness drops and they begin to decimate resources and eventually habitats. This is because without predators, prey species, such as deer, may multiply exponentially. With high numbers of prey animals, common food sources may become scarce, which can lead to sickness and malnourishment. Fear of the wolf drives the deer to maintain optimal fitness and the rest of Nature's components begin to follow suit. In more balanced prey-to-predator populations, ecosystems thrive because the pressures in competing for the same resources are diminished.

We need top predators. To some humans, *we* are considered top predators, and since we are abundant, things should be okay, right? This is a great misunderstanding of our role in the greater ecology to which we belong. Pound for pound, muscle for muscle, natural wit for natural wit, we may not be top predators after all. Without the invention of tools to assist in hunting, we would have no chance against a raging rhinoceros or a Serengeti lion. We need the non-human predators to keep our world alive.

When we ease modern-driven pressures, Nature *will* find and establish a new balance. In places where top predators have been severely decimated, this new balance will be established first from the ground up, in a long process called *upgrading*. This is where we may find ourselves in many of our wild places today. We can facilitate this upgrading by simply stepping aside to allow nature to reach her new balance. This is an extraordinary ability of Nature, the *built-in regulatory system* that constantly strives to regain and maintain homeostasis.

Keystone species are made up of both predators and herbivores. By focusing on the right species, we can boost this process, but only to a degree. *Time* is what Nature will need. Our greater ecology is constantly homing in on a path toward natural balance, from chaos to order, with moments of chaos and order continually overlapping one another. That is truly wild.

When all native species and their environments regain natural patterns of organized abundance and distribution it will promote health and healing for all species. Our great cognitive abilities give us the ability to see and understand this, which gives us the responsibility to be a part of the solution. Through understanding how Nature works, we can be a part of this regenerative upgrading. We can do this "stepping aside" by living within our means, using only what is necessary for survival, reducing and resisting over-consumption, and abiding by a more natural order. It may just be this simple.

Our Watersheds

Simply stepping aside and giving Nature the time needed to recover is *the* most powerful way we can assist this upgrading process, but there are ways we can be active drivers of the natural restorative process. A couple of years ago I returned to a field site to assist in efforts to complete a long-term riparian (wetland) restoration project. The project took place on a private piece of land consisting of around 910 acres. That is not much land in the grand scheme of ecological conservation, but it is enough to see the wonders and rewards of watershed restoration. Every parcel of land that can be restored and preserved counts. The property's boundary encompasses a stretch of a main creek. The creek sits within the Mimbres Valley of New Mexico, adjacent to the Gila National Forest. Driving up to one of the access points of the property, one can oversee the densely vegetated ravine as it sits relatively low within the valley-like setting. The main ravine is met with several side tributaries, many of which have experienced erosion from historic cattle grazing. The beauty of this project is that the owners have donated the land back to nature as part of a conservation easement *and* have retired it from all cattle operations. Just for clarification, conservation easement properties and cattle removal don't necessarily go hand-in-hand. However, on this particular easement, measures have been taken to ensure that cattle do not wander into the area. Fencing keeps cattle out while remaining permeable to native wildlife.

When free-ranging cattle are allowed to graze land within a southwest bioregion such as this one, a troubling cascade of effects takes place that undermine the overall ecology of the land. These events overtime will lead to an overall ecological instability that cannot be reversed if cattle grazing is allowed to persist. The only way lands experiencing this kind of overuse and abuse can recover is by removing cattle indefinitely. Only then, the land may heal over time. Added efforts, such as the watershed restoration techniques implemented in this project can help speed up the process of recovery.

The first human-handed efforts to restoring this piece of land were implemented in 2002. The efforts have been repeated periodically throughout the years until this project's last mobilization a few summers ago. While there, I was hired to assist in the development and construction of natural watershed stabilizing structures throughout the system of natural drainages or ravines. During my first visit to the property, I was pleasantly overwhelmed by the results of previous work. Clearly, the land was healing! It was in a stage of upgrading. It was astonishing to see pools of water within areas of thick, healthy, established native vegetation consisting of sedges and deer grass—and this was in the dry season of the desert southwest! The area had not received rain for months, and the monsoon (rainy) season was still a couple of months away. Viewing the area from the high ridge above you might not have ever guessed there could be healthy, thriving pockets of wetlands hiding within this primarily dry, piñon-juniper-laden property. I was onboard, excited at the prospect of contributing to its ongoing recovery.

The restoration techniques involved were very effective and ideal for land where erosion has occurred from grazing cattle. We worked along the main stem of natural drainages as well as within all perpendicular tributaries. By principle, we would not have considered treating a piece of land without first removing the grazing cattle indefinitely, if this were at all possible. Otherwise, our restoration efforts would undoubtedly be undermined, and a basic functioning riparian system could not have been achievable. In delicate landscapes such as this, removing cattle indefinitely is the only way one can ensure full and lasting ecological recovery. Just as treating the main cause of a disease promotes health, when the culprit of this type of destruction that led to soil instability is removed (cattle in this case) the land will heal itself after initial restoration efforts are in place, and this healing will continue. Accumulated improvements in ecological health can be seen in relatively short order.

Our work on this parcel of land resulted in approximately 300 additional erosion control structures, effectively reinforcing previous efforts. The following summer we returned for the project's final mobilization. This time we were working in and observing the area *during* the monsoon season. As we made our assessments to determine the progress of previously implemented structures, what we found was an area thriving with life!

Many of the previously constructed structures had successfully accumulated noticeable amounts of sediment. This has contributed to greater sub-surface and surface moisture retention as well as a greater density in native vegetation growth. Many of the pools of water were active with native aquatic life, including tadpoles, water boatmen bugs, mosses, Blacknecked Garter snakes (*Thamnophis cyrtopsis*) and more. Signs of other wildlife in the area included Canyon Tree frogs (*Hyla arenicolor*), great horned owls (*Bubo virginianus*), black bear (*Ursus americanus*) and deer.

Newly established vegetation included most notably native deer grass and sedges, especially important plants that promote soil stability, as well as seasonal wildflowers including wild morning glory (*Ipomoea sp.*), wild onion (*Allium rhizomatum*), Indian Paintbrush (*Castilleja sp.*), verbena (*Glandularia sp.*), dayflowers (*Commelina sp.*), trailing four o'clocks (Allionia incarnata), desert four o'clock (*Mirabilis multiflora*), globe mallow (*Sphaeralcea sp.*) and more. Additional note-worthy plants observed included newly established narrowleaf cottonwoods (*Populus angustifolia*) within the main channel and several young Fremont cottonwoods (*Populus fremontii*) within worked tributaries. The establishment of cottonwood is a sign of substantial subsurface moisture. A truly awesome achievement.

Later, revisiting the site revealed an overall greater ecological stability of the watershed with ongoing recovery. The amount of floral and faunal diversity present within this primarily piñon-juniper woodland, along with the presence of a stabilized watershed, proves that restoration efforts like these make significant positive impacts. The property now provides a natural habitat for native plant and wildlife species as well as crucial water filtration resulting from greater sediment and vegetation concentrations.

It is difficult to effectively express the many intricacies of the actual work involved and the signs revealing restorative success, despite my eagerness to elaborate. Much of the work requires onsite observations and learning to develop the skills and techniques necessary for effective restoration. This project has been perhaps one of the most rewarding sites I have ever worked. What we witnessed was the phenomenal process of natural upgrading. For me, this proves that we humans can live in a more regenerative coexistence with Nature, instead of a perpetual existence of downgrading impacts. Again, together we can either do great things or terrible things—human cooperation can be our saving grace or our dis-grace.

Personally, I feel grateful to have been a part of promoting the Earth's upgrading process while also being a part of the whole of Nature. We have the knowledge, and as children of the Earth we must foster the wisdom to turn that knowledge into our practice and livelihoods.

9

The Naturalist

The person who loves birdwatching will most likely notice many other things in the environment relating to the birds they love to watch. By paying attention to various aspects of Nature including habitat, weather patterns, seasons, previous experiences of sightings in particular locations, and of course bird song and calls, birdwatchers collect information that helps them locate the birds. They may also notice the various insects that occupy the habitat in which birds tend to thrive as well as anticipate breeding seasons and the patterns and behaviors of migratory birds. Based on previous observations, they may even be aware of whether the arrivals of certain species of birds are early or late, or if the bird populations have experienced an increase or decline. By noticing that the birds forage or take shelter within certain plant species, birders often recognize when valuable natural resources are in healthy abundance or not and can deduce a great deal about the state of our overall environment and what contributes to a healthy habitat.

I have been fortunate to participate in conducting surveys of threatened and endangered birds along the beautiful Verde River and within neighboring forests in Arizona. The gathering of detailed information about those areas was invaluable in developing a greater understanding of what makes up suitable habitat for the birds I was seeking to document. With diligence and mindfulness, these associations can be made in relatively short order, especially if you care enough to find connections in the living world around you—something I find intriguing.

After familiarizing ourselves with each of our assigned regions, our crew soon developed a sense of which animals we would likely see in different locations. In a particularly dense and buggy area, I knew the chances of seeing Vermillion flycatchers were high. In areas where cottonwood stands were especially thick, the yellow-billed cuckoo could likely be found. Mexican spotted owls are known for occupying old-growth forests, preferably alongside deep ravines thick with vegetation. Certain species will almost always be spotted among thick stands of reeds along the riverbanks, such as the common yellowthroat. Hiking along transitional ecozones are particularly interesting. In an area where the edge of the forest melds with an open juniper woodland means it is very likely we could find sleeping great horned owls. Stands of invasive salt cedar may mean chances for seeing many of the birds we sought were slim, and so-on.

The more time spent in a particular landscape, the more likely one is to gain a sense of what birds and other animals are likely to be seen. But the bird species seen at one location can change at different times of the year, and at different times of the day, for that matter. You begin to sense where, when and what you will likely see or hear. Thus, an intuitive sense is born.

A sudden splash in the water usually means the presence of beaver or river otters, although there is still delight in the unexpected. One time when I heard a familiar splash, experience made me think *"beaver,"* but when I looked, I was delighted to see a spooked raccoon swimming across the river. That bit of information was then added to the collection of possibilities upon hearing a splash. Another time, while traversing a particularly dense area covered in flood bank debris, I came within ten feet of a foraging striped skunk. I stopped in my tracks and watched as the seemingly oblivious skunk continued to forage. The experience made me realize just how incredibly nearsighted skunks are. It made sense that one would have to come threateningly close to succumb to the skunk's smelly defense. After a few more skunk sightings it was clear that they quite preferred to forage this particularly dense location, likely feasting abundantly upon various grubs and insects. The expectation of seeing skunks in this area was verified with even more confirmed skunk sightings.

Not long ago I was taken by surprise to hear the song of a lone male red-winged blackbird outside my home. My home is situated in a fairly arid location. While there are several small seasonal drainages scattered throughout the greater area, it was an unexpected sound to hear. In my mind, I was transported to the water's edge as the song of the red-winged blackbird is a classic tune of riverbanks and wetlands. With eyes closed I could almost feel the cool, humid, river side air on my skin.

No matter how many field guides one might read, these connections are often made only when there has been some sort of previous experience. Those with little nature awareness and experience may not be able to associate a wandering red-winged blackbird with wetlands, but once the connection is made, it is hard to forget.

That is the beautiful thing about our abilities to assimilate and recall experienced information. The endless clues Nature gives us about our surroundings are multifaceted gems of insight into the health and happenings of the web of life. Over time, a naturalist begins to see and hear Nature's moving parts as one, sensing the inner workings of the whole, living, breathing Earth. All because of a love of birdwatching, finding insects, tracking animals or just being in Nature, naturalists see the wholeness in all life.

Evolutionarily we are *all* naturalists, intrinsically evolved to give attention to aspects of our natural surroundings. When we see a cloudy sky, we make the appropriate adjustments of what to wear. When we feel a few raindrops, we might choose not to water our gardens, and so on. While we often do so without a lot of thought, we are aligning ourselves with natural order—because being a naturalist is at the core of who we really are.

~ ~ ~

Many of us have become frozen by *ecological grief* into believing our individual actions contribute little value. You might not think that we could help lessen the effects of the losing of our topsoil from massive food crop operations or help lessen the process of desertification in our public wildlands, but we most certainly can. Knowledge is our key. The more we learn about, see, or experience the effects big industry has on Nature, the more likely we are to align our own lives with efforts that support Earth-benefiting practices. In doing so, we help to inform and inspire those around us through our lifestyles and our actions.

When we no longer cater to the profit-oriented resource misusers by adopting a more minimalistic lifestyle, we will avoid wasting valuable resources. Taking action in this way is incredibly impactful. In living more simply, one is simply living more! Making do with less gives us more freedom and empowerment. Through this empowerment, we inevitably begin fine-tuning our *nature awareness* by finding different, even more sustainable ways to live. Within this newfound resiliency we find that there is space for the human-earth oriented relationship to grow and for the natural world to flourish.

There are numerous ways in which we could ease the Earth's burden of ecological destruction by realigning ourselves with our inner naturalist. Again, it is our culture of affluence that has steered many of us into stressful, over-complicated lives. Because of this, many are realizing that living more simply is the true life of luxury. As writer Adam Gopnik observed, "The variations of abundance die at the moment of crisis, and the old stable dull solutions come to life again."

In seeking simplicity, some people are taking back the power to create their own realities. One way is in guarding themselves against manipulative algorithmic targeting and other modern trappings. Algorithmic profiling has become the technological name of the game that steers people into endless consumerism with endless choices of *stuff*. This kind of manipulation holds us back from fully experiencing life because it distracts us from the needs of our living, breathing surroundings.

In the quest for greater freedom and simplicity, many of us have realized that paradise can be built close to home by minimizing or limiting the number of personal possessions; creating self-subsisting food forests; building *green* rooftops; wildlife-friendly gardening; and natural-material building with onsite or local materials. By endeavoring to do this we can simultaneously ease the cancerous growth of big business by using and buying less and reduce the damage of big agriculture by growing a portion of our household's food use, thus contributing to regenerative and restorative efforts to provide habitat and other resources for native wildlife.

There was a saying during the Great Depression: *Use it up, wear it out, make do, or do without.* In a time of great upheaval, crisis was met by an entire nation. The practice of frugality and the serious management of one's own resources was not suggested, it was imperative. Today, highly conditioned to living in affluence, society often fails to recognize the urgency of change we must all make. We have no other choice than to be guardians of our endangered blue planet. Now is all we have. But we can learn from the past. A close friend of mine says, "Wealth produces waste." A truth many may not want to acknowledge. Yet, here we are, at the precipice where we must redefine the meaning of wealth. Perhaps our greatest wealth of all is a flourishing Earth.

~ ~ ~

I believe there is another way we can reawaken our inner naturalist to help keep the human-earth connection alive. As urbanization grows, many of us are finding it harder to connect with more natural things and places. Nature is falling out of sight and out of mind, which is especially concerning because it causes the sense of our human-earth connection to diminish right alongside this radical disconnect. Communing with Nature is seen today as a kind of pastime, but for our ancestors it was life. When we aren't allowed to commune with an aspect of Nature every day because of a lack of natural spaces around us, we won't consider ourselves a part of it. If we don't consider ourselves a part of it, we won't think to care for it. If you live in a space lacking these luxuries, placing something as simple as a hummingbird feeder out your window or starting a garden can help bridge that gap by inviting the dance of life into *your* life. Seeing a hummingbird at our window can remind us of the living, breathing world that continues to exist alongside our own lives. Gardening can also act as a reminder by inviting various birds, butterflies and more. The smallest of things can do wonders for the nurturing of our human-nature relationship. Every plant or wild creature you see can reawaken your sense of kinship.

There are ways we can connect with and gain a sense of wild Nature every day. People living in cities can take part in community orchards or make a commitment to visit the closest natural park or go for a walk on a regular basis. Bring your living spaces to life with multiple house plants that you must then learn to care for and learn their individual languages and needs. We can also *disconnect to reconnect* by limiting the time spent on smart devices and instead turn our attention to the dynamic world around us. Even if one is unable to gain access to these things, we still have the sky above us, something that is always accessible to us.

It was once common for our ancestors to read the sky on a regular basis. The sky is a part of Nature we sometimes fail to connect with, even though it is right there above our heads all day, every day. You might already be one who looks for various weather patterns in the sky. When done with regularity, you will find that you'll become better at predicting various kinds of weather by learning to understand what different cloud types indicate. While doing so, we can remind ourselves that we too are a part of our sky and weather. Sometimes I can sense changes in wind or weather patterns just by my sense of smell alone. For instance, when I know there are wildfires in neighboring states to the west of me, I can sense the direction the winds are blowing by my sense of smell. Sometimes the sensation in my skin with changes in humidity can indicate changing weather.

Another thing I like to do is "read" the trees outside my window or around my neighborhood. It is a habit of mine to look at the trees wherever I am. They not only act as places to spot birds and other wild critters, but trees indicate wind direction that can sometimes indicate changes in weather. Branches whipping about in many directions often indicates a rainstorm is soon to follow. Since the winds typically blow eastward where I live, I take special notice if the trees in my yard indicate otherwise.

In looking closer to the world around where *you* are, you will find there are a multitude of things you can do to nurture the human-earth connection. After some time and practice, you'll find these connections more and more effortlessly.

I once lived adjacent to a man who lived on a graveled lot with a large tree standing beside his trailer. I knew from living within eyeshot of the tree that it invited a plethora of wildlife that included birds, cicadas, and more. Although the graveled lot itself lacked diversity, the lone tree stood as a beacon for wildlife. Despite his lot's being covered in earth-stifling gravel, he was still able to connect with Nature every day. He had placed hummingbird feeders in the tree and at his window and would sit and watch birds of all kinds visit the tree. Over time he came to recognize individual birds and their peculiar temperaments. In our conversations he could not only tell me about the birds he watched, but about other natural happenings within and around the tree. He was not an ecologist or biologist, but simply a human who remained very much aware of the living world around him.

We often discussed the state of the world. Not being particularly impressed with smart technologies, he believed that in many ways they were not an improvement for humanity, and that they in fact hindered our humanity and our sensibilities. Although he kept a phone to stay in touch with close friends and family, he felt the benefits smart technology offered us seemed especially good at complicating matters by stealing our time and awareness. We are all fans of some technologies, and we must accept that there will always be a thread of hypocrisy that runs through modern humanity regarding our use of and thoughts about these technologies. But increasingly, many smart technologies are failing to enhance our lives. As we embrace these technologies at the expense of our relationships with ourselves and with others, we risk losing sight of our connection to the living world around us.

Upon occasion, I would invite my neighbor on hikes in our local trails. Since he was not bound to a smart device, he could appreciate the world about him. Very few people I knew or associated with took note of the smallest natural aspects around them. Sadly, this not only continues to be the case, but noticing and acknowledging the world around us has become almost non-existent—not because people don't have the desire to, but because our technologies steal and steer our attention away from such things. It is very likely that you, dear reader, because you are reading this book, are one who takes note of the living, breathing world. We can help open the eyes of our fellow human beings in the way we lead our own lives, keeping our sense of connection to this living earth alive by always keeping Nature within view of not only our eyes, but our minds and our hearts.

While backpacking in a favorite wilderness, to experience the last of the day's life-song and dance as the evening drifted into darkness my partner and I lay looking upward toward the forest canopy. Camping tentless was our preferred style and we did so whenever weather permitted. We listened to the lovely song of a nearby hermit thrush, my most favorite of bird songs. Its unusual ethereal song, already echo-like, seemed to bounce off the canyon walls nearby. Bats flew haphazardly in and out of view snatching mosquitoes and other nighttime insects. Stellar Jays bickered among each other as they hopped from tree to tree. In the distance I could hear the persistent churning of the river. As always, I hoped to hear the lullaby of a coyote's song before drifting into sleep. Referring to the creatures we were watching and hearing, my partner said, "Everybody has a part to play out here, don't they?" Bats, birds, mosquitos, moths. and coyotes. With a smile I replied "Yes, they do," marveling in their abilities to maintain such beautiful balance as the dance of life played out before us. The next thing he said provoked strong sentiments I have struggled with for many years. In a wry tone he asked, half in earnest and half rhetorically, "What's *our* part?"

~ ~ ~

One late Fall I collected willow stems along a creek in southern Colorado to be used for wetland restoration. On this restoration project I worked alongside a highly experienced Navajo crew who worked quietly and methodically. Interestingly, the stoic and quiet nature of the Dené (Navajo) people is what I enjoyed most about working with them. I also loved restoration work requiring only handwork versus work that relied on noisy machinery. I believed that whenever one is in wild nature, we should do our part to respect the peace and serenity that naturally exists in the wild as much as possible. The Navajo crew were less talkative, more introspective, and aware than most other people I have worked with. They did not feel the need to fill the natural silence with senseless chatter or music, and simply focused their attention on the job at hand.

As members of the crew emerged from the dense thicket hauling bundles of stems to be tied and placed with the other harvested willow, other crew members disappeared back into the hidden world of willow to collect more. With loppers in hand, we meandered our way through thickets of willow stands. Clusters of the dormant and dominant plant stood anywhere from four feet to an impressive eight feet. Multiple crisscrossing wildlife paths made snaking the way through fairly easy. While ambling about, we sought only the thickest of clusters from which to harvest, leaving behind the smaller, young clusters to grow and thrive. We deliberately chose only the right stems, mindful not to collect dead or dying stems and took only a few per cluster.

I quite enjoy willow harvesting, as the meticulousness involved is peaceful and meditative. Visibility is very limited and sometimes one can hear wandering deer and other wildlife just a short distance beyond. A few rows of willows are all it takes to provide a blanket of security for wildlife. But sometimes one can glimpse a bolting deer bouncing away.

This time I loved how wildlife wandered so quietly though the willows. Inspired by this, I tried to be as quiet as the wild animals who fed and lived there. One could almost come upon a grazing deer. The sounds heard while harvesting were light and benign. Occasional sounds of wildlife, whether deer, nearby ducks and other birds, or random *"snip, snips"* from the loppers and the brushing up against willows as crew members made their way through, was all that was heard.

Willows are extraordinary plants. They generally grow along natural flowing water bodies, providing considerable stability to watersheds while also providing generous habitat and food for countless wildlife. Since they grow quickly, they are a naturally abundant resource and have been used historically for making cordage (ropes), weaving baskets, and making medicine. Today they are an outstanding tool for combatting erosion in wetland restoration and are a tremendous natural asset. What I find fascinating about willow harvesting is not only how much the harvested willow will benefit the area in need of restoring, but also how in some areas the harvesting act itself can benefit the land.

Beaver populations have suffered in many parts of North America, which has led to ecological consequences. In many regions, unregulated trapping and killing have decimated beaver populations to an unsustainable low. They have been targeted unfairly as natural destroyers of environment, although it is widely recognized today that beavers are incredible environmental engineers who aid in creating, expanding, and maintaining healthy wetland habitat. Even so, in many parts of the country their numbers have taken a blow and the consequences are exceedingly evident.

Willows are an extremely important natural resource that provides both habitat and food for wildlife, including many crucial pollinator species. The dance between willow and beaver is a crucial relationship in maintaining healthy ecosystems. When beavers chew on willows, thinning them out, it stimulates regrowth. Since beavers build with willow as well, they inadvertently transplant willow throughout different parts of waterways, creating beneficial sandbars that help induce river meandering—a critical feature of a thriving riparian ecosystem. Much of the same happens when we humans harvest willow where beaver populations are low. Not only are we translocating willow, but by cutting some of the willow we too are stimulating future growth just as the beaver would, had their populations remained stable. Willow harvesting became even more rewarding work as I learned more about its all-around benefits. There is *always* a way to take what is needed, while also giving back.

The wisdom of many Indigenous peoples shines through in this *knowing*. Their livelihoods depended upon treating nature as a part of themselves and not separate. A wise Apache told a story about how his people could take what they needed from Nature in a meaningful way, while also nurturing the health and integrity of the wild. His people collected saplings to be used for arrow shafts. First, they collected saplings *only* when there was a great need to do so. Second, they utilized the knowledge they had gained from watching the forests grow. They understood what constitutes a healthy forest . . . how trees competed for space. They learned how diseased trees looked, and how the disease developed. They took only the saplings found in clusters, allowing the strongest saplings to remain planted. By reducing competition from the other saplings, the tree could grow to be big and strong. Just as the act of beavers chewing on willows stimulates stronger growth, this practice shows that humans too can live in reciprocity with Nature.

Humans are deserving of the awesome generosity Nature provides, but man does not always act in a way that is deserving. Nature gives us everything we need to survive, so why wouldn't we feel inspired to give back—to take care of that which takes care of us? Striving to restore and maintain our worthiness of that generosity is necessary if we are to thrive. The life-dance taking place around us is all the encouragement we need to realize this way of living can certainly be achieved.

Many Native peoples believed when one receives something from Nature that is needed for building, making tools, starting a fire, plants for cordage, medicine or simply obtaining food or water, whatever is received doesn't cease to exist, but rather becomes a part of us—our own spirit. But if taken needlessly, purposelessly, and carelessly without thanks in our hearts for the all-providing spirit of Nature, then it will die or become sick and unhealthy—we become sick and unhealthy with greed and miserliness.

Whether working in restoration or simply traversing backcountry, I have seen what too much senseless, mindless *taking* can do to a once thriving landscape. Although many times these damaged spaces can be restored, these efforts must be done with the understanding that we are tending not just our own needs and resources, but that of wild Nature in return for its giving spirit.

We can and have lived this way. It is a part of our human-nature heritage to live as balanced beings . . . to be the guardians of the garden instead of conquerors of territory. If we wish to continue to thrive upon this giving earth, this must become our fulltime work, our way of life. We must adopt and adapt to a new, yet *not* so new, calling. Our wild calling. To create a new dawning of stewardship we must be guardians of the most diverse garden we know of—our Earth. *This* will be a true testament of our evolution. "Our part" is to be a part of Nature.

Old Ways and Inner Truths

The admiration I felt for the natural world as a child placed me on a path that I have been following not only from my own curiosity to learn, but also from a sense of an inner knowing. I have felt that humanity was unconsciously scrambling to secure a sense of place within natural order. The sense of kinship that we unconsciously seek is awaiting our reunion.

One of my favorite books growing up was about a young teen who finds himself alone in the wilderness after surviving a single engine plane crash. He had nothing but the clothes he was wearing and a hatchet his mother had given him as a gift. To survive, he had little choice but to set aside his intense emotions, which could cost him his life. He had to become fully aware of the elements of Nature that surrounded him in the vast Canadian wilderness. He faced cold nights, weather changes, hunger, and encounters with wildlife. With determination and perseverance, he learned quickly, and in doing so he survived.

It is said that the Apache Stalking Wolf believed that someday, especially in the so-called *end times*, people would give anything to learn the old ways of living as *children of the earth*, abiding by Nature's ruling forces and with respect for this earth we call home. This would become the only way to survive, to know Nature as intimately as many of our ancestors did. It is the erosion of this historic knowledge that has plagued the modern world and caused our great disorientation.

Like atrophied and under-worked muscles, the skills, awareness, and intuitive abilities are still within our grasp, if we choose to use them. We simply haven't been firing the muscles associated with them. These intuitive and instinctual *muscles* are embedded somewhere within the subconsciousness of humankind, standing by and eager to grow. The fact that we have such instincts suggests that we come into this world having everything we need, without all the "stuff" we have so recently acquired.

As I understood that many of the ancient ways of knowing could give us back a sense of resiliency, I often wondered what deep knowledge of those wise elders still existed today. I have realized that when we know ourselves well and are willing to pay attention to what our true needs are, we can allow our inner truths to be our guides. Having spent my entire life between wanting to live by what I always *sensed* to be true and living senselessly by what we've been *told* is true, I've come to recognize that wise elders are not limited to wise *humans*–that wisdom itself is an integral part of the natural world of plants, animals, and elemental forces. Intelligence in Nature is found all around us.

Rebuilding a sense of connection to Nature and to our wild kin has become imperative if we are to secure a more resilient existence and promising future. It is part of our true humanity to feel such connections; deviating from this deprives us of the abundant world we all know is possible. By realizing that Nature is simply an extension of ourselves, we will find the richness in all that is.

"When you know nature as part of yourself, You will act in harmony.

When you feel yourself as part of nature, You will live in harmony."

~ Tao Te Ching

10

No Country for Old Turtles

I was camping with a dear friend in the Baboquivari Peak wilderness, a place considered sacred to the O'odham people, when I was surrounded by what I can only describe as living natural spirits.

It was late. The long drive took us through the whimsical Sonoran Desert toward the setting sun. Silhouettes of ancient Saguaro cactus stood majestically tall and picturesque against the painted sky, creating a breathtaking sight. Living up to 200 years, towering Saguaros give awesome presence to the desert. In reflecting on the incredible legacy of those standing before me, I was overcome by a deep sense of spirit. I was in the presence of living "ancient ones," something I had not experienced before visiting this place, even though living ancestors are always all around us in the form of mountains, forests, oceans, and other natural beings. Among the Saguaros I felt *safe* and *embraced,* as though they were watching over me with great compassion and wisdom.

The desert drive was a typical ride of washboard rumbles and swirling dust. Having left light-polluted areas many miles behind, our visual range in the now fully darkened desert was limited to what our headlights provided.

Emerging from the darkness, a magnificent Great Horned owl landed in a large shrub beside the dirt road. We slowed to a crawl, then to a stop, and observed the large bird's graceful presence.

After arriving at camp, I looked up and saw a dazzling display of stars spilled across the dark sky. Feeling a sense of *collective spirit,* it was as if earthbound spirits were being graced by the anointing stroke of the Milky Way. In celebration, the nighttime brimmed with life song and dance. While listening to the chorus of nocturnal wildlife, a collard peccary zig-zagged its way through our camp, adding to the enchantment of the moment. I could feel life's energies flowing around me.

Torn between sleep and exploration, my mind wandered child-like, absorbed by the exceptional life that seemed to breathe through this place. As my eyes closed, my ears hung on to the melody of life around me until it lulled me into a deep and restful sleep.

The next morning was as alive as the night before. Distracted by this, we spent the morning exploring near our camp before heading out. There was almost too much to take in—countless birds, lizards, insects, peccary, deer, and even feral horses. Eventually we peeled ourselves away from these lovely distractions to begin our upward journey.

The meandering trail toward Baboquivari Peak was lined with newly sprung native vegetation. The earth was painted with hues of young, fresh green. As we gained elevation, views of this verdancy seemed to carpet the earth in all directions. The desert was in bloom.

After much rambling about, a large desert tortoise appeared on the trail before us. I smiled and thought about how old he might be and how fortunate he had been to reach this size. Honored by the encounter, I reflected on the status of his kind: *critically threatened*. I was grateful to see the tortoise wandering in an area that was still wild and undeveloped, and impressed by the location of this encounter that was next to a steep edge, high in the mountain.

Unfazed by our presence, the tortoise never once retracted his head or retreated. Perhaps he was as curious about our presence as we were of his. He stood as guardian of the path, as though he had made a journey back from the sacred peak earlier that morning. After a few moments of admiring the old tortoise, we wished him well and continued our way up the mountain. With bustling life around every bend, the desert mountain continued to dance in celebration of recent rains and new blooms. I was astonished. I was witnessing an aliveness so rich and diverse, something many may believe is unrealistic for a desert. Thanks to the abundance of recent rains this natural space abounded with healthy, vibrant life.

~ ~ ~

In the summer before writing this book I spoke with Kevin Emmerich, a biologist and former National Park ranger of over 20 years, about the devastating implications of *big solar* on Western desert wildlands. Kevin, along with his wife, Laura Cunningham, also a biologist, work diligently to protect the last undisturbed deserts of California and Nevada from the massive solar industry. Areas included the Mojave, Great Basin and Colorado deserts—regions of incredible biodiversity and habitat of many unique plants and wildlife. Not only are these deserts home to federally endangered and threatened species, but they are also home to other natural treasures such as dark night skies and culturally significant landscapes. Laura and Kevin founded the Basin and Range Watch organization that focuses on educating the public about these often overlooked and threatened areas and their unique natural assets.

During our interview Kevin informed me about a 690-megawatt solar power generating facility that was proposed to be built on roughly 7,100 acres of public lands. The proposed location is in the Mojave Desert directly south of the Moapa River Indian Reservation. If approved, the facility would directly destroy habitat for multiple federally threatened and endangered species (including both plants and animals) in irreplaceable desert wildlands.

The desert tortoise is one of these species. Not only are they considered federally threatened, but they are also (supposedly) protected by the Endangered Species Act. Living up to 50 years, they are considered a long-lived species as well as a significant keystone species upon which many other plant and animal species rely. If big solar get its way, the operation would irreversibly impact thousands of acres of prime desert tortoise habitat, contributing to major ecological instability for many other species that rely on the tortoise, including kit foxes, burrowing owls, Gila monsters, collard peccary, Gambel's quail and many more plant and animal species. And because desert tortoises travel long distances, they are valuable seed dispersers of native plant life, which in turn provides food and habitat for other native desert dwellers.

The megawatt solar power proposal claims to ensure that the Bureau of Land Management (BLM) and developers involved will do everything possible to ensure the safety of desert tortoises, including temporary exclusion fencing that will keep native wildlife from entering the site while under development and relocation—efforts many ecologists could tell you are insufficient and futile in the long run.

Both tortoises and turtles have extremely acute navigational senses that aid their strong instinctual drive to return to their place of birth to lay eggs, mate, or hibernate. Removed tortoises will *always* try to return to their home ranges, which puts them in tremendous danger. When this instinct draws the tortoises back to their once prime habitat, and *if* they survive the journey home managing to avoid becoming roadkill, they will find a decimated landscape where all native vegetation has been mowed down to the roots and previously dug dens flattened and destroyed. It would no longer be a place the tortoise could survive.

Sadly, the project to which I am referring, called the Gemini Solar Project, has since been approved to proceed. It is just one of multiple ongoing large scale solar and renewable energy projects proposing to invade and destroy our last desert wildlands.

While nearing the completion of this book, I was informed that the Gemini and Yellow Pine Solar Project had moved forward with its efforts. After a team of BLM and US Fish and Wildlife Service recruits excavated and removed over 100 adult desert tortoises to be relocated, 30 of the tortoises were preyed upon by badgers, a devastating outcome.

The relocation of wild animals often ends in disaster. It is delicate business that involves making objective decisions based on several ecological and environmental factors. Through Nature's intelligence, plants and animals living within a shared and stable ecosystem exist in balance of each other's needs of resources and habitat.

The relocated tortoises had little chance against hungry resident badgers, despite, according to Kevin, "badgers are not known to commonly prey on desert tortoises." But because of recent extreme drought conditions, badgers took the newly introduced tortoises as an extraordinary feeding opportunity. Kevin concluded, "It is possible that drought conditions have driven them to extreme measures." After the fact, BLM and US Fish and Wildlife Service are now considering applying a foul-tasting paste to the tortoise shells as a deterrent for predation. I wonder how the tortoises will feel about that. One could see how extreme measures to remove native tortoises in the first place led to the execution of even more extreme measures. Aristotle said, "the best things are placed between extremes." It is the intelligence of natural order that exists between extremes.

Alternative solar energy *sounds* like a wonderful thing. Who would have thought just how destructive an alternative industry could be? Especially largescale operations such as the Gemini Solar Project. This extraordinary example is one reason I would like to encourage all to question even the things that might *sound* promising. With a better understanding of Nature and the kinship of all that is, the willingness to question these things can become second nature.

Kevin and Laura are not against solar technology itself, but rather the absurd placement of massive solar projects in our wild deserts. Opting for small scale, roof-top solar, as well as less consumption of resources overall, is our most obvious solution to easing the burden from the wilds, wildlife, and our planet. And we must be continually aware that big industry, whether conventional or "alternative" only sees profit.

~ ~ ~

Just like desert tortoises, box turtles like my Pokey remain bound to the invisible perimeters of their home range. Depending on the resources, their home ranges may shift slightly over time. This is when they run into problems of being killed by cars, taken in as pets or preyed upon. Wandering box turtles provide a food source for foxes, coyotes, ravens, striped skunks and more. The juvenile turtles are more prone to predation than adults, as adults have had more time to develop their natural armor and other defense strategies.

Humans, however, are their greatest threat. From cars, farming equipment, and direct removal, from native habitat to the most impactful form of habitat loss . . . the sprawling urban development and housing subdivisions. Due to slow maturation to reproductive age and increased mortality due to modern human activity, the recovery of the box turtles remains in jeopardy. Box turtles are now considered threatened, but the United States has yet to make it illegal to remove the species because of the lucrative pet trade and ownership.

It is becoming harder than ever to determine how to best help these wild creatures. To always presume a wandering turtle is lost is risky thinking. Many people claim they are saving a turtle crossing a road by pointing them back into the direction from which they came. However, the turtle is likely wandering *within* its home range and is heading into a direction with purpose. Whether that is to forage in a known location of resources, mate, lay eggs or hibernate. Yet, their home range may unfortunately be fragmented with roads and other human-made obstructions. If perhaps there does seem to be substantial habitat in the direction they are heading, the best thing to do is simply wait until the turtle crosses safely to the other side. We can still be their ally in watching for incoming traffic.

Another unfortunate way people claim to save and rescue box turtles is to remove them entirely from their natural habitat. A woman I knew had "rescued" a turtle that was well on its way to crossing over a road into the desert, by taking the turtle home. Little did I know she had another turtle she kept in her backyard that she had also "rescued." When she took the second turtle home, she thought placing it with the other would be appropriate. When she did so, the two turtles fought. The territorial misplaced turtles were simply trying to claim their dominance in their newfound disorientation. One of the turtles suffered a massive bite wound to the neck that became infected with maggots.

Much like the attempts to remove and relocate box turtles and desert tortoises in order to protect them, taking my sweet Pokey from her habitat represented a gross misunderstanding of the nature of Nature on my part. Albeit I was very young when Pokey entered my life, but sadly, the adults in my life lacked this understanding and even encouraged such removals. To protect prime habitat, we must help wild places maintain their own agency by leaving both the habitats and their occupants alone. Every time I see people with box turtles and even wild snakes as pets, my heart aches. It is a misunderstanding that directly threatens our living, breathing world. Nature operates best as a whole. Removing Pokey from her home thinking she could live and thrive with me was pure ignorance. She was an element that made her home in the Chihuahuan desert complete. The desert needed her as much as she needed the desert. The wilderness and its creatures do not belong to us, but they *do* belong.

~ ~ ~

The turtle and tortoise have been a somewhat continuing theme in my life. One summer I took part in an archeological dig as a student assistant in a large cave in the mountains of West Texas. As the only student biologist among a crew of archeologists, I was especially fascinated by the recovered flora and fauna specimens rather than with human-fashioned specimens like spears and sandals. Every day I filled my field notebook with descriptions, drawings, and measurements of my recoveries. Anything and everything, from a single raccoon tooth to a rib bone of a frog made it into my notes.

After a day's work in the field, our lead professor could often be seen flintknapping pieces of obsidian in the hot desert sun. At the end of the project, he generously awarded each student with a title and gift as a "thank you" for our efforts. One by one he declared the title he had playfully conceived for each student and handed them a brown lunch sack that held the gift. As he made his way through the students, the titles differed but the gifts remained the same: an arrowhead. When he finally made his way to me, he said, "You are awarded the *Circle of Life* award, for your love of all life." Honored, I reached into the paper bag expecting to retrieve an arrowhead and was deeply moved to find a flintknapped obsidian turtle.

It was so fitting.

Final Thoughts

There is a creek I visit often when I am not able to go deeper into the wilderness. It is a place that fulfills my every niche of daily wonder and curiosity. It is where on the toughest of days and in the sourest of moods I know my spirit can be lifted. A place where my eyes are soothed by the forest's rich verdancy. Where the wafting scent of wild cherry blossoms forces them closed again in admiration of their essence. It is a place where many times I have welcomed the sky to open, releasing healing rains and boisterous thunder. Drenched and happy, I continue to walk in full immersion. It is also where I have walked upon deep virgin snow and have admired Nature's greatest seasonal works of art. Following the creek upstream, Mourning cloak butterflies dance at my feet while the thrush's ethereal song draws both a sigh and smile. Embracing the pace of Nature, it is a place my heart will forever wish to *know* more deeply.

As does Nature, this place thrives dynamically. With each passing month I find myself discovering previously unseen things and beings. Wound-healing plants present themselves in abundance. Plantain herb, yarrow, and Solomon's plume speckle about my path. Alpine sorrels, relatives of my dear old friends the yellow wood sorrels, grow atop moss-carpeted rock ledges. Red-faced warblers draw my attention upward to the bustling canopy of life-song and dance. Wild canyon grapes sprawl high onto the trunks of old cottonwoods and drape down from branches above me. Prickly wild gooseberries, still green, await their last transformation of taking on the pink and red hues of ripeness. I find myself drawn to a particular stand of seven ancient ponderosas gathered together as if to discuss the fate of the future. The stand of ancients is located toward the end of my return hike and always generates thoughts of tomorrow's world of wilds, knowing this place is becoming drier and drier, possibly dictating the ponderosa's own fate. Emory and Gamble's oak are believed to become more prominent in the predicted drier, more fire-prone future, eventually replacing ancient stands of the now dominant ponderosa. I wonder too, just how humanity might look then, if still around, when the natural world has fully adopted this shift. I wonder also where my own personal world might have led me. For now, I continue to honor the existence of my forest friends of fur, feather, and verdancy on their humbling journey toward natural equilibrium.

~ ~ ~

While my own sense of kinship with the living natural world runs deep, I am not an expert tracker, nor am I particularly agile. Although I may try, I cannot walk as stealthily as a fox. I do not claim to have exceptional intuitive senses or instinctual senses, nor are my senses engaged all the time. But I do know where I want to be as part of the greater symbiosis of life and who I am as one who knows that Nature is the only thing that truly matters and is the only thing that is real. I know I want to live as fully human as possible, and I know what kind of story I would like to write and leave behind.

From where I am, there is always inner and outer work to be done. One thing barefoot walking teaches me is to always be aware of my surroundings, that there is always something new to learn. I do not need a wise elder in my life to teach me this. Although when I do wonder if wise elders still exist, I think of those who have come before me, whether plant or animal, who nurtured Nature's continuation. I recall Harold's lesson while we were working on the post-fire restoration project in the Jemez Mountains of seeing the world through a better lens of awareness where not even a sapling among the grasses is missed, and that there still exists a wish and willingness to know and preserve the already known of this wild world. While it is no longer our dominant way, Indigenous wisdom prevails and only by a collective orientation toward modernity do we not learn from that wisdom.

Most of all, my wish is to inspire my readers to always question the narrative being told *to* us rather than discovered *by* us, and a desire to search for the areas that need work within one's own self—striving to really know yourself well as a true human being biologically, physiologically, psychologically, and intuitively. And to be courageous enough to ask, *what is truly optimal for our species and for our living world?*

Wild Nature and its creatures can teach us a lot about who we really are, and while we are so fortunate to have many natural spaces still available to us, let us embrace the opportunities to gain a better understanding of our place here on earth from within these natural temples.

In my own quest, I still trip and fall. I still make many mistakes. And while I know many of them, I cannot tell you all the scientific names to all the native plants, birds, and other natural beings near my home. But I do feel a great sense of connection to them and of my place here on this truly awesome living world. As I continue to foster a greater sense of this belonging, I will take those moments of inattentive "trips and falls" of unconsciousness as lessons, and work to reorient myself toward the things that matter most. All the while, appreciating the life that still flourishes wild and free as extensions of who I am.

In wanting to know more about the wholeness of Nature and how Nature is always striving to find and maintain homeostasis for us—*for all of us*, I will continue to learn all I can about the inner workings that have sustained and supported life for many millennia.

So often people feel that to go into Nature they need to go someplace *out there*—that we are somehow separate and must drive or walk somewhere and *then* we will be in Nature. But Nature is not *out there*. Nature does not begin at the park, woods, or trailhead. We are always *in* Nature. We *are* Nature. Our homes and our cities are not truly separate either, they are simply nestled into Nature someplace on this planet. Which is in turn nestled someplace in our spectacular solar system, galaxy and so on, existing as part of the greater ecosystem.

As I think about Nature in this way, I am reminded of our origins on this Earth, specifically through *abiogenesis*:

that gradual process of life arising from non-life through the evolution of simple to increasingly complex forms, more than 3.5 billion years ago. It is a reminder that we are connected even to non-living aspects of Nature. The thought of it never ceases to astound me.

The most incredible force that will ever exist is *life*. Restoring our sense of kinship to that force can deepen the awareness of our human-earth relationship of reciprocity. As I personally dive deeper into the intuitive knowings that have already come to light, I rest assured knowing that I have the greatest teacher of all . . . Nature herself. And I remember the lesson of solitude; that there is no self, just all that is in the greater symbiosis of life—that we could not *be* without the rivers, oceans, and mountains, because we *are* the rivers, oceans, and mountains.

ACKNOWLEDGEMENTS

To my dear friend Daniel Robleto for believing in my abilities and for his unending encouragement that crescendoed into a tone of urgency over the years. I was listening. Thank you for all the love and support.

To my mother for sharing (as well as being excited about) the little things that Nature brought home to us. I have more memories than you will ever know.

To my partner, Wade Stover, for your loving support and loving interruptions. Tiny-home living can be hard, but I am glad to be living it with you.

A debt of gratitude to Shari Johnson for your invaluable guidance in helping me to express my heart and soul. Working with you has been a delight. I have learned so much. Also, to my friend Edwina Wood for your beautifully balanced way of encouraging others and for introducing me to Shari.

To *all* the special humans who have encouraged me to continue sharing—and for taking an interest in—my stories, including those I have met in my wilderness travels, followers of my online journal, *The Wandering Naturalist*, as well as the following individuals for their contributions and support of this book: Mike Karnahen, Jake Margerum, Natalie Wesley, and my sister Crystal Razo; and to the people whose research aided me on this journey listed at the end of this book. Thank you for your invaluable information.

To Asim Tanveer on Fiverr for formatting and bringing the book's full cover to life.

My *deepest* of gratitude to all my beloved animals: Pokey, Harley, Persia, Sahara, and Dharma. They are the ones who connect me to the *source* of who I am.

To Pokey for sending me on a trajectory of an endless love of wild Nature and for showing me that to love is to be wild and free.

To my sweet Siamese Harley, for truly being my first true best friend. For helping me to realize I had a knack for reading animal body language, especially cats. For your looking out for me as family, and for teaching me that love can be a healing force. I love you and miss you, sweet boy.

My precious Siamese Persia, for everything you were, and *are*, to me. For understanding my absences for work and life, yet always greeting me with pure love and undying affection. For twelve beautiful years of precious companionship. For teaching me a lesson in *oneness*, and for showing me that love is a continuous force between worlds. I miss you so much. I will love you forever.

My sweet Siamese, Sahara, for your sensitivity toward the world's energies, your peace-loving spirit and our special nap-time moments; for continuing to help me nurture my ability to connect with animals in a deeper way and for keeping my desire for interspecies connection alive. I love you, baby girl.

My little Schnauzer, Dharma, for always reminding me what I *should* be doing, in nearly every moment of every day. May we have many more wild adventures together.

To Lyra, a tortoise whose story is yet to be told. For your telling presence in our lives and the lessons that are still yet to be learned.

And to *all* the creatures who have crossed my life's path, whether domestic or wild, for sharing your unconditional love, understanding, insight and wisdom; my warmest gratitude for inspiring a returning to wholeness, and this book.

SOURCES

1: The Beginning and the End

Hannah M. ter Hofstede, John M. Ratcliffe; Evolutionary escalation: the bat–moth arms race. J Exp Biol 1 June 2016; 219 (11): 1589–1602. doi: https://doi.org/10.1242/jeb.086686

Langley, Liz. *Echolocation is nature's built-in sonar. Here's how it works*. National Geographic, 3 Feb. 2021. https://www.nationalgeographic.com/animals/article/echolocation-is-nature-built-in-sonar-here-is-how-it-works

2: The Human Experience

Dunn, R. (2012 July 23). Human Ancestors Were Nearly All Vegetarians. Scientific American. https://blogs.scientificamerican.com/guest-blog/human-ancestors-were-nearly-all-vegetarians

Little, B. (2020 Jan 9). Early Humans May Have Scavenged More than They Hunted. History. https://www.google.com/amp/s/www.history.com/.amp/news/prehistoric-human-diet-scavengers-vs-hunters

Reed, D. R., & Knaapila, A. (2010). Genetics of Taste and Smell: Poisons and Pleasures. Progress in molecular biology and translational science, 94, 213-240. https://doi.org/10/106/B978-0-12-375003-7.00008-X

Huffman, M. A., (1997) Current Evidence for Self-Medication in Primates: A Multidisciplinary Perspective. *American Journal of Physical Anthropology*. Https://www.researchgate.net/publication/254307247_Current_Evidence_for_Self-Medication_in_Primates_A_Multidisciplinary_Perspective

Jardine, K., et al. Volatile organic compound emissions from *Larrea tridentata* (creosotebush), Atmos. Chem. Phys., 10, 12191-12206, https://doi.org/10.5194/acp-10-12191-2010, 2010

Sarantis, H., et al. (2010) Not So Sexy: The health risks of secret chemicals in fragrance. *Campaign for Sage Cosmetics and Environmental Working Group*. Https://www.ewg.org/sites/default/files/report/SafeCosmetics_FragranceRpt.pdf

Li, Q., et al. (2009). Effect of phytoncide from trees on human natural killer cell function. *International journal of immunopathology and pharmacology, 22*(4), 951-959. https://pubmed.ncbi.nlm.nih.gov/20074458/

3: Lost Natural Inheritances

Gooley, T. (2018) *The Nature Instinct*. The Experiment.

Rinpoche, P. (2010) *Words of My Perfect Teacher*. Revised edition; Yale University Press.

Harari, Y. N. (2011) *Sapiens: A Brief History of Humankind*. HarperCollins Publishers

Wynn, T. (2012 December) Fire Good. Make Human Inspiration Happen. *Smithsonian Magazine*. Retrieved from https://www.smithsonianmag.com/science-nature/fire-good-make-human-inspiration-happen-132494650/

Dana Lynn, C. (2014). Hearth and Campfire Influences on Arterial Blood Pressure: Defraying the Costs of the Social Brain through Fireside Relaxation. *Evolutionary Psychology*. https://doi.org/10.1177/147470491401200509

The World is getting wetter, yet water may become less available for North America and Eurasia. (4 Nov 2019). *Science Daily*. Https://www.sciencedaily.com/releases/2019/11/191104112828.htm

Carbon sequestration in soils. (Dec 2012). *Ecological Society of America*. Https://www.esa.org/esa/wp-content/uploads/2012/12/carbonsequestrationsoils.pdf

Chen, C., Park, T., Wang, X. et al. (2019) China and India lead in greening of the world through land-use management. *Nature Sustainability* 2, https://doi.org/10.1038/s41893-019-0220-7

Qiu, L. (2014 Dec 6) The Dirt on Dirt: 5 Things you should know about soil. National Geographic. Retrieved from https://www.nationalgeographic.com/culture/article/141205-world-soil-day-soil-agriculture-environment-ngfood

Foxx, C. L., Heinze, J., Gonzalez, A., et al. (05 January 2021). Effects of Immunization With the Soil-Derived Bacterium Mycobacterium vaccae on Stress Coping Behaviors and Cognitive Performance in a "Two Hit" Stressor Model. *Frontier Physiology*. Https://doi.org/10.3389/fphys.2020.524833

Bogard, P. (2017). *The Ground Beneath Us: From the Oldest Cities to the Last Wilderness, What Dirt Tells Us About Who We Are*. Little, Brown and Company.

Owen, D. (2019). *Volume Control: Hearing in a Deafening World*. Riverhead Books.

Bogard, P. (2014) *The End of Night: Searching for Natural Darkness in an Age of Artificial Light*. Back Bay Books.

Sava, N. (2019). What Can I Do to Improve My Night Vision. *Golden Eye Optometry*.
https://goldeneyeoptometry.com/2019/04/08/night-vision/

Boston Children's Hospital. (2017, September 28). How do we sense moonlight? Daylight? There's a cell for that: Neurons share the job of sensing the ambient light level. *ScienceDaily*. Retrieved June 27, 2021 from
www.sciencedaily.com/releases/2017/09/170928121704.htm

Drake, N. (2019) Our nights are getting brighter, and Earth is paying the price. *National Geographic*.
https://www.nationalgeographic.com/science/article/nights-are-getting-brighter-earth-paying-the-price-light-pollution-dark-skies/?loggedin=true

Savage, M. (2017). Friluftsliv: The Nordic concept of getting outdoors. *BBC*. https://www.bbc.com/worklife/article/20171211-friluftsliv-the-nordic-concept-of-getting-outdoors

Gooley, T. (2018). *The Nature Instinct: Relearning Our Lost Intuition for the Inner Workings of the Natural World*. The Experiment.

Algunas, K. (2018) *This Land Is Our Land: How We Lost the Right to Roam and How to Take It Back.* Penguin Publishing Group.

Harari, Y. N. (2018) *Sapiens: A Brief History of Mankind.* HarperCollins Publishing.

Algunas, K. (2018) *This Land Is Our Land: How We Lost the Right to Roam and How to Take It Back.* Penguin Publishing Group.

Serapiglia, S. (1990). An Educator's Illustrated Guide to Nature's Greatest Engineers for use with the Giant Screen Experience BEAVERS. Stephen Low Productions Inc. https://stephenlow.com/wp-content/uploads/Beavers-Teachers-Guide-web-150303.pdf

KCET. (2018 May 2). *The Art of Basket Weaving.* [Video]. YouTube. https://www.youtube.com/watch?v=DAm1OaW84pM

4. Bioregionalism

Suzman, J. (2017). *Affluence without Abundance: The Disappearing World of the Bushmen.* Bloomsbury Publishing.

Pennisi, E. (2015). Earth home to 3 trillion trees, half as many as when human civilization arose. *Science Magazine.* https://www.sciencemag.org/news/2015/09/earth-home-3-trillion-trees-half-many-when-human-civilization-arose

Soga, M., Gaston, K. (2018 Apr 4). Shifting baseline syndrome: causes, consequences and implications. *Frontiers in Ecology and the Environment.* 16(4). 222-230. https://doi.org/10.1002/fee.1794

5. All Our Relations

Miller, J. (26 February 2020). Slash and Burn: Why in the BLM clearing vast swaths of 55piñon-juniper forests across the West? *Sierra Club.*
https://www.google.com/amp/s/www.sierraclub.org/sierra/2020-2-march-april/feature/slash-and-burn-pinon-juniper-BLM%3famp

Blume, A. W. (2020). *A new psychology based on community, equality, and care of the earth: An Indigenous American perspective.* Santa Barbara: Praeger.

Zych, A., Wing, M. R., (2017 April 20). Life Under a Rock: Bacteria in Extreme Environments. *ScienceFriday.*
https://www.sciencefriday.com/educational-resources/life-hidden-beneath-the-rocks/

Greenbaum, E. (Nov 2017). *Emerald Labyrinth: A Scientist's Adventures in the Jungles of the Congo.* University Press of New England.

Nuwer, R. (Sept 2019). Frogs Make Their Homes in Elephant Footprints. Biology. *Scientific American.*
https://www.scientificamerican.com/article/frogs-make-their-homes-in-elephant-footprints/

6. Our Primal Nest

Tuulari, Jetro J et al. "Neural correlates of gentle skin stroking in early infancy." Developmental cognitive neuroscience vol. 35 (2019): 36-41. doi:10.1016/j.dcn.2017.10.004

Maltz, Maxwell. (1960). *Psycho-Cybernetics.* Simon and Schuster.

Narvaez, Darcia. (2018). *Basic Needs, Wellbeing and Morality Fulfilling Human Potential.* Palgrave Pivot.

Narvaez, Darcia. (2014). *Neurobiology and the Development of Human Morality: Evolution, Culture, and Wisdom*. W. W. Norton & Company.

The Evolved Nest (https://evolvednest.org)

Miller, Robyn. (2016). Potential Therapeutic Benefits of Babywearing. Creative Nursing. 22. 17-23. 10.1891/1078-4535.22.1.17.

Konner, M. "Nursing frequency and birth spacing in Kung hunter-gatherers." IPPF medical bulletin vol. 15,2 (1978).

Konner, Melvin, and Marjorie Shostak. "Timing and Management of Birth among the !Kung: Biocultural Interaction in Reproductive Adaptation." Cultural Anthropology, 2, no. 1 (1987): 1-3.

Harari, Y. N. (2014). *Sapiens: A Brief History of Humankind*. Vintage.

The Great Dance. Directed by Craig and Damon Foster. Produced by Ellen Windemuth. South Africa, 2000.

Hari, J. (2018). *Lost Connections: Uncovering the Real Causes of Depression and the Unexpected Solutions*. Bloomsbury.

Harari, Y. N. (2014). *Sapiens: A Brief History of Humankind*. Vintage.

Gooley, T. (2018). *The Nature Instinct: Relearning Our Lost Intuition for the Inner Workings of the Natural World*. The Experiment

7. An Unnatural Relationship

Wildlife corridors: Conservation and economic solution. Center for Western Priorities. https://westernpriorities.org/wildlife-corridors-a-conservation-and-economic-solution/

Targeting Wildlife Services: Our Campaign to Rein in a Rogue Federal Program Killing Wildlife for Private Interests. (2021). Center for Biological Diversity. https://www.biologicaldiversity.org/campaigns/wildlife_services/index.html

Hari, J. (2018). *Lost Connections: Uncovering the real causes of depression—and the unexpected solutions*. Bloomsbury Publishing.

Harari, Y. N. (2011). *Sapiens: A Brief History of Humankind*. Vintage Books.

Morrow, B. (2021, July 20). Bezos thanks Amazon customers and employees for space flight because 'you guys paid for all this'. *The Week*. https://www.google.com/amp/s/theweek.com/jeff-bezos/1002815/bezos-thanks-amazon-employees-and-customers-for-space-flight-because-you-guys%3famp

Murphy, D. (2020, February 21). How Amazon's Jeff Bezos should spend that S10 billion if he's serious about climate change. *USA Today*. https://www.google.com/amp/s/amp.usatoday.com/amp/4807536002

Waugaman, E. P. (2011, July 8). Names and Identity: The Native American Naming Tradition. *Psychology Today*. https://www.psychologytoday.com/us/blog/whats-in-a-name/201107/names-and-identity-the-native-american-naming-tradition%3famp

Suzman, J. (2017). *Affluence Without Abundance: The Disappearing World of the Bushmen*. Illustrated edition. Bloomsbury Publishing.

Gibbens, S. (2019). Can medical care exist without plastic? *National Geographic*. https://www.nationalgeographic.com/science/article/can-medical-care-exist-without-plastic

Mitchell, S. & Donahue, M. (2018). Report: Dollar Stores Are Targeting Struggling Urban Neighborhoods and Small Towns. One Community Is Showing How to Fight Back. *The Institute for Local Self-Reliance.* https://ilsr.org/dollar-stores-target-cities-towns-one-fights-back/

Zetlin, M. (2019). A College Professor Bribed Students to Give Up Their Smartphones for 9 Days. Here's What Happened. *Inc.com* https://www.inc.com/minda-zetlin/smartphones-use-smartphone-fast-give-up-mobile-phones-ron-srigley.html

Smith, S. (2021). Why more young people are ditching their smartphones
Return of the brick. *HuckMag*. https://www.huckmag.com/perspectives/reportage-2/why-more-young-people-are-ditching-their-smartphones/

Jeong, E., et al. (2017, November 30). Smartphone Addiction Creates Imbalance in Brain. *NeuroscienceNews*.

https://neurosciencenews.com/smartphone-addiction-brain-imbalance-8066/

Harari, Y. N. (2011). *Sapiens: A Brief History of Humankind.* Vintage Books.

Rincon, P. (2019). Homo erectus: Ancient humans survived longer than we thought. *BBC.* https://www.bbc.com/news/science-environment-50827603

Choi, C. (2019). The Final Days of Homo Erectus. *InsideScience.* https://www.insidescience.org/news/final-days-homo-erectus

8. Equilibrium

Hines M. (2011). Prenatal endocrine influences on sexual orientation and on sexually differentiated childhood behavior. Frontiers in neuroendocrinology, 32(2), 170–182. https://doi.org/10.1016/j.yfrne.2011.02.006

Barber, N. (2019 Nov 13) Gender fluidity and hormone disruptors. Psychology Today. Retrieved from https://www.psychologytoday.com/us/blog/the-human-beast/201911/gender-fluidity-and-hormone-disruptors

Blumberg, B. (2018). *The Obesogen Effect: Why We Eat Less and Exercise More But Still Struggle to Lose Weight.* Grand Central Publishing.

Ford, A. R. (2014 November) "Overexposed, Underinformed": Nail Salon Workers and Hazards to Their Health/A Review of the Literature. National Network on Environments and Women's Health. Retrieved from https://aerovexsystems.com/wp-content/uploads/2017/12/Overexposed-Underinformed-Article.pdf

Graham, S. (2005 Feb 16) Air Pollution Can Affect Fetal Development, Scientists Say. Scientific American. Retrieved from https://www.scientificamerican.com/article/air-pollution-can-affect/

Van Cappellen, P. (2003). Biomineralization and Global Biogeochemical Cycles. *Reviews in Mineralogy and Geochemistry*. https://doi.org/10.2113/0540357

Murshed, M. (2018). Mechanism of Bone Mineralization. *Cold Spring Harbor perspectives in medicine*, 8(12), a031229. https://doi.org/10.1101/cshperspect.a031229
Field Museum. "Coronaviruses and bats have been evolving together for millions of years: Different groups of bats have their own unique strains of coronavirus." ScienceDaily. ScienceDaily, 23 April 2020.
<www.sciencedaily.com/releases/2020/04/200423082231.htm>

Boyles, J. Economic Importance of Bats in Agriculture. Science. 01 Apr 2011:Vol. 332, Issue 6025, pp. 41-42 DOI: 10.1126/science.1201366 (retrieved from https://science.sciencemag.org/content/332/6025/41.full)

Kessler, R. (2018) In a World Without Bats. EcoHealth Alliance. Retrieved from https://www.ecohealthalliance.org/2018/10/in-a-world-without-bats

Doucleff, M. (2021 March 19) Next Pandemic: Scientists Fear Another Coronavirus Could Jump From Animals To Humans. NPR. Retrieved from

https://www.npr.org/sections/goatsandsoda/2021/03/19/97931411
8/next-pandemic-scientists-fear-another-coronavirus-could-
jump-from-animals-to-hum

Elliot, D. (2020 Jun 25) Why this sea creature is still a key
ingredient in testing vaccines. World Economic Forum.org.
Retrieved from
https://www.weforum.org/agenda/2020/06/coronavirus-vaccine-
testing-horseshoe-crabs/

Golder, W. (2020 May 21) Saving Red Knots One Crab at a Time.
Audubon.org. Retrieved from
https://www.audubon.org/news/saving-red-knots-one-crab-time

Gleiser, M. (2018, Jan 31) The Microbial Eve: Our Oldest
Ancestors Were Single-Celled Organisms. NPR. Retrieved from
https://www.npr.org/sections/13.7/2018/01/31/581874421/be-
humbled-our-oldest-ancestors-were-single-celled-organisms

Cooper, K. (2017, Mar 30) Looking for LUCA, the Last Universal
Common Ancestor. Astrobiology at Nasa. Retrieved from
https://astrobiology.nasa.gov/news/looking-for-luca-the-last-
universal-common-ancestor/

Doucleff, M. (2017, Aug 24) Is the secret to a healthier
microbiome hidden in the Hadza diet?. NPR. Retrieved from
https://www.npr.org/sections/goatsandsoda/2017/08/24/54563152
1/is-the-secret-to-a-healthier-microbiome-hidden-in-the-hadza-
diet

Schnorr, S. L., Candela, M., Rampelli, S., Centanni, M.,
Consolandi, C., Basaglia, G., Turroni, S., Biagi, E., Peano, C.,
Severgnini, M., Fiori, J., Gotti, R., De Bellis, G., Luiselli, D.,

Brigidi, P., Mabulla, A., Marlowe, F., Henry, A. G., & Crittenden, A. N. (2014). Gut microbiome of the Hadza hunter-gatherers. Nature communications, 5, 3654. https://doi.org/10.1038/ncomms4654

NYU Langone Medical Center. (2015, June 10). Do newborns delivered by C-section face higher risk of chronic health problems later in life?. ScienceDaily. Retrieved June 1, 2021 from www.sciencedaily.com/releases/2015/06/150610092801.htm

Trosvik, P., & de Muinck, E. J. (2015). Ecology of bacteria in the human gastrointestinal tract--identification of keystone and foundation taxa. Microbiome, 3, 44. https://doi.org/10.1186/s40168-015-0107-4

Al-Zalabani AH, Al-Jabree AH, Zeidan ZA. Is cesarean section delivery associated with autism spectrum disorder?. Neurosciences (Riyadh). 2019;24(1):11-15. doi:10.17712/nsj.2019.1.20180303

Are viruses actually vital for our existence? (03 Nov 2015) World Economic Forum website. https://www.weforum.org/agenda/2015/11/are-viruses-actually-vital-for-our-existence/

Carrol, S. (2016). *The Serengeti Rules: The Quest to Discover How Life Works and Why It Matters.* Princeton University Press

Harding, S. (2006). *Animate Earth: Science, Intuition and Gaia.* Green Books.

INTERVIEWS

Ian Frampton
Paul Bogard
Darcia Narvaez
Sailesh Rao
Kevin Emmerich

About the Author

Soraya is a biologist, independent journalist, and wilderness enthusiast. She is the author of *The Wandering Naturalist* online journal where she writes about her personal experiences and observations of Nature. Earning a bachelor's degree in biology with a concentration in ecology/evolutionary biology, she has experience in various field and laboratory projects including assisting in an archeological excavation, lizard and snake tracking surveys, threatened bird surveys, and wetland restoration. She has also hiked thousands of backcountry miles across multiple wildernesses, is a survivor of stage-4 cancer and is a life-long advocate for wild Nature. To support the writing journey visit *Patreon.com/wildroots.*